MEGILAT SEFER

THE AUTOBIOGRAPHY OF RABBI JACOB EMDEN (1697-1776)

TRANSLATED ENTIRELY INTO ENGLISH
FOR THE FIRST TIME

BY

RABBI S.B. LEPERER
AND RABBI M.H. WISE

Baltimore, Maryland
2011 / 5771

Text copyright © 2011 by Rabbi M.H. Wise

Comments are welcome via email to:
Meirhwise@aol.com

Cover/interior design and publisher's introduction
copyright © 2011 Shaftek Enterprises LLC

Cover photo is in public domain and was obtained from:
Chachmei Ahu by Eduard Duckesz; Hamburg, 1908

Published by:

PublishYourSefer.com,
a service of Shaftek Enterprises LLC
4014 Labyrinth Rd, Baltimore, MD 21215, USA
Phone: +1 (410) 696-4611 / Fax: +1 (443) 703-2355
Email: info@publishyoursefer.com
Website: www.publishyoursefer.com

ISBN-13:
978-1-61259-001-1 (paperback)
978-1-61259-002-8 (hard cover)

Library of Congress Control Number: 2010942935

British Library Cataloguing in Publication Data:
A catalogue record for this book is
available from the British Library.

3 4 5   IS   22 23 24

MEGILAT SEFER

TABLE OF CONTENTS

PUBLISHER'S INTRODUCTION..5
ACKNOWLEDGEMENTS..9
DEDICATIONS...15
AUTHOR'S INTRODUCTION...25
CHAPTER ONE..29
CHAPTER TWO..35
CHAPTER THREE...41
CHAPTER FOUR..47
CHAPTER FIVE..53
CHAPTER SIX...57
CHAPTER SEVEN...63
CHAPTER EIGHT...71
CHAPTER NINE...119
CHAPTER TEN..207
CHAPTER ELEVEN...251
CHAPTER TWELVE...295
END NOTES..337
APPENDIX A: PHOTOS AND ILLUSTRATIONS.....................347
APPENDIX B: GLOSSARY...351
APPENDIX C: BIOGRAPHICAL NOTES.................................353

MEGILAT SEFER

PUBLISHER'S INTRODUCTION
ଓ ଚ

When Rabbi S. B. Leperer passed away in December 1995 / 5756, he left this translation in unfinished form. His student, Rabbi M. H. Wise was asked to finish the work of his teacher, and he approached us in the summer of 2010 / 5770 in order to help him publish it. Because of Rabbi Leperer's sudden death, we do not know what his ultimate goal for this translation was. Therefore, we present this work as it was left – with minimal changes from the original manuscript left by Rabbi Leperer other than the work necessary to make it publishable. Due to its inherent incompleteness this translation is not intended to be an exhaustive academic work, and readers are encouraged to consult other sources for further research on Rabbi Emden and his life.

ଓ ଚ

The original Hebrew version of Megilat Sefer exists in manuscript form in the Bodelian Library of Oxford University[1]. Unfortunately, only one copy of the manuscript exists in the entire world, and this copy is incomplete ending in the middle of chapter 12.

There are also two printed editions – the first published by David Kahana in 1897[2], and the second published by Avraham Bick in in 1979[3]. The first was based directly on the original manuscript, while the second was based on a microfilm copy made by the National Library of Israel[4]. There is also a French translation published in 1992[5].

Due to his academic position, Rabbi Leperer had regular

---
1 Cataloged under Mich. 587, Neubauer 1723/2 and Mich. 396 (old catalog)
2 Megilat Sefer; edited by David Kahane, Warsaw: Ahim Shuldberg, 1897. Also available online from Google Books , the HathiTrust, HebrewBooks.org, and the National Library of Israel.
3 Megilat Sefer; edited by Avraham (Shauli) Bick; Jerusalem: Sifriyat Moreshet, 1979
4 JNUL microfilm # F 17754; custodian # OX Mich. 587; JNUL rec # 000065517
5 Mémoires de Jacob Emden, ou, L'anti-Sabbataï Zewi; Paris : Editions du Cerf; 1992

PUBLISHER'S INTRODUCTION

access to the manuscript, and the manuscript was used as a primary source for the translation, with the Bick edition used as a secondary. The Kahana edition was used for comparison purposes only due its inherent unreliability[6].

ᛤ ᛥ

The text is divided into 12 chapters, following the division in the original manuscript. There are also some end notes on the first three chapters, which were created by both Rabbi Leperer and Rabbi Wise.

Rabbi Leperer translated chapters 2-11 and also wrote some of the end notes. Rabbi Wise translated the introduction, chapters 1, and 12, and contributed the rest of the end notes, as well as the glossary and biographical information that appears at the end. Rabbi Wise also typed, proof read and corrected the text, as well as obtained the introductionary materials and approbations.

The publisher added the Hebrew original of the introduction based on the Bick edition, created the table of contents, wrote this introduction, and appendix A containing some photos and illustrations relevant to this work. The publisher also added some footnotes within the text clarifying certain matters such as part divisions, etc.. No changes were made to the text itself.

ᛤ ᛥ

Within the text, editor notes appear as "[Editor note:]" or "[Ed. note:]" and are italicized. Publisher notes appear as "[Publisher note:]" or "[Pub. Note:]" and are italicized. Numbers within the text such as "(1)" reference end notes. The Hebrew originals are referenced as "Oxford MS" for the manuscript, and "Kahane Ed" and "Bick Ed." for the 1897 and 1979 editions respectively.

Due to the terse nature of the original text and because of the large number of idioms and expressions that are sources in

---

6 See the editor's introduction in the Bick edition where multiple examples are cited of how the Kahana edition emblished certain matters, omitted others and made up some as well.

MEGILAT SEFER

Biblical, or Rabbinic sources, source references will appear within the text like "(Prov. 24:26)". When sources are quoted directly, a direct reference appears within the text. When the original paraphrases a Biblical or Rabbinic sources, the source is referenced with "cf" like "(cf. Prof. 24:26).

Because of the unique nature of the original text, it was often necessary to include additional words within the translation which do not appear in the original in order to make the text readable. These additional words appear in parentheses. For example from chapter 1: *"But he (the Golem) damaged his master"*.

Occasionally, it was also necessary to include the original Hebrew term transliterated into English if this term is commonly used in its Hebrew form within English. These terms appear in parentheses as well. For example, from chapter 1: *"remained faithful to God through many generations since the early German pietists (Chasidei Ashkenaz)"*.

Being that both translators are British, the spelling, grammar and other stylistic features of the text follow British English conventions.

In this edition, no indexes of sources, places and people appears. Readers are encouraged to consult the Bick edition for such information. While a glossary is included in the end of the work which explains some of the terminology, it is not intended to be an exhaustive reference.

Baltimore, MD, USA
Kislev 5771

PUBLISHER'S INTRODUCTION

MEGILAT SEFER

ACKNOWLEDGEMENTS
ଊ ଌ

My father, the Elder of the Priesthood, Reb Reuven Hakohen Wise, of blessed memory, who struggled to bring me up to Torah, Chuppah and good deeds, was renowned for his cheerful countenance, patience and forgiving nature. His whole life was devoted to the care of others most of which he carried out secretly. He sent me away from him in my youth, just when he and my mother needed me the most, so that I should sit at the feet of the great Rabbis in London. His self-sacrifice and selflessness should serve as an example to all his descendants.

There was a Jewish man in Yemen, whose name was Yishaya, son of the Admor Elisha the Ramati, a Yemini, a descendant of the exiles who had been exiled from Israel at the time of Yechoniah, King of Judah, whom Nebuchadnezzar, King of Babylon had exiled. And he married Miriam, the only daughter of the Admor Shalom Mowjami. They had a baby daughter called Sarah (Sarit), who was finely featured and beautiful. I am most grateful that they gave her to me in marriage on 10 Adar 5740 in Tel-Aviv-Jaffa. May Hashem prolong their years in good health and tranquillity and may they see Nachat from their children and grandchildren until the coming of the Messiah.

I am eternally grateful to my renowned teachers Rabbi Shlomo Benzion Leperer , Rabbi Moshe Turetsky, Rabbi Elyakim Geztel Ellinson and Rabbi Simcha Bunim Liberman, their souls repose in Eden, may their merit protect their Talmidim and all Israel. Also, may he be distinguished for a long life, to my illustrious teacher, the Rosh Yeshiva of Maaleh Adumim, Rabbi Nachum L. Rabinovitch, may his Torah shed light in Land of Israel just as it lit up the Diaspora.

To my colleagues whom I am privileged to call friends - Rabbis Abraham David, Reuven Fisher, Menachem Gelley, Mordechai Ginsbury, Dovid Halpern, Zvi Rabinowicz, Jonathan Sacks and Shmuel Silberg, my thanks for their unfailing friendship,

ACKNOWLEDGEMENTS

courtesy and support; I wish them renewed vigour and success in the positions that they occupy.

I would also like to thank those who supported this publication by donating dedications, and several friends and supporters who wish to remain anonymous.

To my students whose subtle discussions have helped me acquire Torah (Avot 6:6), to the members of the Raleigh Close Synagogue and Yeshivat Od Yosef Hai, both in Hendon, London - I am in your debt.

It is written in the Zohar - "everything depends on mazal even a Sefer in the Ark". This sefer had great mazal on the day that I found my publisher. He gave of his effort and time beyond the call of duty and his unfailing courtesy to me is an example of the ideal relationship between author and publisher. May the Source of all blessings reward them with health and happiness which they truly deserve. However, I alone remain responsible for any mistakes.

Finally, my debt to my wife who was called "Rebbetzin" even before we were married is too great to be put into words. Since our marriage she has sacrificed days and nights without complaint to allow me to continue learning and teaching. She has kept an open house whilst bringing up our children without help and during this time she graduated twice with honours from Jews' College, London. "Many daughters have done virtuously but you have surpassed them all".

May we see naches from our children, Doron, Rav Shlomi, Helena and Ria, together with their spouses Avital, Eliyahu Eliezer and Aryeh Leib Fivel, and our grandchildren Yael, Devorah, Tamar, Reuven and Miriam. May the words of the Torah never depart from us or them or their descendants until the coming of Moshiach.

I lift up my eyes to Heaven and ask one thing - that I might dwell in the House of the Lord all the days of my life.

M.H.W.; London; Sivan 5770

MEGILAT SEFER

LETTER OF APPROBATION

From:
Rabbi Shmuel Silberg MA
19 Alderton Crescent
London NW4 3XU

Iyyar 5757

    To my dear friend and colleague, Rabbi Meir Henoch Hakohen Wise, shlit"a, who studies and teaches by day and by night, himself the beloved and outstanding pupil of the late departed Rabbi Dr. Shlomo Benzion Leperer zatza"l, Rosh Beis Hamedrash Lerabbonim BeLondon, my warmest greetings and felicitations.

    Rabbi Leperer's sudden demise filled us all with shock and great sadness, depriving us of a friend, wit and scholar, whose work needs no testimony. I am however happy to commend you in your task of fulfilling his wish to bring his work to publication. It will surely be accounted as righteousness.

    Rabbi Yaakov Emden's opposition to Sabbateanism is well known, as is his controversy with Rabbi Jonathan Eibeschuetz. But the fact that his father the Haham Tzvi saved Haham David Nieto of London from the accusation of pantheism is little known. This family's connection to Anglo-Jewry, through Rav Emden's son, Rabbi Meshullam of the Hambro' Synagogue, with descendants in Plymouth and London to this day - and they include the late Stanislawer Rebbe, R.Meshullam Ashkenazi of Stamford Hill - has hardly been documented.

    Anglo-Jewry has been blessed neither with a wealth of native born scholars, nor support for works of scholarship. I hope and pray that Rabbi Leperer's work, of which this is the first to appear, will prove to be a turning point.

Shmuel Silberg
Mara D'Atra

ACKNOWLEDGEMENTS

FOREWORD

by
Rabbi Nachum L. Rabinovitch
Rosh Yeshivat Birkat Moshe
Maaleh Adumim, Jerusalem

One of the most colourful and influential rabbis of the eighteenth century was Rabbi Yaakov of Emden. A prodigiously prolific author, the sheer variety of his writings is staggering, ranging from profound legal scholarship to polemical pamphleteering and from liturgy to literary criticism. Perhaps most unexpected is an autobiography in which he bares his soul. Although it was frequent practice in rabbinical literature to include autobiographical details in the introduction to a scholarly work, it was rare to write a systematic account of one's life and longings, if not unique.

It was gratifying to learn that the late Rabbi Dr. Leperer conceived the plan to render Rabbi Emden's life-story - Megilat Sefer - into English. It was my privilege to work closely with Rabbi Leperer at Jews' College in London, and it is easy to see why he was attracted to this work. For "Megilat Sefer" is a most difficult work to render intelligibly into another language. References abound to the vast range of rabbinic writings of all times as well as literature in other languages. The age was one of great cultural and political upheavals and these are reflected in Rabbi Emden's own experiences. Even the mere geographical spread is challenging, since the author wandered during his life-time through much of Europe. Added to these are the after-effects of the Sabbatean controversy which reverberated throughout the Jewish world, in which Rabbi Emden himself was a major force.

Rabbi Meir Wise has now undertaken to translate Rabbi Leperer's plan into reality by completing the task begun but cut off by Rabbi Leperer's passing. It is an awesome challenge demanding encyclopaedic learning and literary talent. My heartiest good wishes to Rabbi Wise for success in this magnificent endeavour. May the Almighty enable him to see his efforts to full fruition, and may he thus earn the gratitude of all who value Jewish studies.

Nachum L. Rabinovitch
8th of Iyyar 5757

MEGILAT SEFER

PREFACE
by
Emeritus Chief Rabbi Immanuel Jakobovits
President, Conference of European Rabbis

Rabbi Yaakov Emden (1697-1776) was one of the most prolific, controversial, erudite and colourful scholars of the post-medieval period.

Emden became famous above all for his fierce opposition to the pseudo-Messiah Shabbetai Zvi and his bitter controversy with Rabbi Jonathan Eybeschitz whom he suspected of Sabbatean sympathies.

Emden wrote some fifty books, ranging from important rabbinic responsa and a classic commentary on the prayerbook to an autobiography, including details on the life and works of his famous father and chief mentor, the Haham Zvi. There are very few works of this kind to be found in rabbinic literature. Originally published in 1897, it here appears for the first time translated into English and carefully annotated.

The translation and notes are the result of twenty years' diligent labour by the recently-deceased scholar, Rabbi Dr S. B. Leperer who was keen that this should be the first of his writings to be published.

Rabbi Leperer himself had the particular distinction of being born, educated and academically active throughout his life in Britain - in fact in London. In Anglo-Jewish history there are very few such scholars. This volume is also intended as a tribute to Rabbi Leperer's contribution to Jewish learning in this country.

Rabbi Leperer was assiduously helped in this labour of love by one of his favourite students, Rabbi Meir Wise, who served as the last rabbi of the Western Synagogue before its amalgamation, and who has taught at Carmel College and continues to teach at the Od Yosef Hai Yeshivah in London. I hope that this work will be widely distributed and read.

Immanuel Jakobovits, Sivan 5757

ACKNOWLEDGEMENTS

MEGILAT SEFER

ଓଃ ୨୦

DEDICATIONS

ଓଃ ୨୦

In everlasting memory
of my beloved parents

ר' ראובן הכהן וייס ז"ל   מרת יענטא וייס ע"ה
כ"ב תמוז תשמ"ח   ו" כסלו תש"ן

הנאהבים והנעימים בחייהם
ובמותם לא נפרדו

תנצב"ה

ע"י בנם הק" מאיר הנוך

In memory of my beloved mother

Rabbanit Miriam Ramati, of blessed memory,
daughter of the holy Admor Shalom Mowjami z"l

who was brought to rest on
the Mount of Olives
10 Marcheshvan 5659

leaving her husband, children and over 50 grandchildren
all trying to emulate her ways.

"Many daughters have done valiantly
but you surpassed them all"

dedicated by her daughter Sarit

ଓଃ ୨୦

DEDICATIONS

ଔ ଙ

In memory of
Reb Simcha Akiva Burns z"l
17 Teves 5962

dedicated by his devoted wife and children
in London and Israel

---

and sending Bracha veHatzlacha to
his friend Rabbi Wise on his new undertaking

ଔ ଙ

MEGILAT SEFER

ଔ ଈ

In loving memory
of a wonderful husband and father
Reb Moshe Shlomo Hakohen Collins z"l

"What does Hashem require of you but to do justice, to love
kindness and to walk humbly with your God" (Micah 6:8)

dedicated by his devoted wife and sons

In memory of my friend and study-partner

Jonathan Collins z"l
(Reb Moshe Shlomo Hakohen)

"I am distressed over you, my brother Jonathan;
you were so pleasant to me!" (2 Samuel 1:26)

always in my heart
Meir Henoch Hakohen Wise

ଔ ଈ

DEDICATIONS

ଓ ଥି

In memory of my beloved grandfather
Reb Moritz ben Dinah z"l

b. Berlin, Germany   15 Elul 5665
d. New Jersey, USA   2 Kislev 5751

dedicated by Arie Weissmann

ଓ ଥି

MEGILAT SEFER

☙ ❧

In loving memory of
Mrs Rivka Malka Kon z"l

Taanis Esther 5770

devoted wife, mother and grandmother

"A woman of worth who can find
for her price is far above rubies"

from her devoted husband, children and grandchildren

Dedicated to the memory of
a dear friend, counsellor and guide

Marcus Fielding z"l
(Moshe ben Dovid – 24 Adar 5766)

"Whoever is loved below is surely loved above"
(Bartenura to Avot 3:13)

☙ ❧

DEDICATIONS

ଓଃ ଛଠ

In loving memory of our parents

Yitzchok and Soroh Graham   Dov and Gita Zelda Horwitz
Leeds   Manchester

dedicated by their children John and Phyllis Graham
London – Jerusalem

Dedicated to the memory of
Reb Meir ben Menachem Eliezer Tajtelbaum ztl
of Sherps, Poland, Buenes Aries, London and Petach Tikva

A hero of the holocaust, he helped rebuild the Tajtelbaum
dynasty and devoted his life to the service of others

dedicated by his eldest daughter and son-in-law
Dr. & Mrs. Yaakov Wise of Manchester

ଓଃ ଛଠ

MEGILAT SEFER

ଔ ଛୋ

Dedicated to the memory of my father z"l

ר" צבי אריה בן משה מאיר הכהן

who loved to learn Torah

לעילוי נשמת
משה אליהו בנעים בר דוד ע"ה

ଔ ଛୋ

DEDICATIONS

⋒ ⋒

In memory of
Rabbi Reuven Fisher זצ״ל
2 Marcheshvan 5767

Faithful talmid of Rabbi Shimon Shkopf
and Rav Elchonon Wasserman

Loved by all who knew him

dedicated by his children Martin, David and Angie

In loving memory of my dear sister
Feige bas Dovid Yehudah
21 Kislev 5771

from her brother Rabbi Meir Aaronberg

⋒ ⋒

MEGILAT SEFER

ଔ ଚ

In honour of our great Rabbi and Guide
Morenu Harav Meir Henoch Hakohen Wise shlit"a

dedicated by his talmidim

Kenton Cheder	Borehamwood Cheder
J.F.S	Carmel College
The Central Synagogue Nelson Street, E1	The Western Synagogue Crawford Place, W1
Stepney Hillel, East London	Hillel House, Euston
Yakar Educational Foundation	Yeshivat Od Yosef Hai
Raleigh Close Shul, Hendon	Wednesday and Friday night shiur (1977-2007)

ଔ ଚ

DEDICATIONS

ଔ ଞ

בית המדרש לרבנים בלונדון
נוסד שנת תרט"ז

לזכר ולעילוי נשמות
מורינו ורבותינו
הגאונים האדירים

הרב ישראל ברודי זצ"ל

הרב יחזקאל אפשטיין זצ"ל

הרב קופל כהנא זצ"ל

הרב ישראל יקובוביץ זצ"ל

הרב שלמה בנציון לעפערער זצ"ל

הרב משה טורעצקי זצ"ל

הרב שמחה בונם ליברמן זצ"ל

הרב אליקים ג. אלינסון זצ"ל

תנצב"ה
הוצנח ע"י תלמידיהון ותלמידי תלמידיהון שיחיו

ଔ ଞ

MEGILAT SEFER

☙ ❧
AUTHOR'S INTRODUCTION
☙ ❧

AUTHOR'S INTRODUCTION

ଔ ଓ

May (1) He who keeps faith forever (Ps.146:6) / guard you /
Gather and listen to Jacob (Gen.49:2) / so that God will listen to you (Jud.9:7)
God who is your God / and the God of your fathers /

Let me tell of the decree (Ps.2:7)/ and justify my actions /
and say: Many deeds have You done O Lord my God with me /
I will declare and speak of a number of them /

Where is the one who can weigh and where is the one who can count? (Is.33:18)
Even though I have not seen its goodness (2) and it is impossible to force the judgement and delay the hour / (cf.TB.Berachot 64a)
O Lord my God I will extol You / I will praise Your name for you have done wondrously /
Advice from afar God has shown me (Jer.31:2) / Of His accusations and His deeds against my persecutors has He shown me/

May it be His will that in this book my words will be written permanently/
they shall be carved in rock in the writings of the House of Israel (Job 19:23)/
so that children yet to be born will arise and tell their children (Ps.78:6) to the end of time./
Then our mouths will be filled with songs of joy (Ps.126:2) / for evil and injustice will be as naught.

ଔ ଓ

MEGILAT SEFER

೧ ೮೦

אבי ישמרכם השומר אמת לעולם
הקבצו ושמעו אל יעקב וישמע אליכם אלוקים
אלקי אלקיכם ואלוקי אבותיכם

אספרה אל חוק ולפועלי אתן צדק
ואומרה: רבות עשית אתה ה' אלוקי עמדי
אגידה ואדברה עצמו מספר

איה שוקל ואיה סופר
אף כי לא ראיתי בטובה ואי אפשר לכוף את הדין והשעה לדחוק
ה' אלקי ארוממך אודה שמך כי עשית פלא
עצות מרחוק ה' נראה לי ממעשיו ועלילותיו אשר הראני נגד צוררי

מי יתן בספר ויכתבון מלי לעד
בצור יתצבון ככתב בית ישראל
בנים יוולדו יקומו ויספרו לבניהם ליום אחרון
אז ימלא שחוק פינו ולשוננו רנה כי אפס רשע ועוולה

೧ ೮೦

MEGILAT SEFER

CHAPTER ONE

I will start with my father's father, my paternal grandfather, z"l, after whom I am named. He was none other than the Gaon, our teacher, Rabbi Yaakov, son of his honour, our teacher, Rabbi Benjamin (may his merit protect me) Ashkenazi, a descendant of "Zak".(3) This is the way they used to sign the name of their family, for they were the holy seed, the tested and purified (i.e. martyred) children of those who in the days of the evil decrees and persecutions remained faithful to God through many generations since the early German pietists (Chasidci Ashkenaz).

My above-mentioned great-grandfather (Rabbi Benjamin Ashkenazi Zak) was one of the outstanding scholars of Vilna (4) in the days before the Chemielniki massacres (5) and was a student of the Gaon, Morenu Harav Yaakov Av Bet Din in Lublin, who was the father of the Gaon, Morenu Harav Heschel, z"l. He (R.Benjamin) served him (R.Yaakov) in the Yeshiva and he (R.Yaakov) gave him (R.Benjamin) his daughter as a wife.

My maternal great-grandfather was the Gaon and Chasid of the Priesthood, the author of the Book of Responsa "Sha'ar Ephraim"(6) z"l (7) the Head of the Bet Din in the glorious and

CHAPTER ONE

splendid community of Vilna, which was then at peace. He had a genealogy going back to Aaron the High Priest, and was one of the grandsons of the Gaon, Rabbi Elijah Ba'al Shem (8) the Elder, z"l who was the Presiding Rabbi of the holy community of Chelem in those days.(9) Look at the Book of Responsa of my father, my teacher the Gaon, z"l.(10)

He made a Golem(11): One incident that is related about him is that the creature that he had created was without speech and used to serve him like a slave. When the Rabbi saw that the creation of his hands was growing very strong through the name that was written on paper and stuck to his forehead; so that Rabbi Elijah Ba'al Shem was afraid that he would cause damage and destruction. He quickly overpowered him and tore the parchment from him on which was written the name and removed it from his forehead so he fell to the ground and turned back into clay. But he (the Golem) damaged his master, for he scratched him in the face as he removed the parchment and removed the name from him.

My master, my great-grandfather, the Gaon, author of Sha'ar Ephraim z"l, the great Chasid mentioned above, sat all his days fasting, except for Sabbaths and Festivals, apart from a few occasions when he would fast from one Sabbath to the next and other consecutive fasts , but despite this his face was bright like the sun as if he had imbibed strong drink every day. The Torah did not cease from his mouth by day or by night. Whoever wants to know more of his deeds and dissemination of Torah, the depth of his study, his rulings and what happened to him and his only son, should look into the Sefer "Sha'ar Ephraim", which his son, the outstanding Rabbi, his honour Morenu Harav Judah Leib, z"l, wrote when he brought this book of his father's to be printed. My great-grandfather, the Chasid, expired in the place of his glory - Uban (12) which was large and prosperous, at the age of 62. His son R.Judah Leib pitched the tent of his Torah in Jerusalem, may it be built up and established speedily and in our days, and died there with a good name, leaving a wise and great son Rabbi Yedidiyah, z"l, who was married to the daughter of Rabbi Yitzchaki z"l, the Chief Rabbi of Eretz Israel in his day.

MEGILAT SEFER

My great-grandfather the "Sha'ar Ephraim" had one daughter and her name was Nechama (z"l). She was the mother of my father and teacher the Gaon, the wife of my grandfather the Rabbi Morenu Harav Yaakov mentioned above who married her (my mother) to him (my father) for he was perfect in Torah and the Fear (of Heaven). The Gaon Rabbi David Oppenheim (13) and another person, both of whom were his students, related in amazement how he (Rabbi Yaakov) knew all four parts of the Shulchan Arukh by heart and how a great miracle happened to him as I will now relate in detail.

It was in the year 5408 (1648) according to the minor reckoning, a time of trouble for Israel in the Land of Poland, Wolhynia and the Ukraine because of Chemieliki. From there the decree spread to the communities of Lithuania, so that the renowned, refined, holy community of Vilna was banished from its nest, after it had dwelt securely and in tranquillity and grown so wealthy that their household utensils were of silver. In wisdom and in rank it surpassed all the other holy communities and so in every place that they reached in their wanderings and journeys in the land of Germany and other states the scholars of Vilna were highly regarded. This was told me by the venerable communal-leader Reb Behr Cohen, peace be upon him, that they rose above and outstripped all Polish Jewry. Her scholars and men of repute studied by day and by night and were never silent (Is.62:6) from studying laws and decisions nor did they move from the sanctuary of the Great Bet HaMidrash, searching and investigating the quintessential truth of Torah in the Talmud and Rabbinics, so that they did not sleep in their homes the entire week, only on the Sabbath.

Thus they became mighty warriors, lions of the Torah, all of whom merited to be decisors in Israel besides other venerated scholars, personalities and leaders amongst whom was the complete sage, the Rabbi, Gaon and Pious One of the Priesthood the author of "Sha'ar Ephraim" z"l, who was the Head of the Bet Din in Vilna, and the Gaon, the author of "Birkhat HaZevach" (14) and other writings, about whom it was said that he knew the Turim and Bet Yosef by heart and the Rabbi, the author of the "Shach" (15) and the

CHAPTER ONE

pious Rabbi and authority "Bet Hillel" z"l (16). Apart from other geniuses, all of them went into exile, they were spread across the country in order to spread Torah in Israel for they were the great luminaries. Maharshak became Av Bet Din in Fiorda and from there rose up to occupy the Rabbinate of Frankfort-on-Main and then Cracow. The Rabbi "Bet Hillel" was accepted as Av Bet Din in Hamburg and Altona, and the Rabbi "the Shach" in Holischau in Moravia. The Gaon Yaakov, father's father also settled in Moravia with all his family. At first he was the Av Bet Din and honoured guest in the house of the well-known leader called Reich-Kaufman, peace be upon him. There he taught the son of this wealthy man, after which he became the Av Bet Din in the holy community of Broda and afterwards returned to (act as a) father the holy community of Uban as Av Bet Din.

However before they came to their inheritance and resting-place (Deut.12:19) many trials and tribulations passed over them (Ex.12:35); their souls waited in silence because of the oppressive wrath (Jer.25:38).

This is what happened to my grandfather, our teacher Rabbi Yaakov z"l who was then a young man. He was forced to flee suddenly to save himself from this whirlwind of persecution. This perfect man was separated from his brothers and his young wife who remained with her father who fled with his son and wife to another country so that they would not fall in to the pit of distress. Those marauders came across my grandfather, they who had slain many and uprooted several Jewish communities without leaving as much as a horseshoe, who spilled innocent blood of those who were faithful to God by the thousand and tens of thousands, who were slaughtered like sheep by the hands of the oppressors. When they came across that righteous man, the guard of the prisoners (TB.San.104a) ordered him to kneel down and stretch out his neck! He did so; he stretched out his neck to the sharp sword to be slain and give up his life to sanctify the Divine name. Whilst he was still on his knees waiting to receive the death-blow from the sword, his soul nearly expired when an angel of God touched him, for God put compassion in the heart of the persecutor so that he had pity because of his tender years. Instead of drawing the sword across his neck on the sharp side, his pity was aroused so that he gave him a blow, by way of insult, with the blunt side. He said to him: Get up, young dog! Run for your life!

So God saved him from the sword of wickedness in the most miraculous and wonderful way possible. Afterwards he hid amongst the slain so that it was not noticed that he was alive by those passing by there. He was parched by day lying between the dead slain martyrs and puddles of water, covered with a sack and freezing at night (Gen.31:40), he wandered in search of some food and to gather the greenery of a bitter fruit that grows among the reeds by a lake to keep himself alive. In this situation for 8 days until the thirst for blood had passed, he then ran away and escaped from the murderous hordes.

Now when he was amongst the slain martyrs there were some of our people who were also hiding some distance away who saw everything that happened to my grandfather; how he had knelt on the ground under the hand of the persecutor who wanted to smite him. They thought that his head was bowed to be slaughtered and, when they saw the sword lying on his neck they thought that he would not live. After he fell to the ground from the sword-blow, which was not a death blow at all, these people who were standing at some distance and were watching in trepidation and panic, imagined that his head had been severed and fallen to the ground, as the Talmudic Sages said: "it may sometimes happen that he was struck by an arrow or spear and she (his wife) would think that he was certainly dead, while in fact someone might have applied a bandage [to his wound] and he might have recovered. (Yevamot 114b).

Therefore when these people reached the town of Trieves, the place of the Gaon, the author of "Sha'ar Ephraim" after they had escaped from the clutches of the enemies by the Grace of God upon them, and came to the Land of Moravia, a place which was quiet and secure, he (R.Ephraim) enquired as to the whereabouts of my grandfather, Morenu Harav Yaakov z"l. He enquired after him amongst the above-mentioned survivors, whether they had seen him

CHAPTER ONE

alive or dead? They said: "Yaakov is dead! For we have seen with our own eyes that he knelt down to be killed and that his head was severed!" Thus answered those refugees who were honest and upright. They testified about that which they had not clearly seen and according to their words the outstanding Gaon of his generation, his eminence our teacher Rabbi Heschel z"l allowed his wife (Yaakov's) Nechama to remarry. According to the rules of a Rabbinic enquiry and law the matter was very obvious indeed, as clear as the Torah rule "..according to the testimony of two witnesses the matter shall be established" (Deut.17:6); and with an Agunah the Sages were even more lenient.(17). However his wife who was the most beautiful girl amongst women did not want to accept condolences for the living - the husband of her youth.

That righteous woman remained pure, ready to bring forth a great dynasty, an upright blessed generation, handiwork in which to glory (cf.Is.60:21); for after half a year the "slain one" arrived on foot, which was a wonder and miracle in Israel. From then on the Gaon Ba'al "Sha'ar Ephraim" mentioned above did not want to release any Agunah in that generation and in those perilous times, for there were many wives bereft of their husbands who disappeared in that whirlwind of plunder and pogrom. He was fearful of making a mistake, therefore he took upon himself to refrain from being involved in the release of any woman, since this mistake happened under his authority (lit. under his hand) (cf.Is.3:6) for he had permitted a married woman (to remarry), saying that at a time of upheaval like that one cannot rely at all even on two witnesses, so that there was fulfilled in him, "No calamity befalls the righteous" (Prov.12:21)

MEGILAT SEFER

CHAPTER TWO

My father, z"l, the great and renowned scholar, the glorious splendour of Israel (1) was born of this marriage (2) whilst the family were still living in Moravia. Then my great-grandfather (Rabbi Ephraim) moved to Buda that is Ofen, the capital of Hungary, with all his family, including my grandfather Rabbi Yaakov. For some years Rabbi Ephraim was Av Bet Din of that important community, a position to which he brought great prestige. His children and grandchildren married into the most affluent families of Ofen while he taught Torah with such success, that his reputation spread throughout Turkey and Eretz Yisrael and many great Rabbinic authorities addressed their Halakhic problems to him. While my father was still of tender years, he studied Torah assiduously at the feet of both his father (Rabbi Yaakov) and his grandfather (Rabbi Ephraim) and already evinced a fine intellect and prodigious memory. As a young man he went on to Salonika to study the methodology of some eminent Sefardi scholars who lived in the city and became particularly attached to Rabbi Elijah z"l (3). Then my father returned to Buda (4) where he enjoyed the reputation of a great Talmudic scholar although he was very young. Indeed, among my father's letters I found some correspondence between him and his

CHAPTER TWO

grandfather, Rabbi Ephraim, covering the period of my father's stay in Salonika. In his letters, Rabbi Ephraim exhorted his grandson to sit assiduously at the feet of the eminent Sefardi scholars, to be closely associated with them so as to appreciate their particular approach to Torah studies and when he (my father) returns home, to make sure he brings with him some example of their novellae. During these exhortations Rabbi Ephraim showers my father, z"l, with compliments and laudations befitting scholars of the highest repute.

In reality, even as a young man, my father was impelled by a Divine spirit, so that he wrote extensive Responsa on sheets of foolscap. Two of these which were concerned with interpretations of Scripture, are still stored away and presumably, because of their prolixity, my father did not include them in his published Responsa. For several reasons, even I found it difficult to study the latter extensive Responsa. Firstly, I came across them at an inopportune moment. Secondly, they have been handled by other people over the years, so it is possible that part of them was missing. And finally, they are written in Spanish which I can read only with some difficulty. Moreover, if to all these factors you add my preoccupation with many problems, you will appreciate why these Responsa have been a load on my mind. I was therefore compelled to lay them (the Responsa) aside until the "saviour" came and brought them out of limbo. This was a certain Hirschel of Glogau who pressed me to hand them over to him so that he would have the honour of publishing them. Finally, I acceded to his request.

My father was a handsome man besides being pious, even as a youth. Consequently, many important men desired to negotiate marriage between him and their daughters. Ultimately he was betrothed and married to the daughter of a very wealthy man of the community of Old Buda who was generous to my father so that he became one of the most affluent men of Buda. He (my father) then accepted the rabbinate of Sarajevo, Bosnia, a community of many exceedingly affluent people. When Buda was captured from the Turks by the Emperor's forces (5) the entire Jewish community was taken prisoner. My grandparents, with their feet in fetters (6), were taken to Berlin by the Prussian general in whose area they had been captured, but there they became separated. My father however, managed to enter the besieged city of Buda and, miraculously, to leave it. A cannon-ball smashed into his house killing his wife and child at the very moment my father was in an adjoining room. He emerged unscathed, which was indeed a miracle affected by God's mercy! He (my father) was then able to flee the city. It was at that period that my father wrote the responsum which later appeared in his published work (7).

It (the responsum), was in reply to a problem concerning the return of dowry to the family of a woman who had been killed, together with her young daughter, as a result of the bombardment of Buda by the Imperial forces. This incident occurred at a time when the local legal ruling regarding the return of dowries was valid (8).

It was after this that my father was appointed to the Rabbinate of Sarajevo and he served that community until the end of the siege of Buda. In Sarajevo he was highly venerated, but when the city was attacked and besieged by the Emperor's (Leopold I) forces (9) and my father learned that his parents had been taken prisoners, he left Bosnia and went to Germany.(10) Throughout that long and arduous journey he would not accept any material aid, although because of his great reputation, he was welcomed in which ever town he set foot. Nevertheless he managed to survive with the paucity of means at his disposal. When he arrived in Venice he was the guest of the pious and renowned scholar Rabbi Samuel Aboab z"l (11) who showed my father the greatest courtesy and affection. It was in Venice that he (my father) found himself almost penniless but was miraculously aided by a certain Hungarian who was in debt to my father whom he met at some hostelry. The debt was repaid in full so that my father had no need to abandon a pious characteristic which he had cultivated from his youth, that is to spurn the bounty of human beings. This conforms to our Sages' observation, "God assists one to follow the road he wishes to pursue".(12) For indeed, God was with him.

CHAPTER TWO

From Venice my father continued to Ansbach (13) where there was an unseemly incident with a well-known man of wealth. My father was to some extent compelled by Divine decree to come under this man's authority. He now requested my father to permit him to contract a marriage prohibited as incest of a secondary degree (14). Previously this person had sought such a permit from several rabbis and by dispatching an agent (for this wrongful act) (15) to Poland and the agent being well equipped with money, he had succeeded by financial consideration in persuading some of the local rabbis to release him from this prohibition. A few of these rabbis signed the release after receiving handsome gifts, while some acceded to his (the man's) request on the basis of false facts which the agent had presented to them. Now, because of the great respect in which my father was held by that community (16) the man entreated him to subscribe to his release from this rabbinical prohibition. He (the man) wanted to shake my father's hand on the assumption that he was agreeable, but my father dismissed him with a powerful rebuke because he (the man) had had the effrontery to make such an improper request.

The outcome of this incident is well known. For after the man had married the woman (prohibited to him), he was struck with severe paralysis so that it seems Divinely ordained that they (the man and his wife) should be unable to pursue a normal marriage relationship. This was a great Kiddush Hashem (17) for it is indeed quite evident that any infringement of a ruling of our Sages carries a more severe penalty than an infraction of an act proscribed by the Torah. For we daily observe people flagrantly transgressing the Torah, for example by the practice of usury (18), or by robbery (19), extortion (20), the taking of false oaths (21), etc., yet the Holy One, blessed be He, shows forbearance, suffers the insult (to Himself) in silence and does not exact punishment in this world. On the contrary, He pays them (the sinners), their reward to their face to cause them to perish (22). But regarding any infringement of the prohibitive measures or ordinances of our Sages, He is not so liberal or patient, for punishment is not delayed! This is to indicate how beloved they (the Sages) are to Him, "for all their words are like coals of fire" (cf.Pirkei Avot 2:15). Hence we often find that God acts more stringently concerning the reverence due to the righteous than to Himself. Examples of this often occurred and can be appreciated by any Jew who has studied history and who therefore realises that events are not fortuitous. You (the reader) will understand this (fact) more clearly as we continue with our narrative viz. that one who transgresses any ruling of our Sages ultimately suffers either an untimely death, poverty, or terrible suffering which are far worse than death.

MEGILAT SEFER

⊂ҕ ଛ⊃
CHAPTER THREE
⊂ҕ ଛ⊃

Let us now revert to my father's biography. Having left Ansbach, my father z"l v(1) journeyed to Prague with such a growing reputation that Rabbi Yaakov (Reischer)(2) Av Bet Din of Bohemia, wanted my father to marry his daughter Shifrah who had a considerable dowry, but my father declined because she was a widow. He then continued to Berlin and though quite a number of wealthy men who had learned of his great reputation earnestly sought his hand on behalf of their daughters, particularly some affluent men of Hamburg, he was not concerned with acquiring wealth but preferred a member of a noble family. Consequently my uncle R.Ze'ev z"l, arranged a marriage with his sister, the daughter of my (maternal) grandfather the eminent Rabbi and Av Bet Din of the Three Communities, (3) viz. R.Meshullam Zalman Neumark (Mirels) z"l (4). This lady was my pious mother Sarah, z"l. Indeed my mother, an intelligent and deeply sincere religious woman, proved to be a wonderful wife to my father. She was a descendent of the renowned Mirels family which emanated from the circle of the early Orthodox community of Vienna. This family was replete with respected and munificent individuals who were men of deep piety in deed and

CHAPTER THREE

thought as well as being outstanding Talmudic scholars. For these reasons all the eminent scholars of that intellectual generation sought to become attached to the family by marriage, for they (the family) had attained great renown in Torah learning, religiosity, social activity, and general affluence.

My maternal grandfather spent many years of his life in peace and tranquillity as the Rabbi of the Three Communities and used his position with such equity and wisdom that in his day the Communities' affluence and reputation grew rapidly. He (my maternal grandfather) was privileged to see more than one hundred and fifty descendants, whilst a fifth generation was born in Lithuania. Indeed, all my mother's brothers and brothers-in-law were outstanding in both Torah-scholarship and communal activity. Some became Rabbis of communities and others were lay-leaders in Poland and Lithuania. Indeed they were active everywhere and their reputation illumined Jewry.

In Altona my parents, z"l, had five sons and five daughters who are all, thank God, well and flourishing in the present year (1752). May God prolong their days in peace and tranquillity. The Almighty enabled my father to build a truly Jewish home in Altona and to establish a large Bet Hamidrash that is a Kloiz (5) the foundations of which were laid by some important and affluent members of the Three Communities. The purpose of this Kloiz was to disseminate the study of Torah Lishmah.(=for its own sake) My father attracted students and prominent Rabbinic scholars from Poland and Lithuania to his Kloiz and there they studied Torah with great assiduity.

Day and night they studied Talmudic texts with Rashi and Tosefot, the tomes of the decisors of the Halakhah as well as Aggadic texts, so that they became fully conversant in Torah and its ancillary studies. Indeed, under my father's aegis they completed the whole of Shas (6), the Turim (7), the Tenach (8), the Midrash and grammatical works on several occasions. Due to my father's influence they also assimilated concepts of self-restraint, strictness in religious observance, true piety and inner religiosity. For he (my father) z"l, hated unjust gains and even refused gifts which other Rabbis considered equitable.

Throughout his life he did not accept any gifts of money from individuals though on many occasions wealthy and affluent men wanted to make him rich. Many eminent people such as princes and dukes often brought him gifts of precious silver and gold jewels but they were disappointed, for he declined to accept anything. No one could possibly recount his activities, indeed they were unimaginable unless one had seen him and been in his company. Just at the time of writing there are some elderly gentlemen who attended upon him (my father) and remember his deeds, his religious conduct and his Torah studies. These men who, were his friends and acquaintances in years gone by speak of his reputation and the memory of him with passionate joy, for never has his like been heard of or seen in these parts (Germany) for many generations. Thus, he attained a high standard in Torah and ancillary studies which he both learned and taught, for all (his) endeavours in these fields were regarded as a religious duty and not for the purpose of social advancement or for public acclaim. Indeed, his main purpose and desire was to magnify the honour of his Creator and to firmly establish the pillars of Torah (study) with all his heart, soul and might. He possessed a lion's heart, delivering the oppressed from the power of the oppressor, nor was he a respecter of persons in Torah-matters, but fulfilled the precept "You shall not be afraid of the face of any human being". It was due to the latter characteristic that he always found some opposition from certain powerful personalities in the community (Altona), a topic with which, God willing, I will deal shortly.

This opposition was not based on any hatred of my father's personality, God forbid, (except for certain worthless and impudent contemporaries) for everyone acknowledged him to be a man of God. But the very reason they (the opposition) feared him was that he showed no partiality for anything that was unjust. This however should not cause any astonishment, for a person who would not accept any gold or silver, or the most precious jewels in the world would obviously show no favour in pronouncing judgement but only

CHAPTER THREE

do "that which was upright in the sight of God." (Deut.6:18) What however is indeed astonishing is that he (my father) was not consumed by a passion for material things or by a tendency to love money which is the answer to almost all our needs, seeing that he was burdened with sons and daughters whilst his income was so paltry.

For as Rabbi of the Kloiz his fixed annual income was sixty Reich Thalers (9) yet his basic expenditure was far more than that amount. Moreover, my mother never failed to have a child almost every two years and my father was particularly delicate, physically frail and of such a weak disposition that he could not eat any heavy foods.

Consequently, he accustomed his children not only to avoid delicacies so that their natures should not be turbid nor their intellect dense, but he also withheld heavy foods from them as well as luxuries. He subsisted on the basic necessities so as to be independent of human charity for none had such trust and faith in God as he. I will relate only one story (among many) which illustrates his hatred of human beneficence. It once happened that the highly esteemed philanthropist, Herz Hanover (10), visited Altona. It was well known that he was an extremely wealthy individual being worth many hundreds of thousands of Reich Thaler besides the fact that he, was very generous with this wealth and held genuine Torah-scholars in high esteem. He paid a visit to the home of my father z"l, to learn something of his (my father's) greatness as a Torah-scholar and his religiosity. Herz Hanover spent several hours with my father discussing his (Hanover's) affairs and listening to my father's advice. Finally, he asked my father to study Torah for one hour daily on his behalf for which my father would receive payment. This proposition would not have involved any effort or hardship nor would it have been demeaning, for in any case he (my father) zealously studied Torah unceasingly, both day and night, although this was not public knowledge. Therefore all my father needed to do was to say, "I agree", and then he (Hanover) would have plied him with wealth.

But just listen to his (my father's) reply! He said, "God forbid that I should do this, i.e. to study Torah on behalf of another person for monetary gain. My study of Torah is an expression of love for my Creator, to acquire a knowledge of the Torah in order to observe it fully. The respected guest then wanted to give my father a substantial gift, but my father raised his voice and said, "Keep your gifts and give your largesse to someone else." Herz Hanover left the house breathless, for he had failed to achieve his purpose viz. to make a generous gift to an eminent scholar. Indeed, our honoured guest was quite astonished at my father's pride and, later, in his hotel he remarked to Zekli Wiener, a lay-leader of Wandsbeck, "Can we find such a person as this, a man, in whom there is the spirit of God? I shall not rest my head on my pillow until I have made him wealthy." He (Hanover) thought of various schemes whereby he would make my father wealthy for he (Hanover) was the most generous man of his day. However, within the space of three months Herz Hanover, may he rest in peace, passed away.

Nevertheless, his resolution did not come to nought but was fulfilled to some extent, though inadvertently. For following his (Hanover's) demise, differences arose between his widow into whose hands all his estates had fallen, and his son-in-law who wanted them (the estates) to revert to him since he had married Herz Hanover's only daughter who was therefore, her father's sole heir. The widow requested my father z"l to settle the question and he consequently travelled to Hanover and having stayed there for a while made what he considered to be a peaceful settlement which was acceptable (to both parties). My father was given over one thousand Reichthalers to cover his expenses. Some years later when my father passed through Hanover on his way to assume the Rabbinate of Amsterdam (1710) the parties (to the previous settlement) again sought his advice, just as though they were seeking Divine guidance. For they had found his first arbitration most effective, but now other differences had arisen between them so that as he was passing through Hanover they wanted him to settle matters so that there should be no further trouble. Again he, effected that which was requested of him and was given all his expenses. Unfortunately the parties did not heed the advice he had given so that subsequently the situation deteriorated. Having regretted that they had not followed his sound advice the

CHAPTER THREE

parties sought his assistance yet a third time. This happened when he had left the Rabbinate of Amsterdam (1714) and was again passing through Hanover. However, on this occasion they were unsuccessful as I shall describe later on but now I shall revert to the main topic of my narrative.

MEGILAT SEFER

CHAPTER FOUR

For nearly twenty years my father had a Yeshivah and Bet Midrash in the Kloiz of Altona through which he disseminated the study of Torah and religiosity. Its abiding success was acknowledged by a large number of people so that he attained a high reputation not only in the Three Communities but far and wide throughout many countries. Indeed, his impact was felt in Jerusalem. Many German and Polish Rabbinic scholars sent him their Halakhic problems that covered all aspects of Torah, practical decisions (on Jewish law and practice), altercations and difficulties that confronted them, and his replies (Responsa) were regarded as though emanating from the Sanhedrin itself. Even some Sephardi communities sought his Halakhic expertise, so that from him Torah went forth to all Jewry. He also had to deal with Halakhic problems and decisions that concerned individual members of the Three Communities and the Sephardi community of Hamburg, as well as with problems that touched on relations between various communities. In addition, as Rabbi of the Kloiz (in Altona) he played a key role in the (wider) community since he was the son-in-law of the Rabbi,(of the Three Communities) my most revered (maternal) grandfather, who was

CHAPTER FOUR

confined to bed for some years, so that all important problems affecting the communities were thrust upon my father's shoulders. He became a servant of the communities, but received neither salary nor reward. Indeed, he carried their burdens and encumbrances gratis, and even introduced measures for their religious welfare.

He was the first person to obtain kosher wine (for the communities) and so enable them to recite Kiddush and Havdalah. Previously no kosher wine was available, so to redress the situation he, (my father) sent people to Italy and France to arrange for the production of kosher wines. Henceforth, the best kosher wines were available in the communities, and at inexpensive prices. He also introduced an Halakhically-correct method of keeping Shabbat foods warm in the sealed ovens of the local bakeries. Before this people were lax in the observance of this practice and kept the Shabbat foods warm by placing them in hot ashes and consequently infringing a stringent halakhah of the Shabbat. Moreover, before he came to Altona people were neglectful in the production of Matzot to the extent that they may well have eaten Chametz during Pesach. My father therefore introduced a most important measure whereby wherever Matzot were baked, a learned and God-fearing person was to be appointed to supervise the production of Matzot according to the strict conditions of the Halakhah. Furthermore, in order to ensure that both rich and poor would equally benefit without imposing an additional burden on the poor who could not obtain bakers (since they were unable to pay them), he levied a small tax on every litre of flour (for baking Matzot) and a double Tax on the wealthy.

Despite this levy the rich obtained their Matzot far more cheaply than if they hired bakers independently. For with the proceeds of the tax the communities hired communal bakers to provide Matzot for both the wealthy and impoverished, these bakers receiving the same salary from both groups.

My father also abolished the impious custom whereby women, who had to purify themselves after child-birth, would wait several months before attending the mikveh. This harmful practice prevented them from the correct observance of the regulations concerning cohabitation with their husbands, a situation which had serious repercussions. Finally, he (my father) abrogated the prohibition of usury in which many had hitherto sinned. My father was a guardian of the poor and of anyone who was in distress, whilst he groomed the wealthy to increase their acts of charity and benevolence as his counsel was always heeded, particularly since he was so apprehensive for his own self-respect, seeing that God was with him and that he hated the beneficence of individuals. Moreover, since the communities were then enjoying such affluence that people cared little for money, they had so much trust in my father's piety and faith that many of the wealthy entrusted him with large sums of money for distribution amongst the poor whom he considered worthy of such charity. In this way these wealthy men were credited with performance of charity to its highest degree viz. the donor being unaware of the recipient and the latter unaware of the donor.

    These people (collectors) travelled annually throughout Germany, Bohemia, Moravia, Austria, Holland, England, France, Poland, Russia and Lithuania and obtained excessive funds from all these European communities, yet all this great wealth was misappropriated by these communal Robbers who devoured the property of the poor (of Eretz Yisrael). Consequently, the debts of the Ashkenazi poor (of Eretz Yisrael) have so accumulated that, for our sins, the settlement of the Ashkenazim in the Holy Land has all but ceased and hardly a single Ashkenazi now lives in Jerusalem (may it speedily be rebuilt!). Indeed, at the present time the Ashkenazi community of Jerusalem has been uprooted because of the heavy debts that its members have been unable to meet. In fact, an Ashkenazi, who recently visited the Holy Land was seized by an Arab creditor who wanted him to settle the debts incurred by local Ashkenazi Jews! Thus, instead of the latter becoming potentially rich, had all the vast proceeds which were collected annually been properly distributed among them, (but now) the Ashkenazi community (in Jerusalem) is small and poverty-stricken. My father however, in his role as a guardian of his people and always conscious of their needs,

CHAPTER FOUR

also turned his attention to the poor of Jerusalem and made every effort to fulfil his role in the arrangement to the best of his ability.

He sent the proceeds (of this charity), with which he had been entrusted, from Altona to a very wealthy and honest person in Leghorn who, in turn, was to forward the money to a scholarly acquaintance in Hebron. It (the money) would be entrusted to the latter with the utmost secrecy, so that the Arab inhabitants of Jerusalem would not learn about it. My father then wrote to the scholar in Hebron requesting him to involve himself in this important Mitzvah, also setting out how he (the scholar) should implement all the arrangements wisely and unobtrusively, so that the funds should be distributed amongst the Ashkenazi poor of Jerusalem in the best possible way. This would ensure that every poor person would receive the charity he required to meet his essential needs.

In addition, my father also requested the scholar (of Hebron) to perform this important Mitzvah in every aspect, which meant travelling to Jerusalem and seeing that each needy individual was given the right amount (of money). He (the scholar) was also asked to obtain a signed and sealed acknowledgement (of the sum received) from every recipient. The reliable delegate fulfilled his mission to the utmost of his ability. My father adopted the same procedure whilst he was Rabbi and Av Bet Din in Amsterdam, and I myself have seen receipts (stating the name of the poor and needy) which were posted to my father from Leghorn. I also observed the signatures of the recipients some of whom were impoverished (Rabbinic) students, some orphans and others widows. These receipts were signed and sealed by the individual recipient attesting to the sum (of money) received from the scholar (of Hebron) to whom the money had originally been forwarded from the places I have previously mentioned. Such a procedure had never been followed since the beginning of our Exile, and had our European communities initially taken the trouble to adopt such an arrangement, then the settlement of our Ashkenazi brethren in Eretz Yisrael would have been constantly strengthened, enabling them to establish viable communities and Batei Midrashim, and to expand Yeshivot for the dissemination of the study of Torah Lishmah in the Holy Land whose atmosphere is so enlightening. But above all, the Ashkenazim in Eretz Yisrael would have been able to study Torah assiduously.

In fact, there were certain Sephardi communities and affluent Sephardim of Amsterdam, London and Turkey who adopted similar measures to prevent charity-funds destined for Eretz Yisrael from being lost or misappropriated. As a consequence, their (the Sephardim's) Batei Midrashim, Yeshivot and communities have continued to flourish in Jerusalem, Hebron and Safed, enjoying undisturbed progress. In contrast, the sins of our generation have caused the complete dissipation of Ashkenazi charity (for Eretz Yisrael) with the consequent evil affects on those communities. For though a tiny remnant is still there, it is sorely afflicted. May the Almighty have mercy on them and on all those who are in Exile.

On several occasions, my father complained about this situation to eminent leaders of Ashkenazi Jewry and suggested they make a concerted effort to end this immoral activity and halt the machinations of those evil men. Indeed, he maintained that had such measures been adopted by those leaders, then our final redemption would have been hastened! His protests however, went unheeded. For almost every family comprised a charity-collector or was entirely involved in such activities. Furthermore, these families invariably comprised certain powerful members who both, protected and encouraged them (the collectors) to appropriate the proceeds of their collections e.g. to retain the proceeds of charity for their own personal advancement. Thus, vast sums of money have remained in the possession of these people whilst Eretz Yisrael constantly declines "without anyone regarding it" (Job 4.20) until the Lord will be jealous for His Land and have pity on His people for His name's sake.(Joel 2.18) Indeed, even in Altona, my father found the implementation of his scheme was violently opposed, particularly by a certain R..... who would have denied the community the benefits which accrued from the fulfilment of this important Mitzvah. Now the man's family wander about for a morsel of bread (Job 15.23), but

CHAPTER FOUR

no one offers them a crumb (Lam 4.4) nor comforts them (Lam 1.9). For this there are many who are truly sorry.

MEGILAT SEFER

CHAPTER FIVE

We now revert to my father's biography. I have mentioned just a few activities and characteristics of that man of God, for it would be virtually impossible to detail all of them. Indeed, such an exercise would require an abundance of writing paper, ink and quills and even then one would do scant justice to his great reputation. When I was quite young, I wrote a laudation of him and later appended it to my eulogy (at his funeral) which I entitled "Yesiv Pisgom". In short, wherever he lived he laboured for the benefit of the whole of Israel, and his assistance was sought by all who staggered under the yoke of hardship. Moreover, he was fully conversant with the greater part of the Written and Oral Torah, erudition which was coupled with a remarkable knowledge of Responsa literature, apart from the fact that he knew and could converse in several languages viz. Spanish, Italian, Turkish, Hungarian and German. "He could stand before Kings" (Prov.22.29) indeed, God enabled him to find favour with every administration under whose authority he happened to live. God willing, I hope to write briefly about this soon.

My father was a munificent person, so skilled in worldly matters and politics that many benefited from his counsel and

CHAPTER FIVE

practical wisdom. But above all, he was a holy man of God, most saintly in all his ways and humble in all his endeavours. He was an eminent and devoted Kabbalist being well versed in all the major works of Jewish mysticism, Tikkunim, and especially in the writings of the Ari, which he practically knew by heart. He possessed similar erudition in esoteric Judaism, in Tenach, Mishnah, Halakhah, Aggadah, the six orders of the Talmud and the principal decisors including the Four Turim. In addition, he was most erudite in most of the early and late Responsa, in Kabbalah, grammar, philosophy and many other disciplines, indeed, all aspects of Torah were at his disposal. Moreover, his style of speech and writing was most elegant as is illustrated in his published volume of Responsa. (In fact he, left a mass of manuscripts which for many years remained in the possession of strangers.) Originally they had been entrusted to R.Ephraim (z"l) who was to bring them to me, but he died in Lissa so they remained in the hands of people, with whom I was completely unacquainted. It was only after much investigation and cajoling that all the manuscripts were forwarded to me, but I still cannot tell whether anything is missing. Moreover, I was unable to look over them nor to put them in some semblance of order because of my preoccupation with so many things, particularly with the religious duty which I undertook, namely, compiling books and monographs on many aspects of our sacred faith which are of imperative need in these days and which the Almighty inspired me to undertake for the public good.

My brother-in-law, the Rabbi of Amsterdam, still has some of his (my father's) articles in his possession, especially my father's addenda to his (my father's) Responsa which were published in his lifetime.

I must also note that my father perused secular works and books of general interest whenever he, could spare the time. With further reference to my father's sterling religious qualities, he would not have altered his decision concerning any important matter for all the wealth in the world, and though he was of a happy disposition, he never indulged in levity, but was nevertheless able to converse cheerfully with anyone even though he was so God-fearing. He was beloved by all who knew him and they all regarded him as a man of great spiritual reserve and pre-eminence who practised moderation in speech, pleasure and sleep (cf. Pirkei Avot 6.6) and as a person who abounded in spiritual wisdom, religiosity ethics and humility, whose real interests never transcended the four ells of the Halakhah. Indeed his sole delight, both day and night, was God's Torah in which he meditated and through the love of which he grew in stature. Yet despite his zeal for the study and observance of the Torah, he attained renown among those who were close to him and who realised that all his actions were religiously orientated and devoid of any ulterior motives. It was for this reason that his friends and pupils were prepared to sacrifice themselves on his behalf, showed so much concern for his welfare and who devised ways whereby he could obtain a respectable livelihood and not be forced to abandon his high degree of piety to which he had adhered from his youth i.e. not to accept human bounty nor the gifts of anyone in authority. Indeed, he could never be moved from the firm resolve of not to sell his favours by the acceptance of largesse. For there were several affluent men who sought to emburse him and welcomed him with gifts of costly jewellery just as one presents gifts to a revered monarch. (Ps.76.12) but they failed in their main purpose.

Soon after his (my father's) marriage to my mother, z"l, he was given an experienced business-man as a partner. This was to enable him to zealously pursue his studies at the Kloiz whilst his partner would be involved in business with the capital he had been given. But it was not long before he (the partner) fled to Amsterdam having squandered all the capital, leaving my father bankrupt and virtually penniless. Consequently my father was so racked with worry that he was smitten with melancholia that was aggravated by the fear that he would become dependent on human bounty. His illness was so serious that the doctors despaired of his recovery if he remained in Altona. They therefore advised him to undergo a course of treatment at a famous spa situated near the Rhine. He followed this advice and journeyed to the spa for treatment with its hot-spring

CHAPTER FIVE

waters; this was between Pesach and Shavuot. (TB.Shabbat 110a) With Divine assistance he fully recovered from his illness.

It so happened that my father had in his possession a written undertaking that the father of the fugitive partner would be a surety for the money he (father) had invested with his (the fugitive's father's) son, the latter already being in debt throughout the community. The guarantor now fell dangerously ill and my father, feeling that the cause of the illness was due to his (the sick man's) involvement in his son's misdemeanour, tore up the written guarantee and forwarded the pieces to the sick man so that the latter should not take his son's flight too much to heart. Subsequently the man recovered from his illness.

MEGILAT SEFER

CHAPTER SIX

I, Yaakov ben Tzvi, his first son, was born in the middle of Sivan in the period I have just mentioned. My father gave me his father's, z"l, name but I have always called myself Ya'avetz which was indeed my father's wish (a fact to which I allude in the preface to my book "She'elot Ya'avetz). I had been preceded by three daughters which sorely disappointed my father who had almost despaired of having a son, having assumed that the birth of three daughters consecutively had established a chazakah (presumption).

[At this point Rabbi Yaakov Emden added the following footnote: When as a young boy, I once asked my father, the pious and renowned Gaon R.Tzvi, the glory of Israel, why he was called Tzvi, without any patronymic, he replied, "Is not Tzvi and abbreviation for Tzvi ben Yaakov?" He continued without any uncertainty, "if my son, you will one day become a Talmid Chacham and the author of books of Torah learning, you should then call yourself Ya'avetz."]

Immediately before my birth he had arranged for a mohel to

CHAPTER SIX

take his place in the event of the birth of a boy, for he, (my father) might still have been away. However, he managed to return home fully recovered a day or two before my circumcision, and he himself joyfully performed the ceremony. I pray that God will help fulfil the fondest dreams which my father held for me on that occasion and that with God's will I should never act in any way which would bring shame or reproach on my family.

To return to my father's biography. Although he had lost all his capital he did not change his attitude but managed to live in the strictest economy which was contrary to his nature and practice. Indeed, he found great difficulty in obtaining a livelihood, but thankfully there were at that time some generous people in Altona and Hamburg, liberal men who were consistent in their liberality (Isa.32.8). These people replenished my father's purse by taking paltry sums of money from him for certain business ventures. Within a short time they would return him more than double the original capital, but none of the profits came out of their pockets. For my father had forsworn them to refrain from this practice so that they were compelled to comply with his request. Thus, the Almighty blessed their efforts on my father's behalf. For example, if they took two hundred or three hundred Reichthalers from my father with which they bought a string of pearls or a similar item of expensive jewellery at a bargain price, they would bring the said item to my father saying, "we bought this with the Rabbi's money; it is an article which, with God's help, is likely to realise a handsome profit".

Some time later when they would come across a potential purchaser they would take the item from my father and having sold it at a very high price, they would ultimately hand my father eight hundred Reichthalers in lieu of the original capital outlay. These people who on numerous occasions acted on my father's behalf, came from the finest and most renowned families of Altona. First and foremost among them was one who was always the leader of any religious and charitable undertaking, the highly intelligent and scholarly lay leader, the venerable Moses Leibush. Both he and his family belonged to the founders of the community of Altona. He

MEGILAT SEFER

(Moses Leibush) was renowned throughout Germany, a true adornment of his generation, a man who had no peer among the lay leaders of his time. He had studied in the Yeshivah of the great and renowned Rabbi Heschel z"l in a period in which Poland enjoyed peace and tranquillity. This eminent personality was quick to recognise my father's, z"l, virtuous character as soon as he arrived in Altona soon after his marriage to my mother, z"l.

My grandfather was then very old and infirm and although my father was then of tender years, Reb Moses wanted the duties of the official Rabbi of the communities to be transferred to the Rabbi's son-in-law i.e. my father, z"l, since those duties were too onerous for my grandfather. R.Moses had proposed that my grandfather should continue to receive his usual salary and that the communities pay my father a separate salary for assuming the duties of communal Rabbi. Unfortunately, Reb Moses was unsuccessful in this endeavour owing to the opposition of certain elements which, in common with most communities, are always opposed to what is just and correct. Nevertheless, this renowned patron (Moses Leibush) endeavoured to establish a Yeshivah for my father (in Altona) and thus enable him (my father) to disseminate Torah-learning assiduously. He (my father) issued Halakhic decisions and, as I have already stated, was saddled with the more important communal business; all this was done gratuitously. Despite this his sustenance "came flying to him like a bird," (TB.Berakhot 63a) by virtue of the munificence of kind and eminent people, although their generosity towards my father did not affect their pockets. For even if they had so wished, they were not permitted perforce to, do anything for him (my father) which smacked of charity. But as I have already stated, they were instrumental in increasing his capital in that if they happened to come across some merchandise which they considered would ultimately be sold to produce a handsome profit they gave the opportunity to my father and wholeheartedly renounced their share of the profit. Indeed, even if the commodity was purchased at a bargain price they gave the business to my father and took nothing for themselves. May this be accounted to them as a righteous deed

CHAPTER SIX

throughout all generations, for they (I refer to the aforementioned eminent lay-leader Reb Moses together with his noble sons and sons-in-law) acted so magnanimously towards my father.

They were joined by the sons of our in-laws the eminent Rabbi M. Bron and his affluent brother Rabbi V. who acted so generously towards him (my father) when he sent him precious stones and pearls from London which he (Rabbi V) had bought with my father's capital. The sons of Isaac Falk, the renowned lay-leader of Hamburg, were also closely associated with my father, z"l, and were most kind to him. According to what I have been told, the aforementioned lay-leader allocated a considerable sum of money as a dowry for my father's first daughter, my sister, may she rest in peace. It was in this way that my father z"l, earned a sound livelihood for the maintenance of his family without having to rely on anyone's bounty.

Another way in which the eminent lay-leader Reb Moses z"l, assisted my father was in expending several thousand Reichthalers of his own capital to obtain wines from France and Italy. He entreated my father to make every effort to regularise this procedure so that wine should be produced in compliance with the regulations of Kashrut, by sending people from Altona to those countries and (by arranging) that all profits which ensued from this trade should go to my father, z"l. He (my father) helped maintain this trade for some years thereby fulfilling a mitzvah and, at the same time, gaining financial benefit. For he performed an important service for the communities by obtaining the finest kosher wines whilst receiving ample reward for his efforts. In later years the communities did not procure wines of such quality.

On one occasion a great deal of wine was lost because of the soldiers of the Swedish army, this was during a period of economic warfare. The latter had effected an increase in the price of wine to a hundred Reichthalers a barrel, but because the wine had been tampered with by gentiles my father gave orders that such wines should be poured away and the barrels smashed. For he had no desire to sell these wines to gentiles and thus benefit from such transactions. Yet even this loss didn't weaken his determination to gain an honest livelihood by his own efforts and in no way to rely on human bounty even though his annual salary as Rector of the Bet Hamidrash and the Yeshivah was a paltry sixty Reichthalers whilst his basic requirements, seeing that he had to raise a large family, totalled one thousand Reichthalers per annum.

      Nevertheless, as long as his elevated presence abided here (in Altona) the community was blessed. The economic activities of the community constantly expanded and commerce increased so much that the number of rich grew apace. Indeed, in his (my father's) day the affluence and prestige of the Three communities advanced to such a degree that money had little significance, and this affluence daily exceeded that of all the other German communities. This was the situation until my father left Altona, but subsequently the people of God went in to economic decline (cf. Jud.5.11) as I shall explain later. Assuredly, the merit (of his presence), his studying Torah Li'shmah and his religious conduct, induced the abundance of God's favour and blessing to this locality. (cf. Deut.33.23).

CHAPTER SIX

MEGILAT SEFER

CHAPTER SEVEN

Thus he, (my father) was beloved by all people far and wide even though they stood in great reverence of him, and respected him as a holy and godly man. One exception was a certain powerful individual of Altona, namely, the renowned lay-leader Behr Cohen, may he rest in peace. This person was virtually worshipped by the majority of the local community because of his great wealth and attainments. For he had arrived here as a very poor young man wandering around for a morsel of bread, but subsequently he became enormously wealthy. Moreover, he had no children until he was more than fifty years old, so that the community had hoped to inherit his vast wealth. Following the death of his first wife he married a second time and had a son, but then his second wife died so he married her sister and had sons and daughters through whom he experienced much happiness. He arranged important marriages for them for example his eldest son married a daughter of the important Viennese lay-leader Reb Samson, may he rest in peace. Behr Cohen prospered greatly in his old age, enjoying an abundance of wealth and social prestige; indeed, his like had neither been seen nor heard of in that generation. Consequently, the whole community were subservient to

CHAPTER SEVEN

him and obeyed his behest, especially since he was also something of a Talmudic scholar. Truth to tell, he also possessed some fine qualities of character, for example, he diligently pursued his Torah studies whenever he was free of business activities, and established a Bet Midrash in his home and graciously maintained those who studied there with all their needs.

Moreover, his home was the source of charity and kind deeds towards the local poor. Essentially however, these acts of charity emanated from his respective wives and particularly from the last one who performed many acts of kindness unknown to him (her husband) who indeed, was neither extravagant nor liberal by nature though his abundant wealth compelled him to avoid being avaricious. It would therefore seem that even if he so wished, his beneficence would not be proportionate to the great degree of his wealth. He (Behr Cohen) was also an elder who was respected, by the governmental authorities, so that whether it was for their benefit or not, the members of the community of Altona were subservient to him and feared him, for not only was he virtually in charge of the community but he controlled a group of individual business men and merchants who obtained their goods (through him) on a credit basis. Consequently, a person who was in his disfavour found his livelihood endangered even though that particular person may have been on sound relations with the most prominent merchants and creditors. Needless to say (his influence) also operated in the sphere of tax-assessment, and he imposed a high or low assessment according to his caprice.

(Similarly) he would elevate a person whom he favoured whilst he would demote anyone who incurred his disfavour, even though the latter held an eminent position or office (in the community). Moreover, should a person have shown any consideration for the victim then he (Behr Cohen) would exact vengeance and persecute that person for failing to bow to his (Behr Cohen's) authority. Hence Behr Cohen was an exceedingly overbearing communal leader. This powerful individual though (overtly) acknowledging the eminence of my father, z"l, secretly opposed him, even though publicly he displayed great affection towards him (my father). This was because my father neither flattered him (Behr Cohen) nor demonstrated any partiality towards him, on the contrary, he publicly admonished him when he (Behr Cohen) behaved improperly.

There was another family in Hamburg called Fuersten, amongst whom there was a large number of wealthy men. They were however, sadly deficient in Torah-culture as well as in good deeds, all of which was virtually an abomination to God. However, to hide their shame and cover up their misdeeds this family was ostensibly attached to Judaism. Now Israel Fuersten arranged a marriage with the family of the distinguished and renowned Talmudic scholar Rabbi Suesskind Rothenburg, may he rest in peace, who presided over the Bet Din of the community of Witzenhausen and subsequently of Lublin.

> *[Editor's note: According to R.H.Dembitzer "Kellilat Yofi" page 92b (Cracow 1888) R.Moses' father was Mordechai Suesskind Rothenburg.]*

Eventually R.Suesskind's son, the great and distinguished Rabbi Moses married the daughter of Israel Fuersten, the latter however ultimately lost all his wealth in business and found himself in dire poverty, as I shall explain shortly. These two families sought to promote Rabbi Moses and to demote my father, z"l. Following the death of my maternal grandfather the eminent scholar and Av Bet Din, Rabbi Zalman Neumark (Mirels) z"l, the members of the Three communities turned to my father, the son-in-law of the deceased Av Bet Din, and immediately appointed him President of the Bet Din and their spiritual leader i.e. Rabbi of Hamburg and Wandsbeck which were then two separate communities. Thus, soon after the interment of my maternal grandfather z"l, the (representatives of the communities) came to him and proclaimed, "long live our Master, our Rabbi!"

But in Altona there was his adversary Rabbi Moses

CHAPTER SEVEN

(Rothenburg), the son-in-law of Israel Fuerst who, together with his family, had great influence (in the community), for they were affluent and powerful having made common cause with the most influential Behr Cohen. This caused a division in the community, with one half supporting my father z"l, and the other half R.Moses (Rothenburg).

Finally, they agreed that the Rabbinate of Altona should be shared between the two Rabbis, each having authority for six months (in the year). Thus my father was Rabbi of the two communities (Hamburg and Wandsbeck) and shared the Rabbinate of Altona. This arrangement continued until the above-mentioned R.Moses became involved in a scandalous situation, for he participated in a business transaction in which he had obtained a large a mount of goods on credit but had finally become bankrupt. My father now no longer wished to adjudicate together with him (R.Moses) on the Bet Din because of his (my father's) own particular reasons that he stated in a long explicit responsum. An additional reason (for my father's relinquishment of the Rabbinate of Altona) was the death of Mendel Wiener, may he rest in peace, who died on a Shabbat whilst under arrest.

That the latter was cruelly imprisoned was due to R.Moses who was his (Mendel Wiener's) creditor. It was because of R.Moses that Mendel Wiener was arrested by the gentile authorities and was so harshly treated that he died (in prison). However, as far as R.Moses was concerned he had the support of that powerful individual I have already mentioned who whole-heartedly supported them (R.Moses and his family). This was not because he (Behr Cohen) was an admirer of R.Moses but because he was an enemy of my father. Not that he hated my father in his heart God forbid, but because he (my father) showed him no partiality in adjudication thus fulfilling (the Biblical injunction),"You shall not be afraid of the presence of any person". He (my father) showed him (Behr Cohen) no special favour but simply regarded him as one of several lay-leaders. Hence he (Behr Cohen) was afraid of my father. This is what Behr Cohen, may he rest in peace, told me privately when I was a guest in his house, and the following were his very words when he mentioned my father z"l: "I was fully cognisant of the high degree of Torah-learning which your father, z"l, possessed. He was indeed unique in his generation, but he had one failing, he knew his own worth, which says a great deal. He therefore did not highly esteem any other person though he always spoke respectfully to him. Thus Behr Cohen tolerated (my father's esteemed position) since he knew that my father would not show him any partiality which was characteristic of the majority of the community including the Bet Din and scholars for the fear of him (Behr Cohen) made them behave in this way. But this was not characteristic of my father who never thought in terms of fearing any human being.

For his idea of adjudication and communal activities was to treat everyone with equal esteem. It was for this reason that Behr Cohen was not one of his (my father's) followers and was therefore unwilling to allow my father to be the sole Rabbinic authority of the community since he (Behr Cohen) obviously knew that my father would not show any partiality in anything affecting the community or towards any individuals.

That he (my father) wouldn't favour any eminent person was a fact which he (Behr Cohen) had already learned from past experience, (in the period) when his (my father's) father-in-law, my revered grandfather was the Rabbi of the Three communities and my father had assumed his (my grandfather's) Rabbinic duties because of his old age. For on one occasion (in that period), it was on the Eve of Yom Kippur, he (my father) sent for Behr Cohen and when he came to our home my father reprimanded him for his improper behaviour towards certain people whose livelihood had been jeopardised by his (Behr Cohen's) slanderous remarks about them when he denigrated them among the affluent of Hamburg who granted credit to merchants. Indeed, many people complained of the way in which he (Behr Cohen) caused privation to others, apart from themselves, by destroying their means of livelihood. They had informed my father z"l of these facts and it was for this very reason that he (my father) strongly rebuked him informing him of the serious complaints which people had made against him (Behr Cohen) and strongly warning him

CHAPTER SEVEN

to abandon such practices and that if he disobeyed he would bring misfortune on himself and his family. Indeed, my father expressed many admonishments whilst the above-mentioned affluent person listened to everything in silence but retained his hatred (for my father).

Thus, on this occasion Behr Cohen publicly opposed my father, z"l, and so prevented the important Rabbinate of Altona from becoming a decisively inherited position. Consequently, when my father, z"l, refused to sit with R.Moses Rothenburg to adjudicate (in any litigation), the Communal council of Altona sent two lay-leaders as emissaries to my father, namely, Joel Shaw and Elijah Falk, to warn him that if he refused to adjudicate together with the aforementioned (R.Moses Rothenburg) he would no longer be their Rabbi. My father however paid no heed to them nor their message but immediately left the great synagogue of Altona which he had attended from the period he had been appointed to the Presidency of the Bet Din, following the death of his father-in-law R.Zalman Neumark (Mirels), and returned to his former respected position at the Kloiz. To this very day the Yeshivah (Kloiz) is still functioning though a Rector has still to be appointed, following my father's departure from the community; so that at present the Yeshivah exists as a body without a head.) My father's sole position now was Rector of the Kloiz, and none of his well-wishers, friends or relatives could make him change his decision which was based on Torah (principles), for he was already convinced that the whole of the above-mentioned affair was wrong and unjust.

When the two emissaries returned to their associates in the Council-chamber to report on their mission and informed the Council of my father's decision and of his highly dignified reaction, they wavered in their resolution.

For when these communal leaders learned of my father's conduct they were most aggrieved and felt most ashamed of their own behaviour, particularly when they realised that their action did not reflect to their credit since they had planned to dismiss my father, z"l, from his eminent position for no apparent reason. (They were aware) of the widespread reputation of my father and how for many years he had brought renown and honour to the community. Nor indeed, had they found the slightest hint of anything untoward in his behaviour. They therefore cast aspersions on Joel Shaw, which was tantamount to saying that he had defaulted in his mission (to my father) in changing the statement they had (originally) charged him to make to him (my father) since he had added of his own accord the statement to the effect that they (the Council) would dismiss my father, z"l, from the local Rabbinate if he persisted in his obstinacy.

Hence, in Joel Shaw's presence they denied that this message had come from them or that they had entertained such a threat. (They claimed) that they had sent Joel Shaw to entreat my father to sit (for adjudication) with R.Moses Rothenburg as he had done hitherto, but that they had no intention of showing any disrespect to him (my father). This is the statement they wanted Joel Shaw to state (was their original intention) and to offer as an apology on their behalf. For they were most afraid of being "burned by the burning coal" (see Pirkei Avot 2:15) of my father, z"l, since there had been several situations which illustrated that no one could make disrespectful remarks to my father without avoiding punishment. For the Holy One Blessed be He demanded a heavy price (for such conduct) and exacted punishment, even to the point of death. Consequently, when these people saw that the afore-mentioned commission had proved fruitless, they deeply regretted their behaviour (realising) that no Jew should be involved in an action to dismiss from his eminent position such a saintly and scholarly man like my father who had no peer amongst his contemporaries. Hence, they (the lay-leaders) feared for their lives at this conduct which would "render them a derision among their enemies" (Ex.32.25). Thus, it would be in their interest that my father should not abandon his Rabbinate too quickly.

It was for this reason that they wanted to deny the statement with which they had charged their emissaries and thus protect themselves from this potential danger. Hence Elijah Falk the other emissary, did as they wished and deliberately contradicted his fellow-

CHAPTER SEVEN

emissary Joel Shaw, who had accompanied him on the delegation to my father. However, Joel Shaw being a truthful person, kept to his original statement arguing that he had not altered it but had carried out his orders and had taken care to convey the message with which he had been commissioned without any degree of modification, addition or reduction.

Nevertheless, (because of his alleged misdemeanour) Joel Shaw was fined six hundred Reichthalers which he was compelled to pay immediately into the Communal fund, which he gladly did. But besides this (fine) he suffered a cruel punishment for, not only was he expelled from the Communal Council-chamber but he was disqualified from being appointed to any communal office. Nor could he be a member of a quorum for the rest of his life. Moreover, he had, to occupy that section of the synagogue that was reserved for mourners and excommunicates. Consequently he conducted himself in the manner of an excommunicate for several years, and as long as Behr Cohen lived, Joel Shaw was not involved in any communal appointment. This affair has a considerable history and a complete written account of it remained with Joel Shaw and was placed amongst the records of the latter's archives. After this incident my father, z"l, became so seriously ill that there seemed little hope of his recovery, however he recovered after he had been bled. He then realised that the afore-mentioned affair had been the cause of his illness.

MEGILAT SEFER

CHAPTER EIGHT

I now revert to my father's biography. Within six months after the incidents that I previously described and which led to his surrender of the Rabbinate of Altona, he (my father) received a call from the (Ashkenazi) community of Amsterdam. Thus "the Almighty does not withdraw His eyes from the righteous" (Job 36:7). The letter containing the good news was brought to him on the eve of Shabbat Parshat Beshalach as he sat in the synagogue bedecked in a Tallit reading Parshat ha-Shirah from a Sefer Torah. My father, z"l, replied to the invitation with a letter in which he informed them (the community of Amsterdam) that they would have to increase the salary of the Rabbi who would serve them. For hitherto they were accustomed to pay their Rabbi a paltry salary of about five hundred gold pieces (per annum), so that the Rabbi who also presided over the Bet Din, had to depend on a most insecure income, namely, the gifts and benefactions of members of the community. But he (my father) would not accept any human bounty, as I have previously stated, yet his personal expenses were considerable, quite apart from the fact that the cost of living in a city like Amsterdam was high. They would therefore,(he wrote) have to supplement his salary which

CHAPTER EIGHT

would come from the communal treasury so that he would earn a comfortable livelihood. The community of Amsterdam agreed to his terms and to a salary of one thousand Reichthalers (per annum) e.g. two thousand five hundred Dutch Gilders. My father then moved from Altona to Amsterdam where he was received with great acclaim, for the community regarded him as an eminent personality whose (Rabbinic) authority had long been acknowledged by the community's Rabbinic scholars. Indeed, in the past they had submitted to him a variety of problems on Halakhic matters. Incidentally, my father, z"l, had been a protector and mentor to the Sephardi community in Hamburg when he had lived there and was regarded by them with particular affection since they were cognisant of his Godly ways, his wisdom and his sincere pursuit of Torah studies. Moreover, he was able to converse with them in perfect Spanish. For these reasons the presiding Rabbi of the local Sephardi Bet Din (Amsterdam) expressed a particular welcome to my father in a written laudation which preceded my father's arrival in the community.

On his actual arrival he was given an unprecedented welcome by the Sephardim of Amsterdam. In fact no other Rabbi hailing from Germany or Poland had ever been accorded the honour the Sephardim paid my father. For in the past all their eminent personalities used to hasten to visit him and paid the greatest attention to all his statements. Indeed, they did not desist from this practice until the Hayyun controversy reared its ugly head. But until that period all the members of the Sephardi community, both young and old, were beloved and befriended by my father, z"l.

They acted as his protector in the communal struggle amongst the Ashkenazim which was split into two factions, as I will later explain, with God 's help. For the prominent Sephardim were held in considerable repute by the secular authorities who paid the greatest heed to their advice. It was (the Sephardim) who informed the government that my father had no peer in Jewry with respect to wisdom and Torah learning and that he was unique in guiding the Community in equity and justice. That all this had occurred can be attested by the fact that my father was held in such great esteem by the secular authorities and that as long as he remained in Amsterdam the government showed no inclination to interfere in Civil law litigation involving members of the Ashkenazi community. This was despite the fact that at that particular period the Rav and President of the Bet Din did not have the authority to adjudicate in Civil law suits. Nevertheless the authorities adopted this particular policy (regarding my father), so that when the litigants of the Ashkenazi community appeared before them (the civic judicial authorities) they sent them away saying, "Go to your Rabbi for his adjudication." For they (the authorities) were aware of the profundity of his erudition in Torah, his hatred of any kind of bribery and his aversion to any judicial preferment.

Though my father, z"l, was involved in adjudicating cases involving members of the community, he did not accept the fee which was stipulated in the Rabbinic contract for providing such services. Instead, a special community-box lay on his table and when litigants appeared before him the fee which had been fixed by community as part of the Rabbi's income would be inserted into an aperture at the top of this box. Whenever the communal treasurer saw the box was full he and another official would empty the box and take the proceeds to the general communal treasury; this helped in meeting communal expenses. My father had promised to donate this particular income to the community soon after his arrival in Amsterdam. Moreover, he set up a Bet Ha-Midrash for the community where Torah students always pursued their studies. Thus much he had acquired on his own behalf went to the community. He won over a few important personalities among the charitable members of the city who consequently undertook to make annual donations towards the upkeep of this Bet Ha-Midrash. But my father spent much of his income towards maintaining the students of the Bet Ha-Midrash. For example all the fees which derived from Bills of Divorce and Halizah which the community had stipulated as part of the Rabbi's Income. As far as I can remember he was to receive twenty or thirty gold pieces for every Bill of Divorce or Halizah. Hence, my father did not directly benefit from any of the above-

CHAPTER EIGHT

mentioned income during his Rabbinate in Amsterdam. For the fees (for adjudication) were acquired by the officials for the benefit of the communal treasury, whilst the fees deriving from Bills of Divorce and Halizah went towards the maintenance of the students of the Bet Ha-Midrash which my father, z"l, had established in Amsterdam. Indeed, he allocated a particular room in his house for these students. For my father had rented a large house which he himself paid for, since the accommodation that the community had provided was too small to house his family. Consequently, he obtained a small rent from the lease of the Rabbi's house (allocated by the community) and rented a large house for which he paid a high rent (five hundred gold-pieces per annum), but towards which the community made no extra contribution. Nevertheless, he (my father) vacated a large room in this house to accommodate a synagogue and Yeshivah for the students of his Bet Ha-Midrash. The latter also slept there. Every day he delivered lectures to them on Tenach, Gemara, (with Rashi and Tosefot) and the rulings of the principle decisors of the Halakhah.

It was through my father's agency that the community gained a further source of income. For on the night following his arrival in Amsterdam the community had arranged a banquet in honour of the joyful event. My fathers however refused to eat anything until as he stipulated "I have examined the shochet's knife". Consequently the shochet was asked to show his knife to my father who (on examination) discovered that the knife had a notch the size of the tooth of a saw. (see Chullin) He then tested the shochet to see if he could feel what was wrong, but the shochet said the knife was in perfect order. From this incident it became known that the shochet, Lezer, who had held this position for forty years, had fed the people of Israel on "Neveilot" for he could not tell the difference between right and wrong (since he could not feel the notch). My father z"l, therefore dismissed the shochet on that very night and other skilled shochetim took his place. Now the previous shochet had received a salary of 8 gold-pieces for his work, but in addition there was the bonus he obtained from the gentile butchers who gave him (the shochet) the fat, the innards, the head and legs of the animal, all of which was worth a considerable amount. But subsequent to his dismissal and his forfeiture of his position as shochet, the community sold the rights of shechitah to a fully qualified shochet. This meant that not only did the latter not receive a salary from the community, but that he had to pay one thousand Reichthalers as a fee for his appointment. Thus, the arrival of that saintly person in the city made a deep impression, in that the income of the communal treasury increased. Moreover, the arrival of a great Rabbinic scholar brings a two-fold blessing, materially and spiritually. For my father had removed a great impediment from the community which at the same time, resulted in the latter's profit far exceeding the salary they were committed to pay my father, their Rabbi! Then a further income accrued to the communal treasury from renting the Mikveh. For previously they had to pay a salary to the person who supervised the Mikveh and who lived in accommodation attached to the Mikveh free of rent. Moreover, all the proceeds of the Mikveh went into that person's pocket.

But now, as a result of my father's advice, the community benefited by renting the Mikveh. Consequently the (financial) position of the community, was much enhanced, and everyone was delighted with my father, z"l, the newly appointed Rabbi, who was instrumental in effecting these important improvements. But this proved to be a mixed blessing. For apart from the beneficial effects of the shochet's dismissal, my father found himself surrounded by deadly enemies. For since that shochet's income was now sadly reduced it (his dismissal) affected many of his family circle and friends who were dependent on him and were maintained by his considerable income. They now conspired to persecute my father.
But a still greater evil occurred at the period of my father's arrival in Amsterdam. For at that time the community was torn by fierce dissension caused by the notorious incident of the two Chazanim Reb L—and Reb E --. Many lives had been ruined and much money lost because of this quarrel several years before my father's arrival (in Amsterdam). Indeed the situation had reached such an impasse that on Shabbat Shuvah (1709), a year before my father's arrival, during

CHAPTER EIGHT

the Rabbinate of Rabbi Leib Kalisch who presided over the local Bet Din, the two factions who contended as to which of the two aforementioned Chazanim should officiate in the Great Synagogue, came to physical blows. They threw or pushed lecterns at one another and it seemed they intended to cause fatal injury to each other. For our many sins this synagogue, a miniature Temple, became a den of terrorists on that particular Shabbat, a time, when the Rabbi should have been exhorting the congregation to repent. But because of the great trepidation and terror that affected the afore-mentioned Rav on that particular occasion he became seriously ill and, returning to his house he never recovered, for he was struck by a fatal illness. Subsequently, Rabbi Saul z"l was appointed Rav (of Amsterdam) but he died at Glogau as he journeyed to Amsterdam. Following this my father was appointed Rav in 1710. Then the sword of dissension still prevailed within the community, and the discord ascended to the very heavens, leaving little hope of peace. Unceasingly every one planned to destroy the very life of his neighbour. Indeed, they (the conflicting parties) had already laid their several complaints before the local authorities and expended a great deal of their own money as well as that of the communal treasury. The party supporting the Chazan Reb L—seemed to have gained the upper hand, since they were supported by very affluent contemporaries, in particular, the notorious brothers of the family Gokesch, powerful individuals who had obtained great wealth unjustly, but they were to meet an unseemly end. Above all, Aaron Gokesch who, in the latter period of his life was a notorious villain, which was a well -established fact. Indeed, many members of the community were their (the family Gokesch) dependants.

These powerful men fought with the weaker party who supported the Chazan Reb E—amongst whom there were respectable men, who were men of truth and integrity who always pursued righteousness, but who were weary of bearing the yoke of the above-mentioned oppressors, who lorded it over the community for irreligious motives. Indeed, they (the weaker faction) would soon have slept in the silent grave (Ps.94.17) since they could not withstand the insolent men who, in that struggle, expended much money taken from the communal treasury that was under their aegis. Apart from their comparative weakness the other faction was forced to expand their own money in litigation before the non-Jewish judicial authorities. Consequently the struggle went hard for them (cf. 1Ch.10.3) and they were almost brought to their knees and collapsed before the other faction who hated and spurned (cf.Is.66.5) them (the weaker faction) and who had risen against them to destroy them root and branch. Truly, the enmity that exists between two nations of diametrically opposed religions was not as great as the ever growing animosity which prevailed between these two factions supporting these rival Chazanim.

Thus when my father, z"l, was approaching the city (Amsterdam) the above-mentioned powerful party took the first step by sending their representative the Beadle Reb A—an eloquent man, with the object of making my father acquainted with their complaints that he was to stress. He (argued) that my father should associate himself with their cause and vindicate them. Moreover he (my father) should assist them in persecuting the other faction, eradicate them root and branch from the city and so prohibit them from being involved in any of the services of the synagogue. In addition, the deputy intimated to my father, the influence and power of the stronger faction, that they were wealthy, that they enjoyed popular support, and that they had the means of overcoming any opposition. Consequently, (the deputy stated) if my father supported their cause, stood by them and vindicated them, all would be well with him. My father (in reply) promised to assist them (the stronger faction) if right was on their side and that he would act according to the principles of the Torah, and that he would therefore have to hear the arguments of the other faction. Thus, when he, arrived in Amsterdam and heard the arguments of the litigating parties he would be in the position to judge between the parties, as indeed was his duty. However, after several days had passed the above-mentioned powerful faction realised they had not gained that which they sought from my father, for since he loved equity and truth he had no desire to deliver the

CHAPTER EIGHT

weaker party into the power of their opponents who would destroy them. Nevertheless, the stronger faction did not weaken in their efforts to win my father's support in destroying the opposing faction. For they promised to give him ready cash to the tune of twenty thousand gold pieces if he would side with them and, by supporting them, enable them to attain their victorious objective, viz. to prevail over the other faction by utterly destroying their status and so trampling them under foot.

On the other hand, if he still refused to bow to the wishes of the stronger faction he should know that they would become his enemies and in turning the struggle against him, he would not prevail. For (they argued) they had expended vast sums of money in the struggle against their enemies, that they had the support of a vast number of the community, that they had financial resources and that "the gates of the city were hard beset with their weaponry" (cf. Is.22.7) Consequently no one could resist them.

However they grew tired of their devices (and realised) that their efforts to win over my father, z"l, were of no avail. For they (wanted him) to change his whole approach and abandon his religious standards and behaviour. Yet all his life he had proved to be a father to the needy, a bastion of strength to the weak one who "searched out the cause of him he didn't know" (cf.Job 29.6) who "didn't meddle with them that were given to change" (cf.Prov.24:21) who showed no preference in adjudication nor respect from bribes and riches. Indeed he regarded silver as stones and "gold as dust" (cf.Job28:6). He feared no person, nor would he flag in the pursuit of justice for the poor and oppressed; all the dispirited found a sense of security in him; he broke the jaws of the wicked and plucked the spoil from their teeth (cf.Job 29:17). Consequently he regarded their (the wicked's) arguments as worthless, did not respond to their complaints and scoffed at all their offers and gifts. Nor did he show any compliance when they (the stronger faction) increased their bribes. Hence they prepared to battle against him and endeavoured to remove him from the Rabbinate (of Amsterdam) when he had completed just three years of offices. They turned their back on him,

MEGILAT SEFER

"those archers hated him" (cf.Gen.49:23) and even planned to besmirch his reputation with the local authorities. But "many are the thoughts in a man's heart, but the counsel of the Lord, that shall stand"(Prov.19:21). For these men who raised their hand against him found that their wicked plan fell on their own heads, since they were completely rejected from being appointed community leaders so that the evil they had planned happened to them. The latter were the three transgressors of Israel (cf.Amos 2:6) viz. Aaron Gokisch who reared a dog which he called Chacham Tzvi, Judah Prinz and Zalman Caparnes; these were the lay-leaders at that time. However, they lost their status during the period of holding office, so that the hand of the weaker faction prevailed since the secular authorities gave judgement in their favour they were victorious over the affluent and powerful faction. The authorities who could not be bribed gave an immediate order that three lay-leaders of the fullest integrity should immediately replace the former three. As for my father, z"l his Rabbinic contract was fully endorsed and an additional (clause stated) that he could not be removed from office. This was because of his great reputation even among non-Jews, for his scholarship and religious integrity was widely acknowledged.

Above all, the affluent members of the Sephardi community of Amsterdam fully supported my father, may his memory be blessed; at that time, and they were a powerful element in the city, having a close association with the local administration. Hence, the powerful faction in the Ashkenazi community lost their power to carry out their machinations against my father and they were no longer able to oppose him, for the Almighty had removed them from their position in the community, as I have described above. Nevertheless, this powerful group still behaved as wolves and bears towards him (my father) and kindled the fuel of contention and animosity beneath the ashes, so that the sword of discord did not rest peacefully. On the contrary their enmity grew because of the incident of the three lay-leaders, who were of little benefit to the community being men of puny moral status who had been stripped of their high position within one month and suffered the deepest humiliation in

CHAPTER EIGHT

being expelled from authority, during their very term of office, as I have already described. It therefore seemed they no longer had the power to harm him (my father) in any way, which was due to the leaders of the Sephardi community of Amsterdam who gave my father, may his memory be blessed, their fullest support. But the wicked are as turbulent as the sea, standing on guard and craving for the woeful day (cf.Jer.17:16) though their end shall be like a bitter day (cf.Amos 8:10) until sin reared its ugly head and Satan came and confused the world. This was the evil inclination, that snake, that abominable hypocrite Hayyun who confused both the Sephardi and Ashkenazi communities so that the community was divided on all sides. Nevertheless, at the outset every member of the Sephardi community was fully committed to their Heavenly Father. These were the people who had great affection for my father on behalf of whom every one would have given all the substance of his house (cf. Cant.8:7). They (now) came to my father, may his memory be blessed, so that he pronounce judgement regarding this hypocrite, a violent man and that he (my father) should thoroughly examine his (Hayyun's) worthless and defective book which was on the point of being banned because of its distortions.

They wished to rely on my father, may his memory be blessed, since they knew and acknowledged him as a man of true faith in whom resided both scholarship and prudence. From the very first they disqualified their own Rabbi, Solomon Ayllon (from performing this duty) since they already suspected him of Sabbataean leanings. This was because of a certain unseemly incident of a similar nature that had occurred before the present one and which was concerned with the writings of the heretic Cardoza, which were brought to Amsterdam a year before the arrival of Hayyun. These writings were in Spanish, and the whole Jewish community railed against them because of the many heretical opinions they contained made the reader's hair stand on end.

But their above-mentioned Rabbi (S. Ayllon) pronounced them religiously fit stating they were good, holy and pure. However, at that juncture (his pronouncement) was not effective, for the members of the (Sephardi) Council burnt them in his presence, for all these people comprehended these writings since they were written in their native Spanish tongue. Thus, henceforth the above-mentioned unreliable Rabbi was suspected of being identified with the false and offensive doctrines of Sabbataenism. Moreover, according to the "Milchemet Ha-Shem" and the "Shever Poshim" it is obvious that in the past he had been a Sabbataen and although he severed his association with them (the Sabbataeans) and reverted to traditional Judaism the germ of the heresy remained with him, so that it could be reactivated when that heresy recurred (Lit. "The like found its like and was aroused" TB. Eruvin 9a) Thus when the incident involving Hayyun occurred they (the Sephardim) did not want to rely on him (R.Ayllon) from the very outset, for they could not trust him concerning such an important and essential principle of religious faith. Therefore, by a unanimous decision they sent (representatives) to my father, may his memory be blessed, to learn his opinion and to act according to his advice and ruling. For he had a high reputation, and they regarded him as an outstanding authority in matters regarding the preservation of Judaism. They therefore handed the book to my father so that he should spend some time in examining its contents. For in a short time it had come in to their possession through considerable trickery as well as through some coercion, facts which one can conclude from reading the above-mentioned works. ("Milchemet Ha-Shem" and "Shever Poshim")

Thus they (the Sephardim) committed into my father's hands the sword with which to carry out sentence on that man (Hayyun) the enemy of God, who planned to seduce the whole of the Jewish community into his new-feigned religion and who had come forth to tear asunder Israel's ties with its ancient traditions. All these facts were brought to light in every Bet Din of Israel, both in the East and West.

All the latter thanked my father, may his memory be blessed, because of his great zeal for the Lord (cf.1 Kings 19:10) and because he decisively judged that troubler of Israel in banishing him from the territory of Israel. Following this incident many further examples of

CHAPTER EIGHT

his abominable deeds became known, in that he seduced and acted as Balaam in defiling the Holy Land that could not tolerate all his opinions (cf. Amos:10): all of this has already been published in several booklets. However, at that period Satan was dancing among the Sephardi community who still regarded him with almost total disgust when they came to retrieve the above-mentioned venomous book from my father, may his memory be blessed. They accepted his advice and acted strictly according to his behest in expelling the abominable Hayyun from their Synagogue.

But they then had a change of heart and so destroyed all they had (previously) constructed. For they came to hate my father, may his memory be blessed, turned their backs on him and refused to heed his advice in the execution of justice on that person (Hayyun). So that after they had acted in accordance with my father's, (may his memory be blessed) instructions and expelled Hayyun from their Synagogue with great humiliation, and rejected him as my father had ruled, they reconsidered the matter and thus subverted their constructive conduct by permitting him (Hayyun) to join their community and accorded him the highest respect.

The main reason for this (volte face) was because their above-mentioned Rabbi (Solomon Ayllon) who was a fellow conspirator of Hayyun, acted surreptitiously with the connivance of the latter. He visited every member of the (Sephardi) Communal Council in their homes, and throwing himself at their feet wept and implored their favour in stating that he too, had been at fault and had sinned but (asked) whether they hadn't the duty to pay deference to his position which also reflected their position (in the community). Moreover (he asked) where would they bear their reproach, or carry their shame, if they confirmed their suspicion? The status of the Rabbi of the Ashkenazim would then be above that of the Rav of the Sephardim, particularly since they (the Sephardim) claimed that they were far superior to the Ashkenazim! For (he argued) from the very foundations of the community that the Ashkenazim were subordinate to the Sephardim of Amsterdam since the latter were more numerous and influential because of their wealth. social-status,

MEGILAT SEFER

pedigree and quality of character. Moreover, they (the Sephardim) preceded the Ashkenazim (in establishing a community in Amsterdam) through the Marranos who fled from Spain and settled in Amsterdam shortly after Holland had won its independence. For when she (Holland) had freed herself from the yoke of the King of Spain so that all the inhabitants of that country had won their liberty, anyone, regardless of his religion, was allowed to settle there. It was from there (Amsterdam) that Marranos originally found respite through the agency of a Jew from Emden (Jacob Tirado) who brought them to Amsterdam, circumcised them and taught them Judaism. After them (the Sephardim) Jews hailing from Germany settled in the city. Consequently, the latter acknowledged the superior status of the Sephardim in that they should have precedence over the Ashkenazim in all things. This was particularly because of the affluence of the early Sephardi settlers who had brought their considerable wealth with them. It was for this reason that the local administration regarded the (the Sephardim) as important and wealthy men. On the other hand the original Ashkenazi settlers were of a comparatively lower social-status in terms of the contemporary assessment of wealth and its social importance.

But now, (continued R.Ayllon) terrors are turned upon them (cf. Job 30:15) for the whole system is about to be reversed, so that the superiors will become the inferiors, and the converse. This was the mode of speech adopted by that man (R.Ayllon) and so from the outset he deceived those people; who had been in accord with the Almighty with the flattery of an alien tongue (Cf.Prov.6:24) and with the profane mockeries of backbiting (Ps.35:16). He won their support when he asserted that although this in not according to the strict letter of the law nevertheless circumstances demanded this course of actions so that in order to protect their social-status and the honour of their superior community they should not accept the ruling of the Rabbi of the Ashkenazim to retract from their original action which had been completely correct, and that they should now show no partiality in religious matters. Thus, through weeping, supplications, pleas as well as grovelling and many tricks, through soft

CHAPTER EIGHT

words (flattery) they were seduced and prevailed upon to destroy their (former) constructive behaviour based on the original advice (they had received from my father). Instead of resting on firm terrain their feet were now immersed in mud, and soft talk destroyed the peak of perfection (cf.2 Kings 9:13) in that they agreed to behave in a way that was contrary to Judaism. The course of events as they occurred, the stratagems, the variety of unusual weapons, lies and deceptions which were employed in this affair are known and appreciated by those (who witnessed it) and are still alive. For they would remember all the details of that grievous event that occurred less than fifty years ago. Moreover, the affair was also divulged in many publications and tracts which appeared at the time of this grievous struggle, which lasted a whole year. Above all the renowned scholar Hagiz, may he rest in peace, who was the first to enter the fray, published (the whole course of those events) in his booklets "Milchemet Ha-Shem", "Shever Poshim" etc.

Again that I was moved to record this affair in this book was due essentially to my (desire) to acknowledge the wondrous acts and kindness of the Almighty, Blessed be He, both in the past and in the present. (For) the Father makes known His Truth to His sons. (Is.38:19) Moreover, what happened to the fathers recurred in the life of the sons. Hence we could not possibly state all the details of this affair as they really occurred. For these reasons I shall not involve myself in such a task, to record events that occurred more than forty years ago (that is since the appearance of "Milchemet Ha-Shem" and "Shever Poshim," etc.) Yet a further reason (for my reluctance to give a detailed account) is because then I was immature, even though I had begun to flap my wings like the acolytes, a state which would disaffect those who were not of a Rabbinic lineage. Yet I raised my voice, the voice of Jacob, just like junior Levites, and then included myself among a select group to record (in writing) a synopsis of the affair without deviating (from the truth).

For it has been my main intention beloved reader to present to you truthfully and sincerely, as well as to, fully publicise within the framework of this pleasant and genial book, the basic and central issues of this affair so that you should be saved from grievous obstacles; while (at the same time) to confer a blessing on you presently and that you should learn and inform (others) that which happened to my father, z"l, (in this affair) likewise happened to me in the Eibeschuetz affair. They are exactly analogous; what happened to the father happened to the son.

The latter committed the matter into the hands of the (leaders) of the Three Communities so that they should be acquainted with the issue and, the nature of the amulets. But later the superior faction prevailed through lies and evil deceptions (as in this affair), though twice as many were employed in the Eibeschuetz affair. Indeed, it is barely creditable that so similar an affair could have recurred. For by lies and deliberate false words, as well as his (Eibeschuetz's) pen that he wielded against me, they denied, God and profaned the reverence due to Him. Indeed, they exchanged the respect due to the Almighty for their respect of an earthly being which simply has the breath of life and which if snatched away, renders what remains a human-being in material form only. Thus in their folly their hand found the writing pen as a nest, in attributing to me statements which were untrue, and acting without feeling any sense of shame when they strove against the Lord (cf. Num.26:9) and acted arrogantly. Although some who were signatories (to the statements against me) had second thoughts and acknowledged their misbehaviour complaining that they had completely immersed themselves in the mire of folly right up to their foreheads. Hence, some did return to the Lord with all their hearts and might which is a subject I hope to deal with shortly, with God's help.

But to return to the main topic (my father and the Hayyun affair). The Sephardim desired above all to be victors, to attain their goal whilst obscuring their shameful conduct and to exchange the latter for reverence of their Creator. But when they realised they could not compel my father to change his mind despite all their deceptions and lies, they brought the matter to the secular court and sought its decision who was right. Woe to the eyes that beheld such conduct and to the ears which learned to what extent the desire for

CHAPTER EIGHT

victory prevailed over these people who had been reared in the religion of the Lord yet who committed our religious laws into the hands of the gentile courts so that they should adjudicate between Jews and that having weighed up the evidence they should give a decision in favour of one of the litigants! Eibeschuetz acted in a similar way; in fact his conduct was much worse. For he called upon a number of gentile professors from several localities to give evidence against us before the Emperor, may his majesty be exalted, so that he should decide that justice was with him (Eibeschuetz).

He actually behaved this way and published their (the professors' statements). One of the latter wrote to the Emperor stating that he was certain the above-mentioned (R.Eibeschuetz) was a true Christian! This was equally true of his teacher Hayyun, they wholeheartedly concurred in their conception of Judaism according to (their interpretation) of the Zohar. Thus the Emperor, may his Majesty be exalted, was duty-bound to deliver him (Eibeschuetz) from the power of his prosecutors because of his religious views, (just as he (the Emperor) was obliged to declare that the opposition to Eibeschuetz would have to be prosecuted since in opposing him they we were preventing him from converting to Christianity.)

Therefore, when my father, z"l, observed their obstinacy and that the Sephardim who were originally his admirers had revolted against him and had acted with such arrogance that the faction of Ashkenazim mentioned above, who now rejoiced at this calamity (cf. Prov.17:5) were now allied with them (the Sephardim) - "the mouse and the cat (when at peace with each other) had a feast on the fat of the luckless.(TB.Sanhedrin 105a) He (my father) was afraid lest there be a profanation of God since he would be compelled to divulge the fact that in a work published by an author who was regarded as a Rabbinic scholar and which had earned the approbation of some of the most eminent contemporary Rabbinnic scholars contained statements that were anathema to Judaism. Consequently he vacated his position and left the city in which he had acquired great reverence and moved together with his family whom he had earlier sent to the neighbouring community of Emden. It was in mid-winter that we i.e.

my mother, the Rabbanit with her children of tender age made the journey by ship, whilst my father, z"l, proceeded to London at the urgent request of the local Sephardi community who were most anxious to see him and take advantage of his revered personality (before he left for Poland which had been his intention) when that calamitous struggle and ever-growing enmity had begun in Amsterdam.

For they (the Sephardi community of Amsterdam) held my father in great repute. Moreover, he had won great renown (with them) since the time he was Rector of the Kloiz in Altona. For it was just about then that Chacham Nieto who presided over the Bet Din of the London Sephardi community had stated in a sermon on Nature that the latter was to be identified with the Almighty. This aroused opposition to him for there (in London) too, there were two contentious factions one of which as the enemies of Chacham Nieto was looking for the opportunity of discovering in him the germ of heresy. These persons now raised a scandalous commotion in the congregation about the above sermon, but they agreed to the idea of writing to my father requesting his adjudication that he should decide between the two parties and that they would abide by his decision on the problem.

Consequently they had written to him (my father) whose life was dedicated to the Almighty, and he remitted a responsum containing his decision on the problem. The latter can be found in his published work (Responsa of Chacham Tzvi Para.18). When later this highly reputable Responsa was published in a Spanish translation at a time when peace prevailed between the factions, the Council of the London Sephardi Community wanted him to be their Rabbi and to preside over their Bet Din. They promised him a high salary as well as many emoluments; for example he would receive five hundred pounds from the communal treasury and they would stand surety for another fifty pounds. This meant that his salary would be just below one thousand pounds sterling per annum. They hoped that this would be agreeable to him but he declined, arguing he was an Ashkenazi and wanted his children to be reared in Ashkenazi

CHAPTER EIGHT

practices. Moreover he was afraid his sons and daughters would assimilate the life-style of foreigners. For the latter reasons he had remained Rector of the Kloiz at Altona, which brought him an annual salary of only sixty Reichthalers. This had remained the situation until the death of his father-in-law who had presided over the Bet Din of the Three Communities. He (my father) received a similar call from the Sephardi community of Ligorno (Leghorn) inviting him to become spiritual leader and promising him a large salary, but he declined for the same reasons I mentioned above. (For) he was not dominated by ambition nor did he abandon his basic attitude, so that financial considerations did not make him surrender his religious principles to the smallest degree. He chose a strict observance of God's Torah both for himself and his family who might otherwise have fallen victim to an alien life-style.

To turn to the subject of my father's invitation from the London Sephardi Community. Because of this (the Nieto episode) and similar considerations, for he had acted kindly towards the London Ashkenazi Community in which a split had occurred over a get which had been issued by their Bet Din and concerning which the honourable Mordechai Hamburg had made an innocuous remark. The latter's enemies sought to destroy him over this slight matter, but my father saved him from two lions by whose teeth he (Hamburg) was on the point of being torn to ribbons. All these events are recorded in a booklet entitled "Ma'aseh Rav" (by R.Johanan b. Yitzchak Hoellischauer, London 1707) in which my father's kindness receives mention as does his long and unfading kindness to Mordechai Hamburg. When the London Community learned how my father was treated in Amsterdam and of his consequent decision to move elsewhere, they were most eager to see him and welcome his presence among them whereby (they felt) they would fulfil a religious duty. Consequently they looked forward to his visit before he left for Poland. He, z"l, accepted their invitation and travelled alone to London where he was received virtually as a royal personality.

For the leaders of the Sephardi community came to meet him in royal ships, whilst the wider community made long journeys in anticipation of welcoming him during his journey. Indeed, the whole of the great city of London resounded with the noise of the crowds. So vast a throng was gathered to welcome that their gentile neighbours asked them what was the significance of this event, why was this particular day so important, "has your Messiah arrived?"

Thus all the Sephardi and Ashkenazi communities apart from the affluent and prominent leaders accorded him unprecedented honour, each person vying with his fellow-Jew in his endeavour to show reverence and affection for him. They therefore paid early morning visits to his place of residence, the house of the prominent Jew, Joseph Levy, to enquire after his welfare, to bask in the splendour of his appearance and to revel in learning something of his scholarship. When these visitors left they blessed his host one hundred-fold, in that he had merited to have such a man of God staying with him. Moreover, many important personalities and powerful lay-leaders welcomed him with a variety of gifts (each according to his means). They wanted to make gifts of money, "to bring a present to the one whom they revered" (cf. Ps.76:12) merely in order for my father to receive their blessing, hoping, in return that they would receive a blessing from him. Indeed, they regarded all this as offering the first-fruits to a man of God. But he (my father) did not want to deviate from any one of his religious principles even in that difficult period, and he was therefore unwilling to accept gifts from any individual despite his precarious financial situation. For his purse was empty, and he even had to sell the silver-ware he had brought to Amsterdam for a little more than one thousand Reichthalers to maintain his family there. The reason for this was that his salary from the Rabbinate(of Amsterdam) though supplemented by fees for certain duties, proved insufficient to meet the excessive cost of maintaining his family. Moreover, the long journey that he now planned was an additional heavy imposition, since his family comprised more than twenty souls, that is adults, young and tender babies. He was therefore in need of much cash to meet these heavy financial commitments. Consequently, whilst he cast his burden upon the Lord (cf.Ps.55:23) and bowed his shoulder to bear the Almighty's

CHAPTER EIGHT

decree (cf.Gen.49:15), he accepted the gift from the whole of the Sephardi community which was brought to him in one purse and which amounted to five hundred pounds sterling. But the reputable Rabbi Aberle informed me (later) that had my father been willing to accept certain individuals' gifts which they were most eager to make to him and Rabbi Aberle had tried unsuccessfully to persuade my father to do this, for there were a number of affluent men each of whom wanted to him a gift of almost that very same sum (five hundred pounds sterling) e.g. three hundred, four hundred, or as much as five hundred pounds sterling, he could have gained considerable riches there (London) had he shown any dismay for the five hundred sterling he had received from the community in general. Yet he would only accept the above-mentioned sum from the lay-leaders of the Sephardi community that they presented to him on behalf of their congregation and this he accepted only out of dire necessity.

Following this my father left the London community who saw him off with as much reverence as they had greeted his arrival. In the same way, when in later years they learned of his passing, they expressed their reverence at his death. For they blackened the Ark, all the Synagogue was draped in black, and the congregation sat on the floor weeping and lamenting over him just as they would have done for a king or a prince.

There is another incident I should mention regarding my father's visit to London before his departure for Poland. Because of their abounding esteem and deep affection for my father the lay-leaders of the Sephardim requested that he leave with them a portrait of himself painted in Vermilion. This (they said) would be a fine momento and a token of the abiding esteem in which they held him. Yet however much they urged him he would not hear of it for he, z"l, regarded this as bordering on idolatry. But despite this they were neither silent nor desisted in their efforts. Finally, they succeeded in their endeavours and heartfelt desire by a remarkable ruse, which was carried out by an amazing artist who surreptitiously painted his portrait whilst conversing with him (my father), having set up his equipment in another part of the room. My father however, had no notion of this until the painting had been completed and then he discovered a portrait which was the very image of himself. In fact his friends and family found this portrait so remarkable that when I first gazed upon it in London (in later years) I recoiled, for it seemed as if my father was still alive. Copies were made of this portrait and sold at an excessive price, whilst some were available at the London Stock-Exchange. (see my observations on this subject in "She'elot Ya'avetz" No.171)

My father returned to his family from London just before Pesach and arriving in Emden he told us about the miracles which the Almighty had performed on his behalf, for he had experienced a hazardous sea-journey. He remained in Emden until winter had passed, and it was while he stayed in that city that my father, z"l, lost a young daughter. Let me tell you of subsequent events. Soon after Pesach my father journeyed to Poland with all his family. Earlier on he had sent my brother-in-law, Rabbi Leib to pave the way for him (cf.Gen.46:28). At that time the Rabbi who presided over the Bet Din of Prague, Rabbi David Oppenheim, was visiting Poland and my father rebuked him in the presence of all the lay-leaders who were present at that meeting, for assisting Hayyun and secretly supporting him. He (my brother-in-law) together with his family broke their journey at Hanover where they remained for some weeks, in fact till after Shavuot, as he was delayed by Sarhi, the widow of the deceased Herz Hanover.

The latter had planned to detain my father for several months so that he should help resolve certain perplexing problems that had arisen over her son-in-law with whom she was involved in difficult and important legal-problems. This situation was the direct result of her failure to take my father's advice. Originally she had acted according to such counsel and was therefore successful. Later however, she had pursued another course of action and accepted the advice of others who had their own particular approach. Consequently, the whole plan of action which my father had originally counselled her to pursue had fallen through. But now she

CHAPTER EIGHT

was most eager to detain him (my father) in Hanover and ploughed him with any amount of gifts to win his consent. He had already acceded to her request, but on the following conditions: he should be paid fifteen hundred Reichthalers for his being detained for four or six months, which sum he should receive within that specified period whether or not his endeavours on her behalf succeeded. In addition, if my father agreed to stay in Hanover and involve himself in the law-suit she had with son-in-law for the above-mentioned period, then she would be obliged to give him a present of one hundred ducats on the marriage of every one of his sons and daughters. It was on this understanding that my father acceded to her plea. However, this lady (Sarhi) made another unpleasant request of my father viz. that during the period my father, z"l, stayed at her house and was involved in seeing to her affairs, he should send his wife, i.e. my mother the Rabbanit, may she rest in peace, and the family to the community of a small town situated a few miles from Hanover. It was because of this request that the whole arrangement was cancelled. For my father, z"l regarded this condition as most untoward for he would never contemplate sending his wife and family away from him. He then observed that even if she (Sarhi) gave him all her wealth he could not accept this condition. Consequently he left Hanover and continued his journey.

His destination was Poland and while passing through Halberstadt the lay-leader Reb Benjamin accorded him considerable honour and gladly welcomed all his (my father's) for a stay of several days. It was in Halberstadt that he (my father) received a letter from Rabbi Michel (R. Michel of Glogau the author of "Nezer Ha-Kodesh") which contained the latter's critical notes to a responsum my father had given him (R.Michel) to study. My father could not find the opportunity of replying to these critical observations since he was involved with the journey, but I managed to get hold of the letter with the object of studying the contents and giving my reply, should I manage to find a pen.

From Halberstadt we came to Berlin and stayed with my uncle, the fine and saintly Rabbi Wolfe Merles, may he rest in peace, for several weeks. On continuing our journey we were confronted with increasing responsibilities because the army of the King of Prussia happened to be using our route. Therefore we were sometimes compelled to stay at an inn but, thank God, we were saved from any attack or mishap. It was in my uncle's house that I put my hand to writing a responsum to the criticisms of the above-mentioned Rabbi (R.Michel), but did not divulge this to anyone. However when we reached Breslau my father saw my letter and found time to study it with my above-mentioned brother-in-law (R.Leib). He was very pleased with it and kissing me on the head uttered the following sentence: "He kisses the lips that give a right answer" (Prov. 24:26). My observations on Rabbi Michel's criticisms are recorded in my published responsa viz. "She'elot Ya'avetz." I was sixteen years old at the time, but did not compete my responsum then since it was an extensive and highly involved topic. In fact it remained incomplete for several years until I had reached adulthood and had joined the Rabbinate. It was only then that I put my hand to it and with God's help, was able to complete it.

From Berlin my father with all his family continued to Breslau and stayed there for some months until after Sukkot. It was in Breslau that my father arranged a marriage for me. Although (in the past) some highly reputable young ladies sought my hand, some were even the daughters of eminent lay-leaders, my father arranged my marriage to a young lady who was the granddaughter Rabbi Naftali Katz, of righteous and blessed memory. The latter himself was authorised by a distinguished lay-leader of Vilna to scrutinise and question me and then to arrange my betrothal with the promise that I would receive a dowry of several thousand Reichthalers. Rabbi Katz involved himself in arranging this marriage since it was common knowledge that there was a deep affection between him and my father and that they were like-minded. This was particularly manifest after the Hayyun affair as a result of which my father had to leave Amsterdam and abandon his revered position (in that city). Rabbi Naftali too, had suffered deceptions over that religious controversy and he too, had to abandon his position and wander about the

CHAPTER EIGHT

country like a fugitive. It was for these reasons they became very attached to each other and Rabbi Naftali Katz was most eager to become related to my family through a marriage (of a member of his family) to one of my father's sons. When we did meet he was very keen that I marry the daughter of his son Rabbi Mordechai Katz, who then presided over the Bet Din of Broda. (Uhersky Brod, Moravia.) Then my father learned how pleasing and acceptable I was to him. (R.Naftali Katz) and that if my father was agreeable, he preferred his granddaughter to marry me rather than anyone else, for he was delighted with Jacob's son (cf.Gen.29:19). Moreover, the projected marriage was most acceptable to R.Naftali's family.

Hence, whilst questioning each other for example "what kind of dowry are you providing for your granddaughter?" and similar matters they promptly came to an arrangement and, having agreed to the marriage the financial arrangements were documented and stipulated that I would marry the granddaughter of the above-mentioned Rabbi Naftali Katz and that he would offer a dowry to the tune of one thousand Reichthalers. Furthermore, that he should be responsible for my maintenance for four years, and that my father should give me clothes and other presents for the bride as became his status, but nothing else. The marriage to my first wife was arranged for the following year. The above mentioned Rabbi (R.Naftali) found as much delight in me as if he had found a precious object, and be declared that this marriage had been made in the highest of heavens, where the marriage of my wife's name-sake, Rachel to the humble Jacob had been so becoming (cf.Gen.34:19)

With his wife i.e. his family, and all has possessions my father travelled to Poland, to a nation whose language we neither knew nor understood. Winter had already begun and my mother, may her dear soul rest in peace, was with child as she undertook that difficult and hazardous journey. She was now approaching the time of confinement, but harnessed with the bonds of love for the Almighty (cf.Hos.11:4) she wasn't, God forbid, angry with my father for abandoning the Rabbinate of Amsterdam and going into exile with twenty or more souls not knowing where the spirit of the Lord would carry him but searching for a restful abode while encumbered with such a large following. (On the contrary) she fully accepted all this without resentment or fretfulness, unlike women who live at ease but who now tremble for they were confident in the harvest that does not come. (cf.Isa.32:9-10) She however was fully in accord with my father's trust in the Almighty in accepting the burden of complete exile and journeying to Poland. Indeed, she did not refrain from stepping out on the journey although she was in the eighth to ninth month of pregnancy, she followed my father to an unknown country in the winter, when rain and snow fell unchecked. For it also happened to be at a time when she would marry off her daughter viz. my pious sister, Nechama, long may she live, for whom a marriage had been arranged with the grandson of the Rabbi and lay-leader Rabbi Chayyim Weitschitz of Apta. In the meantime however, Apta was burned to the ground, so that my father, z"l, was compelled to become a fugitive and to live in one of the neighbouring villages. It was there my mother was confined with a daughter who was her last child, for having previously borne my father fifteen children she ceased to gave birth to any more. It was also, in the same place that he (my father) gave my sister in marriage (to the grandson of Rabbi Chayyim Weitschitz).

Soon after this a special courier came to him from Hamburg sent by the lay-leader Rabbi Aberle London and his brother-in-law, Ephraim, each of whom was claiming a considerable amount of money from the other. They had taken their dispute to the Communal Council of Altona who decided that the case should be adjudicated by neutral Rabbis, each of the litigants nominating a Rabbinic authority, for they (the litigants) had no confidence in the local Rabbi and his Dayanim's ability to adjudicate in such a difficult and important case in which each of the litigants was claiming a very large sum of money from the other. Consequently, Reb Aberle nominated my father, z"l, whom he had known for many years as one on whom he could rely as on a pillar of iron in that my father's understanding and erudition in Torah was such that the gates of light were revealed to him. That he could be sure of his discerning

CHAPTER EIGHT

judgement, love of truth, feeling of rectitude, counsel and sound knowledge, and in that father constantly sought true justice and was ever ready to vindicate the just. Reb Aberle therefore wrote to my father (stating) he would comply with any stipulations my father made regarding payment for the arduous efforts that the long and hazardous journey would involve. Moreover, (R.Aberle continued) though, it was mid-winter my father should not linger in Breslau, but travel to the Judiciary in Hamburg as soon as possible. My father accepted the commission for a fee of seven hundred ducats (mint-condition) in addition to expenses incurred through travel and accommodation all of which came to a considerable sum. Then my father, z"l, journeyed from Apta to Hamburg accompanied by his son-in-law (R.Leib) and myself, having already been betrothed. It was at the height of the winter and I caught such a heavy cold on the journey that I lost consciousness on several occasions; my (God's) hand was heavy on me in my trouble (cf.Job.23:2) and I was seized by terror and shuddering. My father, z"l, also suffered much on my account, for my illness caused him great anxiety.

We finally reached Hamburg in perfect safety, and subsequently my father became reconciled with the lay-leader, Reb Behr Cohen, may he rest in peace, who had previously been my father's enemy. Until this time, he (R.Behr) had retained part of my father's salary which he had earned as presiding Rabbi of the Altona Bet Din but which had remained in the community's possession because of the above-mentioned dispute. Now however, my father was fully compensated and through the insistence of Reb Aberle they (my father and Reb Behr) became reconciled, my father acceding to the pleas of Reb Behr without the need of the latter's gifts. This was something Reb Behr did not achieve when my father moved from Altona to Amsterdam. For at that time Reb Behr had tried to win over my father with the offer of a large sum of money in fact, a thousand or more Reichthalers, on condition that he (Reb Behr) would be received by my father (before his departure from Altona) so that he would leave my father in a spirit of good-will, having received his (my father's) blessing. But all attempts to affect this had proved unsuccessful, so that all Reb Behr's efforts proved fruitless despite the money he had proffered my father if he (my father) would make peace with him. Yet now he (Reb Behr) had attained his goal without any strenuous efforts and without any cost to himself. Such was Reb Behr's good fortune throughout his life that come what may, he always achieved his aim. So now peace prevailed between my father and Reb Behr who was the tent-peg and corner stone (cf.Zech.10:4) of any significant communal activity that was of a social nature.

Indeed, it was well known that the Rabbi recently appointed to the Three Communities, (Rabbi Ezekiel Katzenellenbogen) would not venture to do anything without the advice and approval of Reb Behr Cohen. If I were to recount just a few aspects of the conduct of the Rabbi who presided over the Altona Bet Din, who because of our many sins, reduced the honour of the Torah to its lowest ebb, then I would have to write a great deal which would require a massive volume. For many tracts would not comprehend his conduct and activities. In short, from the day he arrived in Altona, the course of that community's history changed; God's people in the Three Communities sank in distress. (cf.Jud.5:11) Whereas previously it had been a garden of Eden, it later became a desolate wilderness (cf.Jer.12:10) Already twenty years before his death he (R.E.Katzenllenbogen) had been deprived of the right of jurisdiction over the community of Hamburg in matters affecting Jewish law; whereas previously the administration of Hamburg had granted its Jewish community complete autonomy in this sphere in the same way as the King, may his majesty be exalted, had granted such a privilege to the community of Altona. But the perversion of Justice cried out to the Almighty for in his (R.E.K's) Bet Din bribery was often fully seen so that when the upright administration of Hamburg could no longer tolerate the protestations of these who had been led astray they deprived him (Rabbi E.K.) of the privilege of acting as Dayan in Hamburg with the result that he could no longer compel any member of the Hamburg community to be summoned to his court. Consequently the exercise of Jewish law has had no validity in Hamburg for nearly thirty years.

CHAPTER EIGHT

Let us now return to the main topic. Despite all my father's efforts in the law-suit (between Reb Aberle and Reb Ephraim) to prove that justice lay with the former he did not succeed. He even wrote a responsum on behalf of Reb Aberle in which he clarified the correct judicial decision based on Torah principles, but even in this he (my father) was unsuccessful; he cried like a crane, but he laboured in vain." (cf.TB.Kiddushin 44a) For Rabbi Ezekiel, the presiding Rabbi of the Bet Din, and the other nominated Judge had jointly agreed to find him (Reb Aberle) guilty. Whilst we were staying in Hamburg I was sorely afflicted with melancholia; this was just before Shavuot that is close to my wedding day.

Consequently my father retraced his steps after Pesach and returned (from Hamburg) to Breslau for my wedding. He did not want to postpone my wedding particularly since my intended father-in-law and his father (R.N.Katz) were urging him not to delay completing that Mitzvah. Moreover, they were genuinely frightened by the talk of some idlers who said that it was the intention of my father, z"l, to arrange another marriage for me with the (the daughter) of another lay-leader of Hamburg and it was for this reason (they asserted) my father had taken me with him to Hamburg.

But, God spare my father, he never entertained such a notion. Indeed, he would not go back on his word for all the treasures of the world, how much more so over this affair (my wedding). For he rejected all wealth and even fine gold, since his main purpose (in arranging marriages for his children) was to attach then to the best of people who came from distinguished families. He therefore did not want to delay the wedding of his first-born son, God forbid, nor to hinder the fulfilment of this Mitzvah for all the money in the world. Hence, though he was still involved in a law-suit in Hamburg, he left that city and journeyed to Breslau for my wedding. As we passed through customs in the province of Brandenburg my father's chest containing all the silver-ware I had received in Hamburg as wedding presents was confiscated, and he (my father) had to expend a considerable amount of money to replace them. Eventually we arrived in Breslau for Shavuot and my wedding took place during the days of Hagbalah (the three days preceding Shavuot), but it was not a joyful day for me as since I was extremely weak at the time.

During the period of my wedding Breslau was hit by a flood of considerable proportion which inflicted unprecedented damage to the city, but, blessed be our Saviour and Helper, we were not affected. For several weeks I stayed with my in-laws viz. my wife's grandfather, the above-mentioned R.Naftali Katz. I had my meals in his home and he treated me with the greatest deference. But there is no marriage settlement that does not contain a quarrel. (cf.TB.Shabbat 130a.) For my father-in-law was unable to fulfil his obligation (to me) regarding the dowry which was several hundred Reichthalers short of the promised sum; my father almost forswore me not to forgo this debt. Indeed, though my father-in-law promised to pay me the outstanding balance over a period, I never received a penny of it. Moreover I'm sorry to say, he (my father-in-law) further obstructed me (cf.TB.Sanhedrin 31b) not only in appropriating the customary gifts of the layleaders of Vienna, all of which he retained for himself so that I received nothing, but even one gift which had not come directly to him which the lay-leader Reb A—P—sent to his brother Reb P—P-- (both were my groomsmen) to hand me which he duly did, my father-in-law urged me to hand over to him. For he thought that all the wedding gifts that came from Vienna were really his property. However, in this matter I ignored his attempt to forcibly deprive me of what was rightly mine.

This caused the beginning of a rift between us for he was very angry with me over this matter, and I likewise was angry with him for he was making an unreasonable demand of me as if I were nothing but a fool. In fact, he almost caused a serious quarrel between his daughter, my wife, may she rest in peace, who employed any number of tricks in fulfilling her father's purpose, and me. However, at that time, I knew nothing of all this for this was not the kind of behaviour I had seen or learned in my father's house. For he was most generous to his children with what was his, how much less likely was he likely to have coveted other people's property. In fact when my father, z"l, arranged the marriage of his oldest daughter,

CHAPTER EIGHT

the invitees of the three Communities also gave magnificent gifts worth hundreds of Reichthalers which they intended as a mark of respect for my father, z"l. For to-date, he had not received any tangible benefits from them (members of the three Communities), since throughout his life he would not accept any gift for himself. Indeed, he had incurred many heavy debts over the first wedding he made for his children. For he had issued many hundreds of invitations to the ceremony and wedding meal, in fact to all the important members of the Three Communities with their spouses and children; perhaps one thousand people, and he incurred a heavy debt in suitably entertaining them. Consequently they in turn came laden with fine gifts for the bride and bridegroom. But it never occurred to my father, z"l, to appropriate any single gift. On the contrary, he presented (the bride and bridegroom) with additional gifts out of his own pocket, and for many years he accepted the responsibility of caring for the married couple together with their children. This was particularly true of his first son-in-law. My father gave him what was according to his wealth, a very large sum of money.

Yet he not only refrained from reducing the dowry that he had promised in writing but, for several years, in fact for almost the rest of his life he was encumbered with this obligation. In fact, after my father's death, his first son-in-law was maintained from his (my father's) legacy. I have written this protracted passage at this stage (to describe my father's attitude). Accordingly, I regarded my father-in-law's unusual behaviour in this matter as most strange. My father however, had no idea of all this, but he knew that I had received my dowry of eleven hundred gold-pieces in ready cash. The latter sum my father handed over to Reb P—P--, my attendant, on the assurance that he (Reb P--) would see that the above sum would be invested to yield some profit, no matter the amount, but provided it was gained legitimately. Following this my father set out on his return journey to Hamburg to complete Reb Aberle's law-suit. I was then parted from my father, z"l, whom I never saw again, and together with my wife and father-in-law travelled to Moravia.

MEGILAT SEFER

But to revert to the subject of my father. The above-mentioned law-suit was protracted and since the nominated judges (including my father) could not reach a decision, they had to augment the tribunal with two addition nominees. But all this was of no avail for, "in vain does the founder refine, for the wicked are not separated" (cf.Jer.6:29). For the majority of the court declared Reb Aberle guilty, despite the protests of my father, z"l, that they were treating him (Reb Aberle) cruelly and unjustly, his (my father's) efforts were in vain, for they deprived Reb Aberle of all his estates. I shall not deal at length with this affair since I wasn't there at the time. Moreover, I shall deal only briefly with what transpired when I was originally present (at the trial) with my father, z"l, when he reprimanded the Presiding Rabbi of the local (Hamburg) Bet Din Rabbi Ezekiel Katzenellenbogen, indicating certain errors in his (R.E's) halakhic rulings in other matters some of which concerned marriage and divorce problems. I will just mention that when my father, z"l, was about to leave Reb Aberle and to return to his home in Poland, he addressed the following consolatory remarks to Reb Aberle, "I appreciate that they have put an obstacle before you and have perverted the cause of justice to your disadvantage (as I have already explained above, I cannot give you all the details). However, I am quite sure that in a short time the Almighty, blessed be He, will compensate your loss and you will again begin to prosper for He will place His hand on your head and bless you." My father then journeyed to Poland and lived for a time in a village, and then in Apta, when it was in the state of being rebuilt.

It was at this stage that an untoward situation arose in Apta which was occasioned by a dispute in that community revolving around the very influential family called Weitschitz. Two eminent scholars were hanged as a result of this dispute, mainly through the libel with which they were accused, by the above-mentioned powerful family. As the latter were constantly quarrelling with every one they, acquired the nickname Kor'cham (Ed.note: from Korach who argued with Moses) the name by which they are known far and wide to this very day. Hence when Reb H- Weitschitz was on his death-bed (my

CHAPTER EIGHT

father had arranged the marriage between my sister Nechama and his grandson) he asked to see my father, z"l, before he (Reb Weitschitz) died. But my father refused to visit him stating, "Am I an associate of informers?" His grandson, that is my father's son-in-law, died childless after the passing of my father, z"l, leaving my sister, Nechama a sorrowful widow who declined to marry again for the rest of her life.

After my father, z"l, had settled in Poland, as I have described above, the Almighty stirred the heart or one of the most renowned of Polish lay-leaders, the famous Reb Israel Reitfin who was an official, called "economist" of the great Princedom of Shinevsky. The latter comprised extensive estates in Poland, many townships and a large retinue of serfs. Reb Israel had been appointed supervisor of the estates of this principality and was responsible for all its revenue and expenditure. Everything exported and imported was effected through him hence, Reb Israel was a person of considerable ability. Besides this he was a deeply religious individual, a person of the highest integrity. He now resolved to gain the privilege of fulfilling a Mitzvah by taking my father and his family under his wing. He therefore came to my father and implored him to come with his family to live near him (Reb Israel) in one of these areas over which he (Reb Israel) exercised control for example Sochaczow or Reitfin. He gave my father a large house free of rent, a guard to look after him throughout the day and night and a servant who would always be ready to perform any of the household needs. Moreover, he (Reb Israel) gave him (my father) a number of cows to provide him with enough milk, butter and cheese with which to feed his (my father's) family and so preserve the health of the children. Besides all this he (Reb Israel) provided sufficient wood and heat to meet all his (my father's) domestic requirements as well as a plentiful supply of hens and freshwater fish which came from the lakes under his (Reb Israel's) supervision. All this was provided gratis and met all my father's needs, except for certain commodities which were not basic for survival, and clothes which my father had to buy. But even regarding these commodities the above-mentioned gentleman would occasionally make my mother splendid gifts of perfumes, sweetmeats and fruits, which he was able to import. All these things Reb Israel gave most generously and with the utmost affection. Thus, for several years my father's needs were provided by Reb Israel with love, good-will, and cheerfulness. In fact he did so until 1718 when my father was called to the Rabbinate of Lvov and the adjoining districts. Reb Israel was then distressed because he had forfeited a Mitzvah, for he had played host to the Torah for several years.

Were I to recount everything that happened to my father in Lvov it would have to be a protracted story even though, for our many sins he was not in Lvov for long, in fact, about three months. Nevertheless in that short time he established a high reputation in that city, something that was not achieved by a number of great Rabbis who preceded my father and had served there for many years. When my father was on his way to Lvov to assume the Rabbinate there, a great miracle occurred. For when he was crossing the river Wechsel it was already the end of the winter when the ice (on the river) was fragile and was on the point of melting. The coach in which he crossed was closely followed by another coach laden with travellers, and the ice under the second coach gave way and all its passengers were drowned. It is impossible to describe the great honour my father was accorded whilst he was in Lvov. Indeed, even a skilled writer could not do full justice to half the honour which was extended to my father.

This great respect was not limited to the local Jewish community for even gentiles came to visit him early in the day and stood in reverence in front of his house, laden with presents. During the short time my father held the Rabbinate of Lvov, he introduced some important measures and as raised the reputation of that community. He executed the laws against robbers, and arrogant people became humble in his presence. Moreover, he removed a powerful lay-leader from office, this man being a nominee of Reb Zelig, because the man in question had appropriated communal funds and benefited from what had been plundered from the poor. (cf.Ps.12:6) That person then acted as an informant against my father,

CHAPTER EIGHT

z"l, before the local governing Council. My father, z"l was summoned to appear before them whilst the community was struck with trembling and trepidation, for the Jews of that region stood in great fear of the government. However, my father, z"l, went to the governing Council and standing before them spoke in Italian. The Council accorded him unprecedented honour for they requested the governor to be seated next to my father and that he (my father) should continue to wear his hat. Indeed, the Almighty made sure that my father should make a favourable impression on them, with the result that they granted him almost all the necessary privileges and powers for adjudicating capital cases, should he be so disposed. Thus, my father left the governing Council in great esteem, having been completely exonerated. And so it was that all the informers stood in great fear of my father, z"l, and all local scoundrels were obedient to him and were humble in his presence, for they were sorely afraid of my father. As for the rest of the community however, it was a splendid, glorious and great occasion. Indeed, that other powerful personality Reb Moses Yehiels, who was such a despot that all the community of Lvov trembled at has presence until my father's arrival in the city, he now too, became obedient to my father and accepted his (my father's) rulings and decisions on Jewish law and Practice. He did not think of my father disparagingly but acknowledged him as a saintly person all of whose actions were performed in the belief in the Almighty only.(cf.Ps.33:4) In fact, on one occasion that powerful fellow (Reb Moses Yehiels) was involved in some litigation in my father's court and lost the case. But Reb Moses did not utter a word of protest. On the contrary, he remained a true friend to my father throughout his Rabbinate in Lvov.

A similar event occurred with my father's relative by marriage, Reb Chayyim Leizrel, who had been instrumental in obtaining the Rabbinate of Lvov for my father. He (Reb Chayyim) was a very wealthy person who was highly respected in the community firstly, because of his wealth and his distinguished family, and secondly in his own right, since he was an outstanding personality by virtue of his physical appearance and scholarship.

MEGILAT SEFER

He too, was involved in a law-suit which came before my father's (Bet Din) during which my father tore up a bill of debt which Reb Chayyim had produced against a certain individual. For my father had wisely perceived that he (Reb Chayyim) had allowed "iniquity to make its home with him".(cf.Job 11:14) and therefore showed him no preference but tore up the document in his (Reb Chayyim's) presence. The other Dayanim were astounded at my father's action; he Reb Chayyim) too, at first complained at my father's treatment of him, but he (my father) merely scoffed at him. Subsequently however, he (Reb Chayyim) admitted that the bill of debt was a valueless paper (a sherd) and recorded a debt which had already been settled. Nevertheless Reb Chayyim gladly accepted my father's ruling. Indeed, everyone realised that his (my father's) skill in executing justice was divinely inspired, so that his reputation grew constantly, even among the Gentile population, to the extent that some of them brought their law-suits before him. In fact, some Gentile businessmen came to him (with their problems), each bearing a gift for him and he conversed with them in their vernacular. In short, no Rabbi in Poland had ever been afforded this honour, for he (my father) was held in high respect among the gentiles.

The Jews of Lvov were happy because the leader of Israel kept close watch on the activities of both the community and individuals, making quite sure that the general and the particular were correct and in order i.e. were guided according to the principles of Judaism. Whether it concerned communal activities such as the assessment of taxes, or matters concerning individuals his object was to establish true justice in the community free of partiality. Similarly, in matters concerning Torah-studies, my father resolved to correct that which had become generally distorted in Ashkenazi Jewry. This was particularly true of Poland where the curriculum of Jewish studies had degenerated because they had abandoned the study of Tenach (Bible) to such an extent that the Rabbis had become insignificant because they could not quote a sentence of Tenach. Moreover, they were ignorant of Mishnah, unskilled in the formation at the Halakhah, nor had they studied the Codes of the early

CHAPTER EIGHT

Decisors (of the Halakhah). This situation had worried that saintly personality (my father) throughout his life, so that when the Holy One blessed be He, had found him worthy to be appointed principal Rabbi of Lvov and the adjoining districts he immediately remembered to effect a reform in the curriculum of Torah-studies, so that they should follow the correct and proper procedure as laid down in the Mishnah (Avot 5:24) "at five years the age is reached for the study of Tenach". In this way both young and older students would progress successfully in their studies. Previously all the teachers of the community (Lvov) had called on him (for his assistance) and he had arranged their curriculum, the first subject being the study of Tenach with special attention to grammar.

Had they merited that he should have attended the Council of the Four Lands (of Poland) he would certainly have reformed the curriculum of Jewish-studies for the whole of the Diaspora. In the same vein he intended introducing other significant reforms for the general benefit of Judaism, changes which were undoubtedly worthy of bringing our final Redemption nearer had that generation merited the realisation of his plans by conducting its life in accordance with his Godly qualities of character. But the sins (of that generation) caused his sun to set prematurely. He had held the Rabbinate of Lvov for merely three months when suddenly the destroyer appeared, and on Rosh Chodesh Iyar 1718 the light of Israel in the community of Lvov was extinguished; their light turned to darkness, their joy to mourning. The whole of Poland wept on hearing the tragic news. A unique period of mourning and lamentation was observed for him. Even the rulers of the various provinces of Poland lamented his passing. Indeed, it is impossible to describe in a book the reputation that my father left both in the Jewish and non-Jewish world. You would not believe it even if you were told that, because of our many sins, the rulers were heard to say "the Jews' Messiah came to Poland, but they put him to death". I learned this when I passed through Poland six months later having journeyed to Lvov to visit the grave of my father, z"l. Throughout that long journey I heard people speak of his wonderful deeds, but because of what happened to me subsequently I have forgotten most of them.

When the news of my father's death reached Germany there was bitter mourning in all the communities and people said, "woe to the generation who has lost its leader and steersman." The Sephardi community of London too, paid great reverence to his passing (see above) Again a certain bona fide person who happened to be in Amsterdam they (the community) were observing a memorial service, for my father, informed me that Chacham Solomon Aylon cried out "truly, I sinned against Chacham Tzvi z"l". Moreover a number of eminent Polish rabbis e.g. Rabbi Joshua Falk who then presided over the Bet Din of Frankfurt and Rabbi Eliezer of Brody who later presided over the Bet Din of Amsterdam (1735-1740) rent their garments (over my father's passing) sat on the ground, observed one day of mourning. Indeed, I heard one eminent contemporary Rabbinic authority observe that the world was unworthy to make use of such a holy vessel which possessed the soul of one of the early Tannaim. Alas for our many sins, his life was a tragic one as one can appreciate from a mere glimpse of his many activities, from the unhappy events and frightening periods that he experienced. That, because of his uprightness, saintliness and integrity he was often persecuted and insulted by the thorns of our people who stood at the extremity of the camp, and all because he was no respecter of persons in his adherence to Torah.

That it was because of this Godly attribute which he possessed that an increasing number of arrogant and affluent people were opposed to him, and a variety of archers savagely attacked him, shot at him and pressed him hard. They joined battle against the eye of Justice, they sought to blind the eye which executed strict justice in the world. However, not a single, person who waged war against him was not scorched by his glowing coal, so that in the end they suffered both physically and materially, for the Holy One Blessed be He, demanded that His honour be satisfied.

I cannot go into all the details but merely record all that happened to a number of those people who belonged to the highest stratum of society and upon whom his curse fell, that they became

CHAPTER EIGHT

poor and descended to the lowest stratum. Again, some, may the Merciful One save us, were destroyed together with their families. I will mention only two or three examples for future generations so that they should know, understand and distinctly perceive this, and so appreciate how true are the words of our Sages z"l, viz. "Beware of the glowing coals of the wise lest you be burnt" (Avot 2:16) and "anyone against whom the Sages cast an angry look suffered either death or extreme poverty (TB. Moed Katan 17b) our own eyes have witnessed the truth of these sentiments on several occasions. Therefore, one should pay attention to the fact that to touch the Lord's anointed Ones, his faithful servants, the guardians of His covenant, those who faithfully fulfil His work in reinforcing the breaches of Judaism so as to establish it on its mound, and who study our Torah for its own sake, to touch such people is to effect a raging fire which burns from the soul to the flesh.

Now one person who publicly received his punishment (for his behaviour towards my father) the like of which had never previously occurred and which was known far and wide was Aaron Gekish who was a lay-leader of the Ashkenazi community of Amsterdam-for several years. He was an affluent person whose wealth was more than several hundred thousand gold pieces and was the most powerful individual in that community. We have already mentioned him together with two other men viz. Judah Prinz and Mordechai Cohen. They were the three sinners of Israel who were banned from being elected to the lay-leadership because of their high-handed behaviour in the dispute between the Chazanim which we described above. It was because of this dispute that these three became enemies of my father, z"l, for he would not assist them in their sinful cause viz. to uproot completely the weaker faction and deal with them at their will; all of which I have already recorded at length (see above). From that period they became my father's sworn enemies and committed against him all the despicable and insulting deeds in their power to cause him great distress. This was particularly true of Gekish since such behaviour was in accord with his profoundly natural impudence.

MEGILAT SEFER

Through Gekish's position as a very affluent person they poured scorn on my father. Consequently, Gekish lost all his wealth through disastrous circumstances; as he had come into the world, so he left it. He was the person who reared a dog he called "Tzvi". In brief, these three individuals threatened the very life of my father, z"l.

Regarding the two associates of Gekish mentioned above, they soon met their fate. For soon after the man of God (my father) left Amsterdam they became poor and died in dreadful circumstances. Judah Prinz hanged himself. Yet another lay-leader to whom we referred whose name I will not mention but who was one of a group of my father's enemies, fell from a horse-drawn carriage and broke his neck. But the Holy One, Blessed be He delayed Gekish's fate. He remained in his elevated status for many years after my father's departure from Amsterdam, continued to advance in his business as before, accumulating the wealth of a Korach, but behaving most impudently and arrogantly. Indeed people wondered that since, as they saw it, all the enemies of my father, z"l, had either fallen, had been destroyed or had been caught in their machinations, that the Almighty was indulgent towards him (Gekish) since he had delayed his punishment for more than twenty years after the fate of his colleagues. But his destruction, in the time of God's visitation upon him, came very suddenly. He was arrested by the Judiciary officer of Amsterdam over a mere trifle. At first Gekish was able to pacify the official with the payment of a small compensation, and even later he was able to obtain his release by paying several hundred gold pieces. But "the rich man speaks impudently" (cf.Prov.18:23). For he then wanted to pay ten thousand gold pieces for his release from prison and indeed, the Judicial officer was already kindly disposed towards Gekish since he coveted this large sum, but it was divinely ordained that he (Gekish) should be caught in an evil net from which he couldn't escape so, "when the ox is thrown down, sharpen the knife." (meaning that in critical moments many sins are visited) (TB.Shabbat 32a) For the administration (of Amsterdam) ordered him to be detained in prison, he was put in irons,(Ps.105:18) his feet were put in the stocks (Job 33:11) and he was condemned to

CHAPTER EIGHT

death as if he had been a common thief. He was then brought for sentence to be carried out on a Shabbat, and he was to die just as a villain. Thus, the authorities prescribed whipping for him and proclaimed his death sentence by gibbet close to the court-house in the presence of tens of thousands of people. Subsequently they exercised clemency and allowed him to live a life worse than death, for they sentenced him to other punishments. Thus, they stripped him naked and whipped him, leaving him his life, and nothing more, they bought him back to prison and condemned him to the hard labour of sawing Brazilian timber which is as tough as stone, with a saw weighing several litres, a punishment meted out to those condemned to death but who have been shown compassion.

Thus, he was sentenced to life imprisonment and condemned to the arduous task which I have already described, having to carry out the daily task as they (the authorities) prescribed. He was then a man of over seventy. It was in prison that his life ended after two years. Moreover, he lost all his wealth, for although the administration (of Amsterdam) had not tampered with it, it all went to waste. As for his sons some came to a bad end.

At the initial stage of his ultimate fate he paid little regard to it, for, as I have already stated, it was most insignificant. Indeed it all seemed very much of a joke to him.(Gen.10:14) However, later when he realised the situation was becoming more serious, he gave some thought to his treatment of my father, z"l, and being somewhat concerned he sent a small gift to the community of Lvov so that they should gather a minyan (quorum) to request pardon on his behalf at the grave of my saintly father, z"l. But he received his full and just reward, as I have previously described, and he became a bye-word and an object lesson throughout the world, since because of his great wealth he was very well known in most countries, both among Gentiles and Jews. A number of pamphlets and booklets were published in the vernacular describing this whole affair and in them mention was made inter alia of his treatment of my father, z"l. This effected a great Kiddush Hashem (Sanctification of God's name) throughout the world, since everyone realised and admitted that it was because of the way he had treated that saintly person (my father) that this disaster had befallen him, that my father had done this to him. Hence many who realised this said reverently, "how significant and truthful are the sentiments of our Sages when they say, "the righteous are great even when they are dead". Indeed, the impression that was made by all that happened to that person (Gekish) has no parallel.

Just as my father's curse did not return empty but tore in pieces the powerful men even to their very scalps, and those who felt secure, were either punished or killed similarly, my father's blessing was fully realised and never remained invalid. On the contrary, it produced an abundance of good and plenty, for "the blessing of the Lord brings riches." (Ps.10:22) As an example I will quote two genuine witnesses. The first was my relative, Reb Aberle Norden who administered to my father when he (my father) left Amsterdam. He (Reb Aberle) never moved from inside my father's tent, but did service to the Rabbi without the prospect of any payment even though he (Reb Aberle) had to search around for a living to maintain himself. But he did this rather than derive any material benefit from my father, z"l. Moreover, he (Reb Aberle) had to take care, of his elderly poor parents and provide them with food. Nevertheless, at no time did he abandon my father, z"l, but was ever ready to serve him and to see to his needs as well as those of his (my father's) family to a greater extent than any employee would have done.

When my father, z"l, was on the move and planning to leave Poland that God-fearing young man, rather than abandon the service of my father, wanted to leave his parents and to accompany my father so as to assist him (my father) on his journey to God knows where. However, my father would not allow him (Reb Aberle) to join him but made him return home. Consequently, he (Reb Aberle) remained in Amsterdam, a topic I hope to explain later, with the Almighty's help.

The second witness was Reb Aberle London who was blessed by my father when they parted company in Hamburg where my father had been involved in the adjudication of a lawsuit which Reb

CHAPTER EIGHT

Aberle had with his brother-in-law Reb Ephraim. The former had lost all his estates and assets because of this harsh litigation, as I have explained above. Hence, when my father blessed Reb Aberle he assured him that he had no cause for concern for he (my father) was sure his (Reb Aberle's) fortunes would change to his advantage very soon, and so it turned out, since no promise of my father, z"l, remained unfulfilled. When in a short time Reb Aberle made a profit to the tune of many hundred thousand Reichthalers Reb Aberle himself acknowledged the fact that the blessing of that saintly personality (my father) had been fulfilled to his advantage, so that when he (Reb Aberle) learned of my father's passing he promised a gift of a hundred ducats to my father's family, but this promise remained unfulfilled as I shall later explain, with the Almighty's help.

These are but a few aspects of the character of that great man, my father, z"l, who did not leave his equal in Torah, the reverence of the Almighty, or in qualities of character; particularly in his hatred of bribery and his passion for justice he had no peer on this earth. Moreover, in the field of Halakhic decisions he was unique in his generation so that all his contemporary Rabbinic authorities both in Germany and Poland, draw from the living water of his fountain. Not the slightest variation was made in any of his Halakhic decisions for they were regarded as if one had sought the Almighty's counsel. For all the gates of light were open to his memory, whether it be in Tenach, Mishnah, Gemara, the Turim, the earlier and later Decisors of the Halakhah or in other branches of knowledge. Moreover, he was well acquainted with several languages. In fact, all his knowledge was so ordered (in his mind) that it seemed as if it were set out in a book-case. He had a lucidity of expression, a prodigious memory as well as a fine intellect, and he was both patient and decisive. But towering above all these qualities stood his piety, his sense of holiness and his strict observance of every detail of the Mitzvot. Indeed, he endeavoured to fulfil them with all his mind and body. His main purpose (in life) was to make his people worthy of God's grace. He was zealous in his incessant study of Torah, both day and night. In fact he was always involved in this study for he slept for no more than three or four hours every day. Moreover, his intake of food and drink was no more than that of a small child.

Nevertheless the splendour of his person was like that of a man of God. He was of fine stature, and complexion and majestic in his appearance. His face was almost circular in shape of reddish-white colouring with a large forehead. As to his nose the lower part of his nostril was slightly extended. His mouth was small and always closed, whilst his lips were like rose petals. His jaw-bones were bereft of hair so that he appeared to be shawn, whilst his beard encompassed his face from ear to ear and was like a diadem beneath his cheeks which were like a bed of spices.(cf.Cant.5:13) The pointed end of his chin was long with only a small space between the two points (of the chin), his hair gold coloured and curly, whilst the parting of his hair was uniformly wide. His flesh was soft and tender and there was no hair on his chest. In general he had the appearance of an awe-inspiring angel of God, just as the glance of his eyes was fear-inspiring. He welcomed everyone cheerfully, whilst his speech was lucid and his enunciation clear, and as I have already stated, he was well acquainted with several languages. Similarly, his writings in the Holy tongue were fully lucid and concise. He was kindly disposed to everyone and a merciful patron of the poor. Yet he was as hard as steel when confronted with obstinacy or when it came to shattering the stubbornness of the strong-armed. In the latter's presence he was not afraid to relieve the oppressed nor to break the jaws of the unrighteous and pluck the prey out of their mouths. (cf.Job.29:17)

As a pious man he kept has eyes on those who revered the Almighty, and whilst humbling the pride of the presumptuous and arrogant he spoke harshly to those who indulged in proud talk. He showed no preference in maintaining Torah principles nor did he ever fear any human being. Indeed, my pen would grow weary in writing a full account of his remarkable deeds, his godly characteristics and his attachment to the Almighty in performing His service and safe-guarding His covenant with all his heart and soul. Indeed, I have recorded some of his deeds when I was young and they were published in my pamphlet "Yesiv Pitgom" which was a

CHAPTER EIGHT

eulogy in his memory. Yet even in this I did not succeed in expressing half the honour that was his due. During my father's life time the Holy One blessed be He, granted him the privilege of publishing the first section of his Responsa (which appeared) in the finest type and on excellent paper. This was during the period my father held the Rabbinate of Amsterdam. The above work was highly esteemed by the intellectuals who regarded it as a Responsa of one of the eminent medieval Rabbinic scholars, and it therefore fetched a high price. My father also left a collection of manuscripts containing Talmudic novellae, Responsa, Talmudic commentaries and homilies on the Torah. But they remained in Lissa for some considerable time. After my wife, z"l, had brought them (to me) I still did not touch them and they remained with her for twenty-seven years, right up to 1757, just like a stone which had not been upturned.

The Rabbi Hirsch (Levin = Hart Lyon) who had been appointed Presiding Rabbi of the London Bet Din visited me and urged me to give him these manuscripts so that they could be published in his name, so I committed them into his safe-keeping. As I have previously stated my father was occasionally involved in arguments in honour of God with contemporary Ashkenazi Rabbinic authorities, as one can see in his Response Para.2. In particular he was involved in an acrimonious correspondence with Rabbi Eleazer Broda when the latter was Rector of the Prague Yeshivah.

I will now explain the issue which was the cause of disquiet between then, having heard it from the very lips of my saintly father, z"l. Rabbi Eleazer of Broda's son was affianced to the daughter of Israel Pirshut and was in Hamburg for his son's marriage. At that time my maternal grandfather Rabbi Zalman Merles held the rabbinate of the Three Communities and had arranged a dinner in honour of Rabbi Eleazer, z"l, his son and the latter's father-in-law. My father, z"l, did not attend the dinner as he was in the year of mourning for his father, z"l. However during the dinner my father, z"l, though uninvited, went to his father-in-law's home to pay respect and welcome the scholarly visitor. My father brought with his most outstanding students of the Altona Kloiz and together they welcomed Rabbi Eleazer Broda. The latter then asked my father, "Why didn't you pay your respects till now, why didn't you welcome me in Reb Israel Pirshut's home?" As soon as my father, z"l, realised that he (R. Eleazer) overtly claimed special distinction in the presence of all the bye-standers he became excited but wisely replied, "I am acquainted with the following Talmudic text which is contained in the first chapter of the Tractate Hagigah (p.5b) and which records that Rabbi (Judah the Prince) and Rabbi Hiyyah were once going on a journey (when they came to a certain town) they said, "if there is a Rabbinic scholar here we shall go and pay him our respects." They were told, "there is a Rabbinic scholar here and he is blind." They went to visit him etc... From this incident (my father said) we learn that it is the duty of the visiting scholar to pay his respects to the local scholar first. My father then continued, you must admit that you are not as eminent an authority as Rabbi Judah was in his generation, whereas I am sure that I am no less a scholar in this generation as that blind scholar was in his. You must also admit that Rabbi Judah was completely unaware of the existence or the name of that Rabbinic scholar since he had previously asked if are were a Rabbinic scholar in this town? So that Rabbi Judah could not have known of his (the blind scholar's) existence. Whereas you, Rabbi Eleazer, at least know that I live here (in Altona), it was therefore your duty to pay your respects to me (first). For Rabbi Judah had asked, "Is there a Rabbinic Scholar in this town, so that we can go and pay him our respects?" Thus even though Rabbi Judah was the Patriarch of the whole of Jewry he wanted to pay his respects to the local Rabbinic scholar, whoever he was.

Consequently, you Rabbi Eleazer have made an improper request, whereas I have acted beyond the strict line of the law, in visiting you on this occasion so as to explain my absence from the dinner to which I had (originally) been invited and which was attended by a Rabbinic scholar. For I am forbidden to attend a private dinner since I am in the year of mourning for my father. Nevertheless, I have come to pay my respects to you. When Rabbi Eleazer, z"l, realised that my father, z"l had overwhelmed him with

CHAPTER EIGHT

this irrefutable argument he continued the conversation by stating "you, Chacham Tzvi, should have sent your students to welcome me. I once acted in the same way towards an eminent rabbinic scholar who happened to visit my town. I myself didn't visit him, but I sent my students to deputise for me, and pay him my respects." "But," my father, replied, "I haven't any students." Rabbi Eleazer then asked, "then who are these people who accompanied you, learned Rabbi?" "These are my associates," replied my father. This reply brought the conversation to a close.

Then my father, z"l, turned to the subject of the previous day's sermon, for on that Shabbat Rabbi Eleazer had preached in the Altona Synagogue where my father, z"l, was present. My father had listened to the sermon but had turned towards the wall and made no comment, for he didn't want to be involved in any arguments in the Synagogue. In fact this was how my father reacted to preachers, in general he showed little concern as to whether they preached well or badly. However, on this occasion he heard something which made him take note, for my father was conscious of any suspicion of human arrogance.

Consequently, my father said to R. Eleazer, "in your sermon yesterday you gave a solution to a certain problem (I can't remember what the problem was - author) but your solution was incorrect. They were then involved in argument until, R. Eleazer growing tired called to his son (the bridegroom) saying, "Moses you answer him." At that time my father, z"l, had no son but my young sister happened to be present at my grandfather's house so he (my father) said, "Miriam my girl, you come and answer this." They then parted in bad spirit. Nevertheless, in the end amity triumphed, for the following morning Rabbi Eleazer, z"l, sent a scholar to my father to ask his forgiveness. Furthermore, the rabbi's deputy informed my father that he (R. Eleazer) had committed himself to fast for one day because he had annoyed my father. From this incident one can see that R. Eleazer, z"l, was a truly pious person although he lacked humility. Henceforth, the two Rabbis were reconciled and at peace. Yet when a responsum of R. Eleazer, z"l, came to my father he said, "he (R. Eleazer) has already lapsed (in his behaviour)" suggesting that he shouldn't have acted so arrogantly towards my father.

Since I am dealing with this topic I mention a further incident. Once when Rabbi Ezekiel (Katzenellenbogen), the son-in-law of Mordechai Cohen delivered a sermon his son, Rabbi G , rebuked him stating that he believed that sermon contained serious defects. Whereupon R.E. scoffed at him observing, "if what you say were true and I had said something improper, then Chacham Tzvi (my father, z"l - author) would not have remained silent, for it is well known that he shows no partiality when Torah principles are involved and he was present when I delivered my sermon yet made no comment." When my father, z"l, learned of this incident he said, "I have not been behaving correctly, for people will be misled by my silence (on these occasions) and will think that because I make no comment I agree with what has been said." Henceforth, he (my father) did not attend synagogue when a sermon was being delivered.

Here ends the biography of my father, z"l, though it merely comprises the gleanings of my memory for I knew, but have since forgotten, many more facts. Moreover, there is much about my father's life of which I am completely ignorant for I was only seventeen when I (finally) parted from him, may his memory be blessed. Furthermore, so many of my father's experiences occurred when I was a mere youngster, which is an additional reason for my ignorance of so much of his life. Again, when I had attained the age of Barmitzvah he (my father) was already over fifty and my attendance on him lasted no more than four or five years.

CHAPTER EIGHT

MEGILAT SEFER

CHAPTER NINE

I myself experienced much distress caused by the straits of dispute, and much time was spent in the harsh wanderings of exile, in serious illnesses and in any number of ever changing situations, so that I have forgotten much which I had learned about my father's life, for the alarming changes of circumstances which I experienced were such that the very mention of them makes me distraught. Indeed, I suffered so many terrible experiences that I doubt whether I can recount all of them, and even if I could "they are more in number than the sand." (cf.Ps.139:18) Hence if I were to record all my experiences then innumerable pens, papers and ink to fill a river would prove insufficient. I will therefore record them briefly , beginning with my childhood. However before I begin my biography I must truthfully inform my readers that my intention is not to enhance my reputation or for self-praise, since I am well aware that I have not attained any renown by virtue of my Torah learning or worldly wisdom, nor have I inherited any great status of which I could boast or claim distinction. Indeed, I hope I won't pen my shortcomings but all and sundry know that I have always opted for

CHAPTER NINE

modesty. Indeed, from the time of my adulthood I have known my own worth and my defects. So for this very reason I am not at all concerned about writing my life story. My lack of arrogance is universally acknowledged, for my sole love is the truth. However, three reasons prompted me to undertake this autobiography and not to hesitate in informing my issue of all the facts of my life to the best of my ability. Should I not completely succeed (in this task) I will, at least record all that I can remember of a particular period (of my life) and in general my experiences up to the present time.

The most cogent reason for writing this autobiography is to record the Almighty's kindness to me from my childhood, although my suffering was such that one would hardly credit it if it were described. If a strong person suffers one in a thousand afflictions yet complains, " is my strength the strength of stone, or is my flesh brass" (Job 12:6) then how much more so does this apply to me who as my parents tender and delicate child constantly suffered every misfortune and dangerous illness. Nevertheless, the Almighty blessed be He, delivered me and has helped me to the present. Indeed, "he sorely chastised me but didn't deliver me to death."(cf.Ps.118:18); He did not forsake me, so that I should be consumed, God forbid, but favoured me as does a father his son (cf.Prov.3:12) and "He set my foot upon a rock".(Ps.4O:3) "When I said my foot was slipping" (cf.Ps.94:18) then the exalted hand of the Lord sustained and supported me. Therefore I am determined to declare God's glory to my fellow Jews and family, so that I should not forget His mercy and kindness but loudly proclaim His praise for standing at the right hand of the needy and "saving me from those who would judge my soul"(cf.Ps.109:31). Indeed, I must inform future generations of His wondrous acts on my behalf, "for one who is the least important in his family." (cf.Jud.6:15) Listen therefore, all you who revere the Almighty whose deeds on my behalf are constantly on my mind, for my mouth will praise the Almighty with joyful lips (cf.Ps.63:6) and with my pen I will pour forth His abundant kindness, and loudly proclaim His praises, so that future generations should learn, and children yet to be born should arise and declare it to their children, so that they in turn should praise the Almighty whose kindness endures for ever. For He saved the soul of the needy from the power of the wicked.

My second reason (for this autobiography) is to strengthen the weak, the contrite in spirit and the humble-hearted, those who are insulted and persecuted for not being involved in wrong-doing. Indeed, just as I presently find my neck under persecution (cf.Lam.5:5) by those who hate me for no reason, who repay bad for good and who detest me instead of pursuing what would be to my advantage. Let every one take note and consequently gently show reverence and trust in the Almighty; let them set their hope in the Lord (cf.Ps.78:7) and not forget His actions. Let not their spirit weaken because of the many oppressors or the odium of the archers.

My third reason (for this autobiography) is to permit the sun of my vindication to shine forth and that no cloud settle upon it (cf.Job 3:5) because of the wicked who have striven with me (cf.Ps.17:19) my deadly enemies who have surrounded me and who, have made many false accusations against me in order to destroy my reputation in the world (cf.Gen.34:30) and with sword in hand destroy me with their lies and arrogance (cf.Jer.23:32) which, to their shame, has pervaded the length and breadth of the world. Indeed, their forged writings have been in existence for some time and consequently I am compelled to clarify my actions before God and mankind so that He may bring forth the justice of my cause as the light (cf.Ps.37:6) and deliver the island of the guiltless (cf.Job 22:30). For the truth is still on my side, and it shall be a covering of the eyes for me and my children, may God be blessed.

I now therefore begin the story of my life so that people should learn the righteous acts of the Lord for whom those who await Him shall suffer no shame nor those who trust in Him endure eternal reproach. For He is a very present help (cf.Ps.46:2) in trouble as my own eyes have so often witnessed. Even when I said in my haste I am cut off out of the land of the living, surely darkness envelops me and the light about me is night (cf.Ps.139:11). Even when I complained my foot is moved, yet Thy kindness O Lord has

CHAPTER NINE

supported me. For though I dwell in darkness the Lord is my light, He will relent his anger and give me solace. Therefore in my mouth will He place a new song, even praise to our Lord.

So may the Almighty place His word in my mouth and may He be with my lips and pen so that His praise should be acknowledged by future generations. Now I have already noted above that when my mother was pregnant with me my father was inflicted with such a severe attack of melancholia because of the loss of all his assets that the doctors despaired of effecting a cure. But God's tender mercies sustained him (my father) and restored him to full health just a few days before I was born. He then made his way back from Emsbad where he had received treatment from the spa waters during the period between Pesach and Shavuot, and eventually arrived in Altona after his wife, my mother the Rabbanit was delivered of me on the fifteenth of Sivan 1697. He himself circumcised me after a change of plans because the Mitzvah had been promised to another person. However, my father initiated me into the Covenant of Judaism with double joy. First, that he had been restored to health and second, that he had acquired a son after he had despaired of so doing, for at that time he had daughters only. Yet a further reason for my father's joy was that he was granted the opportunity of circumcising his own son, his fourth child but his first son, the tender child of my parents who followed after the birth of three daughters.

It was for this reason my parents showed such concern and anxiety over me, and I was reared as a dandled child providing much pleasure (to my parents) and being subject to much tenderness and deep feelings. Nevertheless my father, z"l, was quick to enrol me in the (local) Jewish school when I was only three years old so that by the time I was five I had completed the Mishnah of the Tractate Berakhot. In fact I was so diligent a pupil that my young contemporaries tried to compete with me but didn't attain the stage of reading the Amidah fluently. In later years however, my father desisted from enrolling my younger brother into school when they were of such tender age (three years) for he believed that in so doing he had helped to make me so frail. Were I to attempt to record all the events of my childhood it would be a protracted story, apart from which there are certain incidents which I have completely forgotten. I will therefore mention just the serious illnesses with which I was inflicted in my tender childhood. The first was an illness which first affected my face and then every limb of my body so that I was so seriously ill that (the doctors) despaired of my recovery. However, the Almighty sent forth His word and my health was restored to the extent that my face showed no signs of any previous infection, nor were there any scars. The second illness was when my membrum virile was affected by a terrible rash and for a time the urinary canal was blocked, so that my parents were very worried and concerned for me. My third serious illness was when all my legs were covered with boils just like that suffered by Job, and this too, was accompanied by terrible pains. But the Almighty delivered from all these illnesses apart from other bouts of ill-health to which children are prone, e.g. blisters, chicken-pox, measles teething problems.

Moreover, I was constantly subject to tonsillitis, catarrh, diarrhoea and bladder infections. Occasionally, I was also affected by small boils and heat bumps quite apart from welts which were inflicted by my beloved teachers into whose hands my education was committed. On the whole they were very spiteful and punished me mercilessly. Then there were other aches and pains which I experienced from my early childhood. Indeed, "many a time have they affected me from my childhood, yet they have not prevailed against me."(Ps.129:2) Whether it was the loss of teeth or the pain of new teeth coming through, or the compression of the finger nails and similar pains all of which are too numerous to record here.

When I grew more intelligent I sensed my father's distress and the insults he tolerated, how some people planned to endanger his livelihood and remove him from his high office. Subsequently my father, z"l, suffered a severe attack of jaundice which was caused by an excessive amount of yellow bile. This illness which was really caused by the controversy which broke out in Altona, was of such a serious nature that for a long time the doctors despaired of effecting

CHAPTER NINE

a cure. Hence my sisters and I fasted on a Monday and Thursday in one week, although I was then only twelve. When ultimately my father received a call to the Rabbinate of Amsterdam my exile and wanderings then began in earnest. My family travelled (to Amsterdam) at the close of the winter of 1710, a period of very heavy snow-falls, so that the coach which accommodated all the women and children appeared to be on the point of disintegrating and of falling into the water and sweeping all us away. But our cries ascended to Heaven, had not the Almighty saved us then the water would have carried us away and the torrent swept over us. (cf.Ps.124:4) So we arrived intact in another country viz. Holland, a country which we had not known previously, to a new environment, to a new way of life. Thus we experienced many changes until we became used to the character of the country though the food and drink was not as good as that to which we had been accustomed. But, above all, our peaceful life didn't last very long; "this was not the rest which was to give respite to the weary".(cf.Is.2:) For very soon there began the quarrels and persecutions between the two powerful factions which I mentioned above whereby each fact wanted to swallow up its rival alive. My father was crushed between them and because he was unable to effect any harmony between them, nor possibly have justified both factions, he defended the weaker faction so that they were not trodden under, as they prepared to war against him (my father). The archers, i.e. the opposing stronger faction savagely attacked him, shot at him and planned to remove him from his high office as I have already stated. However the Almighty was his Helper and Shield, for at that time the Sephardi community (of Amsterdam) were his strong supporters. Nevertheless, because of his father's suffering, this was a distressing and perplexing period for Jacob.

    Moreover, this contention impeded a great deal of my Torah studies even when I had already attained the age of Barmitzvah, so that the cool twilight I had longed for viz. the light of the Almighty (Torah study) became a terror for me (cf.Is.21:4). For it was a period of gloom, distress and darkness; a time of anxiety, sorrow and worry;

circumstances which did not afford me the opportunity of poring over a sefer, nor to correct my deficiencies in Torah learning, or to acquire the blessing of Torah learning. Hence there was no respite in my lack of tranquillity. Then the sins of that place, Amsterdam were responsible for the arrival of that snake, the hypocritical and hateful Hayyun, one who confused all the Jewish world so that my father, z"l, became involved in a terrible struggle in opposing the powerful and arrogant members of the Sephardi community (of Amsterdam). The latter had abrogated their previous bond of friendship with him (my father) and had become his enemies by involving themselves in a dispute which was not their concern. This was all because they wanted to cover up the shame of their leader and the sins of which R.Solomon Aylon was guilty, that ultimately my father, z"l, was compelled to leave Amsterdam as I have already stated. So he bent his back for wandering once more on the wings of exile and hastened his, as well as his family flight from Amsterdam.

In mid-winter 1714 my father, z"l, travelled to London (where he stayed) for several weeks whilst he sent us, his family by ship to Emden, where we remained as guests until after Pesach. This small community paid us the highest respect and treated us handsomely. The scholarly lay-leader, Reb Leib Emden, my he rest in peace, wanted me to marry his daughter who was so learned and intelligent that she literally had no par in the whole of Germany. He was prepared to give me a large dowry for he was extremely rich as well as being learned in Torah. Moreover his daughter longed to be married to a Torah scholar who was at the same time of a renowned lineage. However, because of a certain defect in her family my father withheld his consent to the marriage although from my point of view I was sorely tempted to consent. For I was sufficiently intelligent to weigh up all the facts, and it was obvious to me that the projected marriage was most suitable. For Reb Leib Emden was unique among German Jewry both in wealth and in possessing a fine daughter so that to me the union seemed right in every way. Moreover, I would have obtained complete independence, (as a result of the marriage), for I fully appreciated that my father, z"l, couldn't make any

CHAPTER NINE

provision for me and that he had enough worries in seeing that his family didn't go wandering off to some unknown destination. Again, Reb Leib Emden and his family had a great affection for me and literally begged me to consent to the projected betrothal and so fulfil their fondest wishes for my welfare.

Nevertheless I had no desire, God forbid, to cause my father any distress though I myself felt inclined to agree to the (marriage) proposal and not abandon this favourable opportunity. Moreover, the defect in Reb Leib Emden's family was not so serious that he should be rejected, for it wasn't God forbid, an essential disqualification. Indeed, all the most respectable lay-leaders of Germany, had attached themselves to Reb Leib's family which enjoyed an unsurpassed reputation for generosity and was considered a family of high rank. Again, such a proposition (for marriage) doesn't happen even day. Yet I didn't disclose what I really felt about it but bowed to the wishes of my father, z"l, out of my love for him. Ultimately I came to the conclusion that the Almighty had not destined this young lady to be my marriage partner, for in respect of the latter I was destined for a more important marriage in terms of family repute. In the meantime, as I shall later explain with the Almighty's help, I experienced a period of trouble and distress. However, the above-mentioned young lady (the daughter of Reb Leib) whose wish to marry me was unfulfilled, was later to show me great kindness when the Almighty designated me to the Rabbinate of Emden. She made strenuous efforts on my behalf so as to enable me to obtain that Rabbinic position and was most kind to me and my wife, may she rest in peace, so that the special affection which my family had for her (Reb Leib's daughter) was like that of a sister or any other close relative; as I shall describe later.

My father, z"l left Emden with considerable responsibility on his shoulders, for my parents, z"l, then had five sons and five daughters all of whom were born in Altona. Only one, of my parents' children, a little girl who was born in Amsterdam, but she was no longer with us having died on the journey. My sister Rachel was then staying with her mother-in law in Eisenstadt whilst, my elder sister together with her husband and family were with us in Emden. My mother the Rabbanit, z"l, was then with child so we were compelled to take with us a maid and a man-servant. Under these circumstances we had to travel with large fully-laden coaches but because of the presence of many soldiers on the roads, we stayed at the house of my uncle, z"l, for several days. It was there that the Almighty prompted me to write an answer to the criticism which Rabbi E- had made of a responsum of my father, z"l for he (my father) didn't have the opportunity of examining the criticisms whilst he was travelling. At that time I made a point of scrutinising and carefully considering those criticisms and it was there (in my uncle's house) I wrote some of my reply. It was the first learned responsum I had got up, with the Almighty's help, but I neither mentioned it nor showed it to my father until we reached Breslau. He then read what I had written in his defence and he was very pleased with my thoughts on the topic.

Kissing me on the head he declaimed the Scriptural verse: "Every man shall kiss the lips of the person who gives a right answer" (Prov.24:26). After a stay of several weeks in Berlin we made for Breslau. The journey proved to be hazardous for the Prussian army was travelling on same road, so that although a state of war didn't exist at that time all those roads were dangerous travel on. Thus we were occasionally compelled to stop. In fact we did actually come into contact with some of those soldiers and that we managed to extricate ourselves unharmed from their clutches was indeed a miracle. Finally we arrived in Breslau at the end of the summer of 1715.

At the beginning of the winter of 1715 we travelled from Breslau to Poland, and it was during this period that my father, z"l, gave my sister Nechama in marriage. However, the latter because of our many sins proved unfortunate, for her husband, the grandson of the lay-leader Reb Weitschutz was killed. We continued our wanderings under great distress, and for a time we stayed in Apta and then in small towns close to Apta for the latter suffered a severe fire.

CHAPTER NINE

Indeed "we were weary and were granted no rest" (Lam.5:5) until an emissary arrived from Hamburg and informed my father, z"l, that the lay-leader Reb Aberle London had nominated him (my father) as a member of the court which was to adjudicate the quarrel between him (Reb Aberle) and his brother-in-law Reb Ephraim, as I have already described above. Taking me with him, my father then set out for Hamburg and we made this long and hazardous journey in mid-winter. It was then I suffered the first serious attack of shortness of breath and this still further increased my father's worries and distress. I received a number of different treatments on the journey e.g. at Berlin, but they all proved ineffective. In fact it was only after suffering many years from this affliction that I came to realise it was caused by weak blood circulation, which had to be drastically reduced. Owing to my illness my father was constantly attending me until one of my haemorrhoids was opened, with the Almighty's help, and this gave me some relief. However, I was then affected by Melancholia and in this state I travelled to Hamburg where I remained until after winter. Then, at the beginning of summer my father made the return journey with me to Breslau and subsequently arranged my betrothal.

    Following my marriage, time effected a separation between me and my father, z"l, and I was not privileged to see him again. His departure for me was like the soul separating from the body, particularly since I was then a tender youth of seventeen lacking the necessary completion of my Torah studies. For hitherto "I had skimmed from the knowledge of my father, my teacher, as much as a dog lapping from the sea". (cf. TB.Sanhedrin 68a)

    This was because of the harsh circumstances which I experienced from the beginning of my adulthood, as I have previously described much of which involved me in distress, sorrow, anxiety and long periods of wandering to and fro in different countries. I was now making my way to a hitherto unknown country viz. Moravia of whose language and people I was completely ignorant and to whose life-style I was in no way accustomed. Yet my greatest distress was the feeling that I had not attended my father, z"l,

MEGILAT SEFER

as much as I should have done. For when I was very young I convinced myself that there was still time to achieve a degree of perfection in my Torah studies. I therefore failed to pay full attention to my teachers' instructions. Again, when I was anxious to study I was unsuccessful in my search for a teacher and mentor. Moreover, my father, z"l, was fully involved in the severe dissension which I mentioned above nor could he afford to maintain private teachers for his younger sons, since rents in Amsterdam were very high whilst my father would not accept any gift and was consequently short of money. Hence when I was about fifteen, the most receptive age, I had to teach my two younger brothers for my father couldn't afford to maintain a suitable teacher for them. This was quite apart from the fact that I myself no longer had a teacher and mentor.

When I left my father, z"l, I travelled to Moravia with my wife and father-in-law, z"l; this was in the first year of our marriage. Arriving tired and weary from the journey, we found the whole of Moravia had been affected by plague which had spread to Broda where we were staying, for my father-in-law had returned to his home (in that city). When after a few days the plague had spread through the greater part of Broda, we fled the city and remained near some neighbouring villages so as to facilitate further flight. We found ourselves abandoned in the countryside and, for several weeks during the winter we had, to shelter under the trees of the forest and to endure nightly frost. This situation continued until, with God's mercy the villagers took pity on us and allowed us to stay in their houses at exorbitant rents. Having surmounted this problem I then became more aware of the difficulties which confronted one who had come to a new country with its own particular characteristics and lifestyle. Moreover at that time thing were proving very difficult for my father-in-law and I was compelled to seek a livelihood contrary to my soft nature, lifestyle and to the pursuit of studies in my parental home. But I immediately experienced something more bitter than death itself for my wife, may she rest in peace, became irascible though I could have appeased herewith a kindly word, (cf.TB. Yevamot 63b) for she was essentially a pious lady, but my misdeeds occasioned this

CHAPTER NINE

behaviour. Moreover, I was no longer maintained my father-in-law, z"l, and they (my wife and father-in-law) were "ploughing with my calf in order to discover my riddle. (cf.Jud.14:18) i.e. they searched for my purse in which I kept the little money I had, for I had no intention of allowing my money to be spent wastefully.

Hence "when the barley is gone from the pitcher, strife comes knocking at the door" (TB.Bava Metzia 59a), so that my wife and I were constantly quarrelling and were on the verge of separating. All this robbed me of any peace and tranquillity; indeed, I haven't enjoyed a peaceful day since my early youth, the blossoming of my childhood, from the womb of the dawn when I should have enjoyed the dew of my youth. But my childhood and youth was spent in affliction for I was constantly confronted with distress and torment, with considerable worries both at home and in the world at large, so that any joy I experienced was tinged with darkness.

Nevertheless, the precepts of the Almighty are right, bringing joy to the broken and contrite in heart (cf.Ps.19:8). They (the precepts) gave me joyfulness of heart and restored my spirit. Indeed, not Thy Torah proved my delight, then I would have perished in my affliction." (Ps. 119:92) However I have omitted; an essential fact viz. that at that particular time my library consisted of merely four volumes of the Tur which I had brought with me and were a present from my uncle, z"l. I studied these with the application which the good hand of the Almighty granted me. But apart from these I didn't have any tractate of the Talmud which I wanted to study unless I borrowed one, and that proved difficult. Although my father-in-law had many sets of the Talmud and his house was full of costly and important seforim I couldn't employ then for my studies since I wasn't allowed to use them and study them to the degree I wished. Yet notwithstanding all these problems (which inhibited my Torah studies) people were attracted to my youthful personality, and both married and unmarried Torah students were eager for me to teach them. Hence, although I was more concerned to study than to teach I couldn't, the Lord forbid, ignore their constant pleas to assist them.

Moreover I convinced myself that I would gain more from my students (than from my teachers) for they would keep me on my toes as far as Torah studies were concerned. Thus, I bowed my shoulders and became a bondsman in the service of the Almighty together with associates who paid me the greatest attention. Young men and reputable students met under my auspices and I taught them Gemara with Rashi and Tosefot, Tur Orach Chayyim with the commentary of the Bet Yosef, Tenach , Halakhah and Aggadic texts. The students found my teaching most acceptable and I for my part, found my association with them both gratifying and pleasant, sweet company indeed. Eventually they (my students) wanted to give me a regular salary which would have been more than ample to meet the cost of living, for their fathers were wealthy and prominent Hungarian merchants. However, I adamantly refused, though in a jocular fashion, for I wouldn't take any money or its equivalent. However, this period of rest and joy didn't last very long, for in these three years of service I had assumed the status of a daily worker since I didn't leave my students to themselves after I had finished my daily Rabbinical discourse, for they had to revise the lesson in my presence.

This applied in particular to my lectures on Decisors like the Tur with the commentary of the Bet Yosef, for I wouldn't dismiss my students until they were fully acquainted with the topic of my daily discourse. In fact occasionally I was so involved in supervising them that I developed a sore throat and had to bandage my head (because of headaches) brought about by the strain of having to explain the texts so that they should be fully conversant with them, that the latter should be logically marshalled and free from any irrational errors.

However, when I learned the news of the death of my father, z"l, the spoiler had suddenly entered my tent and "all my cords were broken" (Jer.10:20) my purpose went, even the thoughts of my heart (cf. Job 17:11) Terror overwhelmed me, (cf.Is.21:4) fear took hold of me (cf. Ps.48:7), the twilight I longed for became a terror (cf.Is.21:4). Indeed terrors were turned upon me (c 30:15) the wheel turned over me, it turned me on my back and rolled me as a ball to a spacious

CHAPTER NINE

land viz. Poland. I made the long journey through country hitherto unknown to me, a hazardous journey in which I was accompanied (on the coach) by Poles. The journey of well over a hundred miles was fraught with perils. Thus, on one occasion as we were leaving the hostelry, we sensed we were joined by two highwaymen on horseback who accompanied our coach until we reached wooded country. They (the highwaymen) constantly rode back and forth scrutinising us as though they planned to attack us. (This continued) until our coach met up with another coach carrying some armed Gentile merchants who were travelling just ahead of us. When the above-mentioned highwaymen saw the other coach they retreated and didn't harm us, blessed be our Deliverer.

Thank God I arrived in Lvov at the end of the summer of 1718 and found my family in deep mourning (for my father). Indeed, the whole of Polish Jewry were lamenting this terrible loss for which they could find little consolations as I have already mentioned above.

I re-aroused the mourning by delivering a eulogy at the grave of my father, z"l, in the presence of a vast crowd. For all the highest dignitaries of the community together with a large throng of the general community came to honour the deceased and listen to my pleasing address which (helped) gain me a fine reputation. The whole assembly found my speech most appropriate. I entitled the eulogy "Yetiv Pitgom" because of the tombstone (Mazeivah) which I had arranged for my father, z"l, and which was erected on the same day on which I delivered this eulogy. In fact the erection of the tombstone was the subject of my address which also incorporated some apt verses of the current Sidra of the week, so that the eulogy was profound and pleasing and everything fitted in so appropriately that everyone realised it was original. It also comprehended original comments and elucidation of (verse) of the Torah, whilst the main theme corresponded extremely well with the current weekly Sidra. I was therefore encouraged to publish this eulogy in a special booklet and, with the Almighty's assistance, it has already been printed.

In Lvov too, I experienced both joy and sorrow, for I studied

(Torah) with my younger brothers and with the son-in-law of the contemporary Rabbi of Lvov, the son of Rabbi Bezalel who was the brother of my father-in- law and presided over the Bet Din of Ostrov. The above-mentioned son later became Rector of the Yeshivah in Ostrov. At that time the community of Lvov did me the honour of offering me the position of presiding Rabbi of their Bet Din, in fact they had previously wanted me to accept the position of (communal) Rabbi as well, provided I grew a beard. This indicated their great affection for the family of my father, z"l, for they believed his sons were sure to emulate him. However, I was then very young whereas "it is a multitude of years which teaches wisdom," and I was an insignificant personality and, although people regarded me as important, I didn't contemplate pursuing any elevated position in the community. Nevertheless, because of their great love and affection for me they made this gesture of presenting me with the splendid and honourable mantle of Rabbi of the Bet Din, a position second only to the Presiding Rabbi of the latter institution, thinking thereby that I would permanently settle in Lvov.

Indeed, all the community would bless themselves through me and my family and I only wish I would see the realisation of all the blessing, I heard behind my back whenever I walked through the streets. There, in the shops, women sat selling all kinds of food and drink and as we passed them they would bless themselves through us. Moreover, the martyred and saintly Rabbi Chayyim Reizes, the presiding Rabbi of the Bet Din, may the Almighty avenge his blood, planned to retain me in the city and begged me to settle there so that I could study with his brother who also the father-in-law of the saintly Rabbi, may the Almighty avenge his blood. Again, reputable rabbinic lay-leaders like Henoch and his brother-in-law Reb Nathan, may he rest in peace, wanted me to settle in Zolochav and study in their Bet Midrash (promising) to provide me with an ample livelihood. In fact I was quite content settle in Lvov, particularly in view of the deep and abiding affection and respect which the community evinced towards my family and the fact that we would be

CHAPTER NINE

living in a good and spacious country whether from the aspect of obtaining an easy livelihood or the marriage prospects (the country offered) my father's sons and daughters who were very young at the time. For though my father, z"l, who was survived by seven young orphans viz. four sons and three daughters, was not so anxious to become affluent through marriages, they (the prospective suitors) would indeed have made us rich.

For all the eminent people of Polish Jewry were anxious to become closely attached to the children of my father, z"l, and would have expanded as much money in the way of dowries and other gifts as we wished, besides plying my mother, the Rabbanit, z"l, with considerable presents. Indeed, even if there had been seventy children to marry off, this number wouldn't have proved adequate to meet the desire of all those in the community who were anxious to arrange marriages with the children of my father, z"l. Hence not only was there no need for us to offer any dowries but they were prepared to make up any deficiencies in the dowries we were prepared to offer and even to supplement them with any number of gifts. They were also ready to make gifts to me, a young man, though the eldest son, were I to agree to the proposed betrothal, and all this apart from the gifts that promised my mother, z"l. Nevertheless, we were reluctant to agree to any marriage arrangements with these affluent people who were constantly urging us and sending their friends and deputies, Shtadtlanim and marriage-brokers, with the object of attracting us to their wealth. For even if they were prepared to open up their purses and conciliate us with large amounts of money it would have proved of little consequence, unless we considered the proposed betrothal as befitting our status. Indeed, just as my father, z"l, rejected wealth as a prime consideration in the betrothal of his children, as he had demonstrated in my case and that of my elder sister, so we emulated him in paying little consideration to wealth, but rather to pedigree.

It was because of this attitude (of ours) that a number of the most powerful personalities in Polish Jewry became our enemies. In fact on one occasion my mother (may she rest in peace) and I suffered a harrowing experience. It happened that one of the local lay-leaders was most insistent in marrying into our family and was extremely anxious that we would consent to the betrothal of his daughter to one of my brothers. To this end he was ready to provide a very handsome dowry whilst at the same time he involved so many mediators (to help gain his object) that we hardly had time to sleep. But we couldn't consent to the proposed betrothal for an obvious reason viz. that a child of my father, z"l, might thereby fail to preserve a principle for which that saintly person (my father) would have given his life. What then could we do in order to be relieved of that important person's pressure (on us)? We decided to arrange a marriage between that brother and the daughter of a Rabbi of a highly distinguished family who were, at the same time, affluent as well as highly reputable. (We did this) despite the fact that this betrothal brought us no immediate financial gain. The lay-leader who had made such strenuous efforts (to betroth his daughter to my brother) realising that all his efforts had been in vain and all his plans rendered fruitless, now became our sworn enemy.

He even opposed us over a bill of debt which he had issued against the province (of Lvov) and in addition to this, he made every effort to bring about a cancellation of the marriage-betrothal we had arranged. We thought the latter would lead to a cessation of his activities but he had other ideas and, as I shall describe later, he proved successful.

This appeared to be determined by the Almighty, for soon after my mother, z"l, passed away following a very serious illness. Ostensibly her death was due to excessive sorrow and worry, for she was inconsolable over the death of the partner of her youth, since she and my father were of a similar age, though she was his second wife, as I have stated above. When my father, z"l, died she was about forty one, so a number of eminent Polish Rabbis wanted to marry her. But, God forbid, for even if a person began to hint to her of re-marrying she would virtually have attacked him because of the bitter feeling this proposal evoked. This was due to her compassion and affection for her late husband, z"l, whose piety and saintliness had no peer in his generation. Hence from the moment her dear husband

CHAPTER NINE

was taken from her she was constantly tearful and in her loyalty to him she wouldn't remarry for all the money in the world. Though people would try to console her by referring to her children and observing "why are you so worried and tearful, haven't you the joy of having his children for whom you have no cause to worry?" On the contrary they continued, her children were a new lease of life for her and would give her much happiness in her old age for every one was anxious to arrange (marriages for her children) so that she would become a rich woman through them. She however paid little attention to such sentiments but remained tearful and worried so that all her joy was darkened. This continued until she became seriously ill and this caused me much anxiety and distress for her passing would have been a terrible blow. Our prayers (for her recovery) ascended to the Almighty, but because of our many sins, she died about three or four years after the passing of my father, z"l. On the following day my little sister aged three also passed away, so that my mother's burial was surrounded by unusual circumstances. Subsequently, I became so ill that the doctors almost despaired of curing me, but the Almighty observed my affliction and sending forth His word He restored my health.

When the news of the death of my mother, z"l, reached Dukla where my brother-in-law Rabbi Leib, my eldest sister's husband, was Rabbi, he immediately travelled to Lvov and finding me extremely ill, he assumed control of all the family business as well as the affairs of my brother. He cancelled the latter's betrothal which I previously mentioned, and taking my brother under his wing he went to Zolochev. Whilst staying there he arranged a second betrothal for my brother, whose previous betrothal had terminated, with the man who had shown such insistence with me, as have described above, and who was prepared to spend a considerable amount of money in order to attain his fondest wish. Moreover, this man promised my brother-in-law, may he rest in peace, that he would make every effort to obtain an important Rabbinate for him (my brother-in-law). In this way that person achieved his earnest wish after he had despaired of so doing.

MEGILAT SEFER

In the meantime I, who had stood surety for my brother's first betrothal, remained in Lvov. When my brother-in-law's arrangements for my brother's betrothal in Zolochev became public knowledge, the family of the Rabbi with whose daughter my brother's first betrothal had been agreed summoned me to appear before Rabbi Joshua who had recently been appointed to the Rabbinate of Lvov. The summons was issued on Shabbat for they (the Rabbi's family) had learned that I intended to leave Lvov at the termination of that particular Shabbat. Consequently in agreeing to this summons Rabbi Joshua had removed all restrictions. My surety didn't involve my brother's person he was already an adult and could act independently, but my surety did concern the expenditure on certain gifts, clothes and other items required for the proposed marriage. After considerable difficulties I managed to emerge unscathed for they (the Rabbi's family) realised that I was not at fault. Incidentally, I should mention the marriages which my fathers, z"l, arranged during his life time for my three elder sisters. First he arranged the marriage of my eldest sister Miriam, may she rest in peace, with my brother-in-law Rabbi Leib, the son of Rabbi Saul, z"l, whose genealogy could be traced back to the eminent Rabbi Heschel, z"l. This marriages involved my father in considerable expense viz. seventeen hundred Reichthalers. He (my father) could have arranged a marriage with any one of a number of affluent German Jews whose sons were very fine young men and who were most anxious to be married to my father's daughter even if she had no dowry. For since she was so beautiful, the loveliest and most intelligent young lady, these people were prepared to expend any amount of money (if my father consented). My father however, paid no attention to the proud who floated in wealth but gave his tender daughter a dowry far above his means in order to become attached to a family of eminent pedigree. Quite apart from the dowry he had to meet other considerable expenses including maintenance, for some years (after the marriage), whereas Rabbi Leib's father only had to meet the cost of clothes and other gifts.

CHAPTER NINE

In the course of travelling to their younger son's wedding Rabbi Leib's father died in Glogau. He had recently been appointed to the Rabbinate of Amsterdam and planned to go there after his son's wedding, but he was not destined to witness his son's wedding ceremony for the hour of his passing had intervened. Subsequently my (future) brother-in-law together with his mother and brothers arrived (in Lvov) and my father made the wedding at very great expense, as I have already stated. After his mother, brothers and brother-in-law had left Lvov the young bridegroom remained under the roof of my father, z"l, just as a new-born child and for some years he battened on my father's wisdom, pouring water on his (my father's) hands and exercising the duties of secretary in transcribing my father's writings and correspondence. My father also taught him grammar and other subjects. Yet despite his close attendance on the Rabbi (my father) my brother-in-law didn't succeed in acquiring a fine and lucid style in Hebrew, but he did gain some expertise in logical argument, in arriving at decisions on Jewish law and Practice and in the conduct of communal affairs. All in all he lacked very little. From the very outset my brother-in-law was most assiduous in his studies which was due to my family's kindness and overwhelming consideration (towards him), advantages which not one in a thousand eminent rabbinic scholars ever merited. His wife was a fine lady possessed of sterling qualities of character, who loved wisdom, who was sincerely religious, modest and profoundly pious. Moreover, in addition to her beautiful and dignified ways she had a deep affection for her husband which was blended with humility and modesty. She was highly skilled in womanly activities and in keeping her home spotlessly clean. In addition to all these advantages he (my brother-in-law) was held in deep affection by his in-laws, my parents, z"l, who saw to his every want. Hence all my father's interests revolved round him (my brother law) and he endeavoured to rear and educate my brother-in-law so as to enable him to succeed to the best of his ability. They (my parents) even made sure that he had the right type of friends, and all this was because he was the first son-in-law, the husband of their beloved daughter. Virtually all my father's toil and efforts were directed towards his (my brother-in-law's) interests not only during my father's life, but even subsequent to it, for he had arranged that after his death my orphaned brothers and sisters should stay close to him (my brother-in-law).

As my brother-in-law was about to leave Poland I handed him the whole of the bequest which my father, z"l, had left him viz. cash, chattels, books and government bonds. Had he taken what was presently available he would have lost a considerable amount of money, amounting to many thousands of Reichthalers so, as the eldest brother-in-law I arranged to have a bill of debt drawn up with Reb Hendele of Altona which the latter would ultimately be paid. In this way I discharged my obligation regarding the above-mentioned bequest. For Reb Hendele realised he would recover the equivalent of the loan once all the items of the bequest had been collected viz. the cash, the books, many of which were scattered around different place e.g. Danzig and Breslau, apart from he government bonds which had to be redeemed. In fact after I left Poland all this had been effected so that Reb Hendele received full payment. Nevertheless for several years he incurred considerable expenses in maintaining my brothers and sisters until, with the Almighty's help, they were all married. Yet with the exception of my sister Leah, he (my brother-in-law) didn't have to give any dowries.

For Leah was betrothed to the son of the Rabbi and lay-leader Rabbi Chayyim Lisrel, a very fine young man. My brother-in-law gave this fellow a considerable sum of money and assisted him in obtaining the Rabbinate of Lvov. During his life time my father, z"l, had committed himself to giving this young man a dowry of a thousand Reichthalers , apart from other customary gifts. He (the young man) proved to be a stubborn creditor so that my brother-in-law had to discharge this debt, although to this day I don't know how much he had to spend on my sister Leah.

However in respect of my four brothers he didn't have to expend anything. On the contrary, he gained considerably from their marriages, and in particular, from the lay-leader Reb Joseph Ostrow, with whom I had been instrumental in arranging the betrothal of my

CHAPTER NINE

youngest brother and his daughter. As long as my youngest brother remained under his aegis my brother-in-law did very well out of him. This was also true of the marriage which he arranged for my brother who had previously been betrothed to the daughter of the Rabbi, as I have already described. In this case too, my brother-in-law made considerable tangible gains, but it was this very betrothal which involved him in certain problems arising from a specific Rabbinate and resulted in considerable enmity and rivalry between my brother-in-law and the above-mentioned R.Joshua. The recent appointment of the latter to the Rabbinate of Lvov was effected through the efforts of members of his family who resided in that community. In fact his appointment involved a degree of secrecy and bribery which had become customary among Jews and non-Jews but which was contrary to Torah law. Indeed there were a large number of people in Lvov who were friendly disposed to the family of my father, z"l, and who would therefore have wanted my brother-in-law to be appointed to the Rabbinate of Lvov were it not for the powerful group who had bribed the authorities. Moreover when the Rabbi and lay-leader R.Nathan of Zolochev became attached to our family and with my above-mentioned brother-in-law who had helped R.Nathan to satisfy his earnest wish of gaining my brother as his son-in-law, he (R.Nathan) also wished to assist my brother-in-law in obtaining the Rabbinate of Lvov. All this resulted in aggravating the rivalry and dissension between my brother-in-law and the above mentioned R.Joshua and they persecuted each other over a long period.

In the meantime R.Nathan endeavoured to obtain the Rabbinate of Tarnopol for my brother-in-law, a position which was already held by a member of my brother-in-law's family. The latter had to give way to my brother-in-law because of R.Nathan's efforts, for he enjoyed considerable influence with the local authorities. As a result the former Rabbi lost his position and was replaced by my brother-in-law. Some people said my brother-in-law should not have allowed himself to become involved in this affair since he was not a Rabbinic scholar and was therefore unqualified to act as a Rabbi.

MEGILAT SEFER

But as it transpired, this affair resulted in my brother-in-law acquiring a host of enemies including some members of his own family who lived in that locality. The latter had at first favoured and supported him, but finally they violently opposed him and caused his endless trouble, for they felt he had involved himself in a nefarious business in tormenting his own kith and kin solely for monetary gain. Consequently they persisted in their opposition until they forced him abandon the above-mentioned Rabbinate. Thus they behaved in exactly the same way as he, for they argued, does Poland require such a person who at first had emulated his Rabbi and mentor Chacham Tzvi, who was like a father to him whose every deed had a religious motive, who loved to see equity and justice pursued by everyone, without vacillation and who never looked for advancement or self-aggrandisement. For this reason many of my brother-in-law's former admirers became his enemies. Nor was he successful in obtaining the Rabbinate of Lvov, especially since it was already occupied by the above-mentioned R.Joshua, and possession is the primary consideration.

As long as he (my brother-in-law) occupied his first Rabbinate viz. the small community of Duka, he was zealous and successful in his studies, but subsequently he became very involved in seeking advancement in the Rabbinate and received a call from the community of Reischerg and here too, he wasn't free of problems; then he obtained the Rabbinate of Glogau. It is my opinion that in these places he failed to make any substantial progress in his Torah-studies, although he did advance in those spheres in which the Rabbinate is unavoidably involved viz. the conduct of communal affairs, experience in Halakhic decisions and the duties of Dayan of the Bet Din. This progress, was due, in particular, to the fact that these communities had eminent Rabbinic scholars and learned Dayanim all of whom liked my brother-in-law. In any case, apart from the struggle over the Rabbinate of Lvov, my brother-in-law was very often involved in personal difficulties, for he had considerable expenses which couldn't be met by the salary he obtained from any one of the above-mentioned Rabbinates. But when he was older he

CHAPTER NINE

succeeded in obtaining a position by which he honoured both his father and teacher (my father), for he received a call to the Ashkenazi community of Amsterdam, to which there was no opposition. He remained there for fifteen years being well provided with worldly goods and receiving more than an adequate salary. However, in Amsterdam too he couldn't avoid the occasional strife which prevailed among the two local factions which I already mentioned above. Although for a time he managed to control some of them, occasionally there was a resurgence of the old hatred of him, as well as enmity which arose from a new direction. For it was during his Rabbinate that the community was once again split open over the support of the two Chazanim.

At first over the Chazan who was later appointed to the community of Glogau and subsequently over the Chazan who was later appointed to the position at Schweidnitz. All this resulted in a further clash of opinions, although the factions didn't get the better of my brother-in-law since he knew how to avoid the complaints and seditious murmurs which his enemies hurled against him.

My brother-in-law also established a new Bet Ha-Midrash (in Amsterdam) and so emulating the example set by his teacher, my father, z"l. But he was unable to undertake a great deal of teaching (Torah) since he had become very weak and suffered much towards the twilight of his life. So that when I left Lvov and visited him in Amsterdam ,he (my brother-in-law) was beyond recovery, yet as soon as I entered his house he seemed to gain a new lease of life and lived until Pesach 1755 i.e. about two years after the passing of my sister, his wife, may she rest in peace. He left his estate to his sons and daughters, whilst his oldest son succeeded to (his father's) Rabbinate. I know feel duty bound to laud his virtues for he was a very generous person, as indeed was my sister, his wife, who constantly showered innumerable kindness on her family and others. This was why they merited that which the pillars of society failed to merit. Indeed, my brother-in-law's life was a complete affirmation of that Rabbinic sentiment, "the service of the Torah is greater than the study thereof." (cf.TB. Berakhot 7b) For his attendance on my father was akin to that of a servant, and it was this virtuous conduct which made him merit two scholarly sons, who in some respects resembled their mother's brothers, all of whom are scholars, authors and pious men, may the Almighty preserve their lives.

My father's second daughter married the son of the eminent R.Meir who presided over the Bet Din of Prossnitz, and this son-in-law too, proved successful in the Rabbinate of several Lithuanian communities. They had a one and only son who proved to be a scholar. This sister's marriage too, incurred my father in considerable expense. May the Almighty prolong their lives favourably. My third sister married the grandson of Reb H.Weitschuetz, but was of short duration, for only a few years after the marriage he was murdered in some woodland. Apparently, this husband was in debt to his father and uncles and they therefore, were instrumental in the murder of two fine and good men, as I have described above. He left no children so that my sister remained a widow, completely on her own, for she had no wish to re-marry, and though many important contemporary Jews were prepared to marry her she preferred to remain a widow for the rest of her life.

As I have previously stated my father married off my elder sisters during his lifetime and he likewise arranged a marriage for me, his first son and fourth child.

As for my younger sister, Leah, my father arranged her betrothal to the son of the Rabbi and lay-leader R.Chayyim Lazarus and he also gave her a considerable dowry. However, he wasn't destined to witness her marriage which took place after the death of my father, z"l, and which absorbed all my father's bequest, as I have already stated. This marriage didn't last long, but she did have a fine son from it. Subsequently she married Reb Meir, a son of the eminent Rabbi Eleazer of Broda, who presided over the Bet Din of Amsterdam and who later emigrated to Eretz Yisrael. This marriage too, didn't last very long but, may the Almighty be blessed, she had a fine son from this husband, z"l. My youngest sister, Deborah, may she live long, was married to a grandson of Reb Joel of Ostrov and both her father-in-law and husband held rabbinates in Volhynia. My

CHAPTER NINE

four brothers, long may they live, were all married after the death of my father, z"l, having been betrothed to the daughters of prominent Jews. The only exception was my brother, Reb Nathan, who was married to the daughter of a prominent Rabbi. The Almighty has graciously granted them fine children, who are scholarly and intelligent; they also have fine son-in-laws, may the Almighty be blessed. However, since I am not acquainted with them or their names, I won't say anything more about them.

    Now, with the Almighty's help, I shall revert to the story of my life and begin from where I made the previous interpolation.

I was eager to settle in Poland with my family, "for how pleasant it is for brethren to dwell together" (cf. Ps.133:1). I therefore stayed there from the end of the summer 1718, when I first arrived, until after Pesach 1719. During this period I wrote to my wife (asking her) to join me in Poland and (stating) that it was a fine country, especially since many Rabbinic scholars lived there, and that it was a land where one could obtain a livelihood as well as a social status. Moreover, (I wrote) it would give us the opportunity of obtaining the right marriage partners for our children, particularly if (like ours) they came from families of the highest pedigree, for people would be so anxious to attach themselves to such families that they would more than compensate their parents. However, I did not succeed in this endeavour for my wife would not accede to my request. Nevertheless, "the counsel of the Lord, that shall stand" (Prov.19:21), for the Almighty planned it to my advantage as I shall shortly explain. My wife was very young at the time and therefore was prepared to leave her parents to go to another country. Consequently, I was compelled to return home after I had experienced a full measure of serious troubles, apart from that period when I remained in Lvov during the year of mourning for my father. During that time we hardly slept, and none of us enjoyed any tranquillity, because we suffered much distress. For it was in Lvov that on the second of Shevat 1719 I buried Sarah Rivkah, may she rest in peace, that is my pious mother, who was quite young, in fact little more then forty. On a few occasions she had appeared to be on the point of death, but on hearing our constant weeping, she recovered somewhat. Moreover, all the family fell ill, and I too, though my illness was more severe in that I was almost on the point of death. However, the Almighty issued His command and I fully recovered though I gained my life (and nothing more).

I left my family in Lvov after I had arranged the betrothal of my youngest brother to the daughter of the lay-leader, Reb Joel Ostrov. I also left all my father's bequest viz. chattels, books, and credit-notes amounting to some considerable sum with my above-mentioned brother-in-law, may he rest in peace, and with my family. For as I have stated, this bequest was dispersed in other places. I was given several copies of my father's Responsa which had been published in his life time but only a few of which had been sold. Consequently, my family obligated me, as the eldest son, to take them and distribute them amongst Jacob that is to sell them to our fellow-Jews. Incidentally, the family also gave me bills of exchange which my father, may he rest in peace, held on Reb Hendele Cohen, and his brother and brother-in-law in Hamburg, and which they (my family) felt should now be paid. Consequently, I left my father's house at the beginning of the summer of 1719 and returned safely to my home in Broda where I remained for some time. It was during this period that I again fell very ill as did the serving-man whom I had brought from Poland. However, the Almighty in His mercy restored me to full health.

As soon as I felt better I had to plan a long and arduous journey to fulfil my promise to my family viz. to sell (my father's) Responsa and to obtain as much cash as possible from the debts which people owed my father, as I have already stated. For in this way I would assist my orphaned brothers and sisters in meeting the cost which suitable marriages would incur. They would have nothing to do with any money which was wrongfully acquired, this being a characteristic they had inherited from my grandfather and father, z"l. I thought I would also get a certain sum as my share once I had finalised the accounts, and on this consideration I accepted the

CHAPTER NINE

obligation of settling an outstanding account of my father's to Malkah, may she rest in peace, the daughter of R.Meir, may he rest in peace, who had died in Altona and had entrusted her estate with my father until her children grew up. I therefore spent a further one hundred Reichthalers out of my own pocket on the security of the Sefer (my father's Responsa) and the debts (bills of exchange) due to my father which I had taken with me.

I therefore set out on my travels again, having first written to Hamburg and corresponded with the lay-leader, Reb Handele Cohen, who was the principal person involved with the financial affairs we had in Hamburg. I set out my opinions to him in writing with (particular) reference to the above-mentioned debts which at first seemed certain to be repaid. However, Reb Hendele had to give pride of place to obtaining a considerable sum of money from the estate of Reb Mordechai Cohen (his brother). During his life-time the latter had been prepared to come to some compromise and to repay Reb Hendele almost thirty thousand Reichthalers. However, Reb Hendele would not accept for his brother owed him considerably more. Since Reb Mordechai was a powerful person Reb Hendele could not obtain settlement of the debt according to Jewish law, for Reb Mordechai was far more powerful than he (Reb Hendele) both in the community (of Hamburg) and with the Jewish judicial authorities (Bet Din). Hence Reb Hendele could not obtain repayment (of the debt) as a result of the verdict of the local Bet Din and was therefore compelled to take his case to the court of his majesty the King. Therefore, in a letter that I posted to him (Reb Hendele) I enquired as to the present position. He replied that the decision of the King's court was still pending, but that as soon as the verdict was given I would receive payment of the debt that amounted to almost one thousand Reichthalers.

It was when the news of the passing of my father, z"l, and the neighbouring areas, that we heard from Reb Aberle London who had again become very wealthy. Since he wrote he had heard of my father's passing and that the sun of so saintly a person had set prematurely and that he had left young orphans, he (Reb Aberle) had undertaken to give my father's orphans one hundred ducats. This gift was in special appreciation for the blessing which that saintly man had bestowed upon him and for its realisation. Therefore, he (Reb Aberle) had asked his sons to write and inform us that one of the family should come to Hamburg to collect the money he had promised. I received this information from a trustworthy person to whom Reb Aberle's sons had written about this promise. This made me excited and I said to myself "harness your coach and go to up Germany so as to fill the cup of contentment and collect all the debts owing to your father, z"l, for the Almighty has sent you to preserve the lives of your family (cf.Gen.45:5); therefore, quickly begin your journey, and do not tarry. So I took the road on which the Almighty had sent me, a difficult and hazardous journey involving me in much expense, for from my home in Broda to Hamburg is a distance of one and fifty miles and I travelled by special coach. All the expenses came out of my pocket, nor did I have a proper meal on the way, Frankfurt-on-Main and Berlin excepted, where I stayed with relatives. However, I incurred expenses with this stay for I had taken a serving-boy with me.

    I arrived in Hamburg without suffering any serious mishap and was the guest of the lay-leader Behr Cohen, may he rest in peace, who welcomed me honourably and cheerfully. I had immediately made for his home before I had informed anyone else of my arrival since I realised he was the pivot on which all the business I had in Hamburg depended and because of which I had left my hearth and home and made a long and horrid journey. I also realised that my father, z"l, had made his peace with him (Reb Behr). I therefore took this step since I had previously made certain enquiries of him and could not therefore forgo my stay with him and look for other lodgings. However, by the time I had arrived in Hamburg all the money which had been left by the above-mentioned Mordechai Cohen had been spent, for just as he had acquired his wealth by unjust means so it was worthlessly expended. When he (Mordechai Cohen) died he had left ninety thousand Reichthalers in cash and this sum had been stored away in a tightly sealed iron chest in his home

CHAPTER NINE

and protected by guards who were especially appointed by the communal authorities, but his worthless sons left no stone unturned (to obtain the money) and finally bribed these guards and so inducing them to steal the chest with all its contents and divide the latter between them (the sons). Thus, all that vast wealth was unfortunately lost, for within a short time the sons had got rid of it all, aimlessly spending it as it came. Hence, the sons were left without a penny of their father's estate. Consequently, some of them fell into bad ways whilst all his children and grandchildren became beggars, apart from one son Reb Joseph Cohen, one daughter in Hamburg and two daughters in Prague and Nickolsberg respectively, who were married to well-known gentlemen. Moreover, another daughter who had married twice (and on each occasion to) a Rabbinic scholar and had been the Rabbinate Creasier (Kromertz), had been prepared to become a beggar, but was maintained by strangers who were friendly to her family by whom they had at one time been maintained, and they treated her equally well. This lady was the best of (Mordechai Cohen's) sons and daughters, for she endured her poverty and wretched state with affection regarding it as an atonement for her sins; she consequently had fine sons. As for the rest of Mordechai Cohen's family apart from the above-mentioned son and daughters they fell into bad ways, as did most of the children of the other three Cohen brothers viz. the above-mentioned Mordechai, his brother Nathan, otherwise known as Nat (Z), and Wegrin Jacob, who after their demise left chests brimful of worms, except for a few valuable objects which the children of Wegrin Jacob inherited.

Hence it was for nothing that the starling Eibeschuetz followed the raven because he was of the same genus (cf. TB. Bava Kamma 92b.) for "the rod of the wicked shall not rest upon the lot of the righteous" (Ps.125:3). Consequently he (Eibeschuetz) had to make peace with that family (Cohen) by the most shameful means. However, he was worse than all of them put together, for none of them provoked the Almighty as did the fore-mentioned. However, I will not dwell on the subject at this stage.

To revert to the story of Mordechai Cohen; just as he was the cause of the impoverishment of the family of his brother the lay-leader Reb Hendele Cohen, so he was for his own family. For almost all his children and grandchildren wandered around for bread (cf.Job 15:23), except for the few who had attained the status which I had previously mentioned, so that the expectation perished (cf.Ps.9:19). However, as far as the family of the above-mentioned Reb Hendele was concerned, they came from good and righteous stock. Though they came to depend on other people for their sustenance because of the above-mentioned sinner Reb Mordechai who had frittered away much of their wealth they nevertheless remained steadfast in their Judaism. All of them were religious and endured the pangs of poverty more severe than death itself because of their love for their Heavenly Father. Consequently, they remained respected by everyone. May the Almighty have mercy on them amongst the other poor of His people, and may the sun of their success rise again.

I now revert to the topic of my above-mentioned financial affairs. By the time I reached Hamburg all the bequest of Mordechai Cohen had been liquidated so that I was unable to collect the debt of one thousand Reichthalers I had previously mentioned.

I then sought payment of a second debt of eight hundred Reichthalers in notes from Nathan Cohen for which his brother-in-law, Reb Behr Cohen, may he rest in peace, was guarantor. He himself (Reb Behr) claimed that the bill of indebtedness had been settled. I did not know the exact nature of this debt although the document clearly included the signatures of the above-mentioned two gentlemen, nor indeed did they deny this. Moreover, I had not found this note of indebtedness among others which had been settled. Yet in some way I understood from the above-mentioned that either they had inadvertently forgotten to tear up the note of indebtedness (after it had been paid) or to obtain a receipt attesting the settlement. For it was reasonable to assume that my father wouldn't have allowed that debt to remain unpaid over so long a period, (particularly) since Reb Behr Cohen was in the favourable position of being able to pay the debt, and he, (Reb Behr) was his, (Reb Nathan's) guarantor to whom my father had originally handed

CHAPTER NINE

the money (for Reb Nathan), except that the folds of the note were torn because it was an old one.

On the other hand, I had reasonable and convincing arguments for validating the note of indebtedness. For firstly, there is the presumption concerning a Chaver that he does not let anything untithed (unprepared) pass out from under his hand (TB. Pesachim 9a), and this is a principle which can be relied upon in prohibitive matters as the Talmud states, "If a Chaver dies and leaves a storehouse full of produce even if they are but one day old, they stand in the presumption of having been tithed (properly prepared) (ibid.). How much more so would this principle apply to such an eminently pious person like my father, z"l, who was so meticulous in all his actions. Secondly, one couldn't argue that the death of my father had unavoidably prevented (the loan from being contracted) for according to Reb Behr Cohen the debt had been paid whilst my father still held the Rabbinate of Amsterdam, so that there had been an interval of some years between the (alleged) payment of the loan and my father's passing. Thirdly, the problem was compounded by the fact that Reb Behr Cohen was unable to give exact details of the (alleged) payment i.e. how and when it was paid, or by whose agency, for there was no note of such a payment in Reb Behr's journal. Moreover, a more cogent argument than the latter was: why hadn't he (Reb Behr) at least asked for a receipt of my father, z"l, when the loan had been repaid, or when he (Reb Behr) had visited Hamburg in connection with the above-mentioned lawsuit, if at that time the note of indebtedness was not available, so that it could be cancelled or handed to Reb Behr Cohen? For Reb Behr was most orderly in the conduct of his business and it therefore seemed remarkable that he (Reb Behr) should have acted so flippantly regarding the debt and was in no way apprehensive lest there be a further demand for payment which would have been illegal.

Consequently, (in view of all these considerations) I claimed that either there must have been some stipulation concerning the loan which had not been fulfilled, or that the payment had not been completed. Nevertheless I could not bring myself to summon Reb

Behr Cohen (before a Bet Din) for adjudication since he appeared to be a very honest person and a good Jew. I was therefore apprehensive of causing any trouble. For though I could have taken an oath to the fact that I did not find (written) among the documents of my father that this debt was paid (cf. TB. Shevuot 45a) or I could have made him (Reb Behr) take an oath (that the debt was settled) for at any rate he would not have been exempt from the latter, I did not wish to be involved in such a procedure. Hence I abandoned the use of the document and regarded it as defective so that it could not be used for collecting the debt, but nor could it be torn up. I hoped the situation would be clarified in the future particularly since I was not the only one involved, for who can absolve the debtor from their share in it? So I was unable to absolve Reb Behr from the debt nor to tear it (the document) up, and that is the position at present i.e. the validity of the document cannot be decided until the advent of Elijah, for I decided not to demand payment through the agency of a Bet Din.

However, regarding the above-mentioned second debt Reb Hendele owed (my father) I was convinced without a shadow of a doubt that it was completely valid. For it was during the period when my father, z"l, was in Hamburg for the above-mentioned adjudication that he clarified his financial dealings with Reb Handele and when my father, z"l, made him the additional loan which exceeded the previous loan (which my father made him) when he (Reb Hendele) was in dire need of cash. My father gave him a bill-of-exchange dated 1715 with the guarantee that he (my father) would collect the debt from the indemnity of Mordechai Cohen which was about to be realised. The above-mentioned promise of Reb Aberle London whereby he had ordered his sons to give my father's heirs a hundred ducats also came to nought (and this) despite Reb Behr Cohen's efforts to obtain the money. For though he wrote to Reb Aberle reminding him to fulfil his promise he (Reb Behr) achieved little success. Meanwhile Reb Aberle's journal came under scrutiny for he had sent his eldest son to Paris and round his neck he had hung a bag of precious stones worth a considerable fortune. His (Reb Aberle's) intention was to train his son in business though have had been forewarned that his son could

CHAPTER NINE

be regarded as a destroyer of estates. The son was like a blight of snow in the time of harvest (cf.Prov.25:13) and proved to be an envoy of destruction to those who had sent him, continuing on his journey and returning empty handed. For he frittered away all his father had given him, for the hundred thousand (Reichthalers) his father had handed to him he spent on the price of a dog. For he brought home a small dog in exchange for the above-mentioned merchandise. Hence the enormous wealth Reb Aberle gained over the previous years by virtue of the blessing of my father, which I described above, was completely lost in disastrous circumstances because Reb Aberle had delayed fulfilling his promise (to my family). Hence Reb Aberle lost all his wealth and reverted to his former state (of poverty).

This affair left me disconsolate too, for I did not know whether I had covered the expenses of my journey. It was only in Frankfurt-on-Main and in the Three Communities that some people bought a number of copies of my father's Responsa which, as I have previously explained, I took with me on my journey. Apart from this I refused to accept any gifts from anyone, so that even when the lay-leader Behr Cohen graciously sent me a present whilst I was his guest over Purim I would not accept it but sent it back with the emissary. Nor did I send any copies of the Responsa as tokens of esteem to particularly renowned lay-leaders which was customary among contemporary authors. They used to send these lay-leaders copies of their work in order to obtain handsome gifts. I however, refrained from this practice throughout my travels although then Germany was such an affluent country that I could have become wealthy through this publication of my father, z"l, had I followed the above-mentioned custom. However, I was very careful to avoid such a practice i.e. to impose a duty on anyone, for I believed one should be a free agent in this matter. It was because of this attitude that I sold only a few copies of the Responsa. In fact, I could have left many copies in Hamburg were I not apprehensive concerning the honour of the Torah, for it is not proper for the Torah to beg entry to a family where its study is not hereditary. (TB. Bava Metzia 85a) Moreover, I had to consider my own self-respect, although many people liked me and had equally affectionate memories of my parents.

It was at that period that a person who had been an ardent admirer of my father, z"l, became my enemy without real cause. (I refer to) the lay-leader Joel Shaw, and all because I stayed with Reb Behr Cohen who was Joel Shaw's inveterate enemy. Even though I bore this person no animosity but rather the greatest affection he inwardly nursed a profound grudge and animosity towards me for several years as I will explain later, with the Almighty's help. (Incidentally) whilst I was staying with Reb Behr Cohen I lost an expensive watch, probably through theft.

From Hamburg I continued to Hanover taking with me several copies of the Responsa of my father, z"l, I lodged with Gumpel Hanover whose brother, Ephraim and he still appeared to be abundantly wealthy and eminent persons at that time. I stayed with them for several days and they accorded me the highest respect even assigning me one of their best rooms. It was then that Gumpel's brother, Ephraim arranged a dinner to celebrate (his son's) circumcision which was virtually a royal banquet. However immediately after this, in the very same week, the brothers made a hurried flight (from Hanover) because they were heavily in debt to the local authorities and representatives. For they had lost the vast wealth they had inherited from their father and squandered a great deal of other people's money by indulging in worthless pursuits, indeed they were hardly concerned with activities which were socially beneficial. They (the brothers) left all their business affairs in the hands of their servants, accountants and many employees who had become rich through the brothers, whilst the latter went into hiding, having had to flee at night. When the news was learned on the following morning everything in their house was sealed by decree of the royal judiciary. I hardly had time to flee the house before the judicial officials arrived to seal everything which remained in the house subsequent to the brothers' flight. These officials appropriated

CHAPTER NINE

all my possessions including my chest, all of which were regarded as part of the brothers' estate. I quickly escaped for my life and obtained lodgings in a local non-Jewish hostelry. However, before the brothers fled they had ordered an official whom they left in the house to give me six Reichthalers. This official was ready to carry out this order, but I did not want to accept anything.

From Hanover I travelled by mail-coach to Frankfurt-on-Main which was then the most affluent and splendid Jewish community, indeed, the crown of all the German Jewish communities in terms of wealth and importance. However, I had barely arrived there when I learned that it had suffered a serious fire and that the greater part of the Jewish quarter lay in ashes. Consequently I accomplished nothing in Frankfurt particularly since I was reluctant to employ the book (my father's Responsa) as a source of livelihood by sending it as a gift to lay-leaders which, as I already stated, was a contemporary custom. It was because of this attitude that Rabbi Ya'akov Katz, z"l, who presided over the local Bet Din, was most annoyed with me for he wanted to act on my behalf and ensure that all my travelling had not been in vain. However, the Frankfurt community made the excuse for not buying copies of the Responsa (by stating) that since their main quarters had been burned down they could not impose an extra burden on certain individuals. In fact, these people remained very affluent and would not have been rendered penniless. Indeed, had I sent a copy of the Responsa to them they would have paid a very generous price for it particularly since my father z"l, was held in great esteem and his publication was likewise regarded with much acclaim.

The above-mentioned Rabbi was prepared to do what he could if I were to accept his advice and emulate contemporary authors. However, his advice was wasted for I could not bring myself to accept the opinion of the Rabbi. He almost quarrelled with me stating, "how can I possibly endeavour or expect lay-leaders to come to you or that they should send their deputies to purchase a copy from you (particularly since I too, regarded the price which my father, z"l, had fixed as rather high, yet I had no intention of reducing that price for wealthy people). Such a practice, the Rabbi continued, is not followed in these times or in these localities. He then quoted examples of several eminent Rabbinic scholars who, though they themselves sold their own publications, were compelled to adopt this procedure (of reducing the price) for otherwise they would not have sold their works. How much more so, the Rabbi argued did this apply to me who was not the author of the work, who was still of tender years and an unknown personality; hence no alternative procedure could be considered. If however, (I remained adamant) it would have been better for me to have remained at home and not to have undertaken a long, hazardous journey which had involved me in such heavy expenses. The Rabbi continued to advance many such reasons for adopting the procedure he suggested, but I stood by my original resolve and no earthly wind would have moved me. Whatever would happen to me I could not be shaken from this resolve. However, some eminent lay-leaders and Rabbinic students sent deputies and bought a copy of the book at the full price i.e. fifteen ducats. I therefore decided to return home since I realised I was not suited to this kind of activity. Though I was advised to proceed to Mannheim, Metz and adjoining communities which were important as well as affluent, and was assured of obtaining considerable financial gain from this journey, I paid no heed to this advice for I realised from experience that the journey would be full of troubles since all these communities were involved in their own problems. Consequently, I resolved to return home empty-handed i.e. without capital or profit.

When I was already determined to return home news came from London regarding Mordechai Hamburg who had returned from East India where he had lived for ten years. He had arrived there poverty-stricken, having left his family, an expectant wife with nine children, quite destitute. His arrival back in London had caused quite a stir for it was a unique and remarkable event that quite an elderly person should have travelled for almost a year from our cold climate to a country possessing a hot climate, and that having remained there for such a long period, had succeeded in becoming extraordinarily wealthy. Now he had returned home with all this wealth and had

CHAPTER NINE

gained an extra bonus in that he had left a family of nine (children) and on his return discovered he now had ten children all of whom were enjoying good health. Moreover he had brought back a treasure of precious stones, one in particular being an onyx which was more valuable than any (similar precious stone) throughout the whole of England. He had also brought back incomparable golden jewels of greenish colour. The news of this man's adventures was published in the London daily newspapers and had spread to Frankfurt-on-Main. For when I was visiting that community the news came in a letter to that fine religious lay-leader Reb Benedet Hamburg, Mordechai Hamburg's brother-in-law. Now Reb Benedet was very attached to me and he therefore immediately sent me a large cup of wine with he announced the good tidings to me, and urged me to delay my return to Broda until I had first travelled to London. He assured me that as from that moment the payment of the outstanding debts of Reb Hendele and his brother Reb Nathan Cohen were secure, for since the honourable Mordechai, their brother, was his brother's partner they shared one purse. Moreover, (he assured me) Mordechai too, was a true adherent of my father, z"l, as was all his family, so that he (Mordechai) was particularly indebted to my father for the good offices he (my father) had executed on his (Reb Mordechai's) behalf.

This was when that insincere Rabbi viz. Uri Feibush and his clique plotted against him (Reb Mordechai) regarding a certain Get which had been secretly arranged by Uri Feibush on behalf of a Cohen. (see p.109 ff. D. Kaufmann "Rabbi Tzvi Ashkenazi and his family in London" Trans. J.H.S. Vol.3) This Get had many questionable aspects and Reb Mordechai had made some jest regarding granting such a questionable Get which appeared to have no validity. For to the honourable Mordechai who was the scion of a highly reputable family, as I have noted above, had grown up in a reputable community, the circumstances surrounding the Get presented a number of difficulties. Consequently the faction who supported Uri Feibush who were Mordechai's antagonists for other reasons, found an opportunity for stirring up strife against him (Reb Mordechai) and schemed to ruin his family for no substantial reason. They therefore ruthlessly persecuted him, expelling him from the Synagogue and his children from the communal school. Thus they prevented him from participating in communal affairs. Such a persecution of a fellow-Jew and an honourable man was unprecedented in Jewry. For Mordechai's obiter dicta (regarding the Get) were expressed quite innocently, yet his enemies would have swallowed him up alive had not the Almighty been with him and prompted him to inform Hamburg of his distress i.e. to contact my father, z"l, and to ask him whether his conduct warranted a punishment worse than death. However, by the Almighty's kindness, my father let his ink fly off the quill and in response completely exonerated the honourable Mordechai from this accusation. Consequently, Mordechai's persecutors ceased their activities and he went on to establish his own independent congregation. This whole incident was recorded in a pamphlet entitled "Ma'aseh Rav" and was published by Johanan Holleschau.

To revert to the main story; it was because of the latter incident that I was convinced the honourable Mordechai would remember the past affection and acknowledge the kindness which he had received gratis from my father, z"l, by showing consideration to the orphans of my father, z"l, by at least paying the above-mentioned outstanding debts (particularly) in view of the great benevolence the Almighty had shown him through the wonderful and miraculous events which I have previously described. I therefore took heed of Reb Behr Hamburg's advice and undertook another hazardous journey in sailing through a region hitherto unknown to me. I had to expend a considerable sum in hiring the services of another man-servant before I began my journey. Whilst on board I suffered a raging fever and the ship too, was in a perilous position when it was hit by such a torrential storm that it was on the verge of sinking. However, with the help of the Almighty we managed to reach port, though I was so weak because of my illness that I could hardly stand, and consequently had to hire a covered coach.

When I arrived at the honourable Mordechai's home I was received respectfully and graciously, and was assigned a room to meet

CHAPTER NINE

all my needs and requirements. Reb Mordechai and his honourable wife and family cheerfully saw to all my requirements and when the Almighty blessed be He, restored me to health I spoke to the honourable Mordechai indicating the purpose and urgency of my visit. When I showed him the bill of indebtedness respecting his two brothers he observed, "I recognise my brothers' signatures, but I will not settle their debts for were I to do so then all the other creditors would quickly descend on me like the fowl of Bet Bukyah (see Yevamot 84a) so that I would have to spend all the wealth I brought from the Indies and I would again become bankrupt." I however, pointed out to him that the amount he would have to spend on behalf of his brothers was very small, that thereby he would be fulfilling an important Mitzvah and that I would hold my tongue and not inform anyone else. Nevertheless, I did not succeed in all my efforts to allay his fears, whilst he behaved like a wily snake remaining deaf to my pleas and leaving me in despair for all my exertions and efforts had proved to be in vain.

The journey made me ill for I had to travel through uncultivated regions, apart from the fact that I was involved in considerable expense, now all had been wasted. Indeed, if the winter had not already set in I would immediately have hurried back home, but the Almighty had decided otherwise. I was compelled to remain in Hamburg and to prolong my exile in frustration and anger. The loss of time and money was most distressing and I was concerned as to when I could provide for my family. Indeed, I endured a long period of anxiety in Hamburg. Even when I had been restored to health on one occasion, it was the night of Shabbat, when I happened to be in a room on the ground floor, I fell ill. This caused a considerable commotion for it was in the early hours of the morning when every one else was asleep. I was immediately given a medicine which with the Almighty's help, proved to be effective. This was what I experienced during my stay with the honourable Mordechai (Hamburg) who gave me a few guineas to help me on my journey. I was compelled to accept this (gift) to meet the expenses of the long journey.

MEGILAT SEFER

Regarding Reb Aberle (London) who had promised a gift to the orphans of my father, z"l, as I have already explained he had been reduced to poverty before my arrival in London. Hence I was deprived of both alternatives. Soon after Pesach I boarded a ship and travelled by way of Amsterdam. When I arrived there on the eve of Shabbat (I learned) that my relative Reb Aberle Nordon heard the splendid news that he had won a prize in a lottery. This happened at a time when Reb Aberle's family, including his in-laws, were in serious financial straits. However, henceforth their good fortune continued to flourish so that that fine God-fearing and intelligent gentleman, Reb Zalman Nordau, may he rest in peace experienced a new lease of life. He was most successful in his old age particularly in the religious merit which he gained through his performance of Mitzvot and charitable acts towards his family and others. He also succeeded in marrying off his sons and daughters who then numbered eleven. Previously he had arranged the marriage of his eldest daughter to Reb Aberle, though he (R.Aberle) barely received a dowry. Subsequently, he (Reb Zalman) was able to arrange marriages for all his other children. I had to lodge with that fortunate person (Reb Zalman) who looked after me like a father. Indeed, I must acknowledge the abundant affection which I received from him and his children. In fact, all his family looked after me when I unfortunately fell victim to a second bout of fever which affected me for several months.

Thus, on two occasions I was prevented from returning home as promptly as I had wished. Many close friends particularly the above-mentioned relative (Reb Aberle Nordau) who for some time had to ensure that I had a doctor and mendicants and who attended to all my requirements. During the long period of my illness a worm several cubits in length which had been gnawing at my innards emerged from my back passage. For almost a year I had felt that some living creature was pecking away on my right side in front of my loins and close to my kidneys, but I had no idea what it was. Hence my fever proved to be a boon, for as a result of the constant emptying of my stomach carried out by my doctor the purpose of

CHAPTER NINE

which was to remove the fever by getting rid of the turbid elements, for the possibility that there was a tape-worm inside me never occurred to him, it appeared that the worm was the cause of my fever. The long tape-worm emerged with my stools and I had to extract it with my hand for it could not emerge completely but remained suspended from my back passage just like a piece of string. This caused me much trepidation for I imagined my entrails had emerged, for one could never have believed it was possible for such a long worm to grow in the human stomach. It was indeed a wonderful thing that such a scourge was removed from me, may the Almighty be praised. Because of these events I spent almost the whole of the summer in Amsterdam.

Subsequently I made the return journey homewards without any delay for during this long trek the Almighty delivered me from so many accidents that they are too numerous to record. However, I will mention just a few examples of the Almighty's kindness to me. Whilst travelling from Fulda to Landeshut (Silesia) I forgot to stipulate with the coach-driver about stopping on Shabbat so that I had to spend that day in an inn on the road and hire a special night-coach to catch up with the covered-coach (in which I had previously travelled) which was going to Prague. Subsequently I was told that there were bandits on that road as well as in that inn. Again, the second coach which I had hired at an exorbitant fee at the termination of Shabbat took a road on which no Jew had previously journeyed, unless he had a special pass. I felt as though I was laid in iron (cf.Ps.115:18) and my whole body was convulsed (Job 21:6). Through the Almighty's mercy the Toll official was not at home but only his maid and she was so touched by my weeping and protestations that she overlooked my offence.

Most remarkable things happened to me in Prague too, which I cannot fully describe but just as drippings of a gutter will touch on a few of my adventures, troubles, and distressing moments (there) and how I was delivered by the constant mercies of the Almighty. (Thus) when I entered Prague which was more dangerous than other cities, mainly because of the black priests and their disciples, the customs official confiscated some copies of my father's Responsa which I had with me. It was a risk to bring Rabbinic literature into Prague at that time for the government had prohibited this practice. Eibeschuetz was then at the lowest ebb of his reputation in Jewry, for some time in the previous year news of his infamy had emerged, initially in the community of Frankfurt-on-Main in particular and then in other communities in general. Although when he realised his precarious position he had the arrogance to deny what was an obvious fact. Moreover, contemporary Rabbis who initially zealously opposed him lost their enthusiasm through "dread of the enemy and the fear all around them" (Jer.6:25) and because of Eibeschuetz's family as well as that of his wife who were very influential in Prague. This influence was particularly strong among the Catholics whom he (R.Eibeschuetz) had befriended and those activities he emulated. They (the Catholics) therefore admired him and because of his attachment to them he forcibly obtained half of the preaching allocation. Consequently, the Rabbis ceased their opposition to him becoming reconciled by a false oath which he took on the night of Kol Nidrei. Nevertheless he was despised by the community who had long realised his dissembling and trickery. Indeed, his previous admirers, including members of his own family, hated and contemned him. In fact, my uncle, may he rest in peace, who was a person of integrity, assured me that even his (R. Eibeschuetz's) own father-in-law (Reb Yitzchak Spiro) wanted to disinherit him. Hence his only supporters were such friends like Popros and other members of his Bet Ha-Midrash. However, he was held in high repute by the Catholic clergy, whatever that reputation was worth. At that time too, he was involved in adjudication in the state courts, pleading on behalf of anyone who was the victim of a creditor, or who was in distressed or hard-pressed. In this way he (R.Eibeschuetz) increased his incomes. I was shown through the widow of my uncle, may he rest in peace, how he (R.Eibeschuetz) moved as swiftly as a hind through the highways and by-ways, but I had no desire to look upon his person, though he sent a messenger to inform me that if I wished to show him respect by visiting him at his home he would endeavour to

CHAPTER NINE

rescue the books (copies of my father's Responsa) which, as I previously mentioned, had been confiscated, and to see that they were returned to me gratis. But I did not want to see him, in fact I found it easier to lose those books than to pay my respects to so arrogant a person. I visited the Rabbi who presided over the local Bet Din (R. David Oppenheim) who arranged a banquet in my honour and who detained me the whole of the day. He accorded me the greatest respect and showed me much esteem besides expressing his strong affection for me in the presence of all his guests. He held my hand throughout the day and showed a fatherly delight in me that was apparent to all. In the presence of the august assembly who filled the house the Rabbi incessantly praised my father, z"l, stating unequivocally that my father, z"l, was unique in his generation and that his type no longer existed.

In Prague I experienced a challenge similar to that of the (Biblical) saintly Joseph, in fact mine was somewhat more challenging. I was then a passionate young individual who had been separated from his spouse for a considerable period. I therefore longed for female company which I had the opportunity of fulfilling in the person of a lovely young lady viz. my cousin, who kept me company and who was audacious enough to evince a special affection for me, in fact she almost embraced me. Indeed when I was resting in my bed she came to see if I was well covered, in other words, she wanted me to embrace her. Had I yielded to my baser instinct she would not have denied me anything. On several occasions I almost succumbed, just as a flame is attracted to stubble, but the Almighty granted me strong will-power as well as an abundance of dignity and courage (cf.Gen.49:3) to prevail over my burning passion. For on those occasions of which I have spoken there was no one in the house except the two of us, nor were they likely to return (at that time of the day) since they were in their shops all day to gain a livelihood. Indeed, on one occasion I was on the point of yielding to my desire were it not for the Almighty's abundant kindness which helped me resisting a temptation that is greater than any other. For I was a (young) man in the full prime life and a young lady was present who on many occasions had manifested the greatest affection for me. Moreover, she was a young unattached relative who had recently lost her husband and would have made herself available had I so wished. In fact, had I succumbed to my baser feelings she would not have breathed a word about it. However, I subdued those feelings and stifled my passion and my deepest emotions, so blessed be the Almighty who gives strength to the faint. I did not succumb but was delivered from that flaming fire. As a recompense I pray that I and my family should for ever be saved from the fire of the evil inclination and Gehinnom, may it so be the Almighty's will, Amen. This generally was my prayer at various times and circumstances from the hazards of which the Lord delivered my family and me from any serious mishap. In particular from the dreadful power of the evil inclination and the many nets it spreads for*one's feet.(Lam.l:13) The struggle is not at all easy for, to my mind the evil inclination is always ready to pounce in the sure knowledge that it will not be recognised. Praised be the Helper and Saviour Who came to my aid in the above-mentioned situation for then I really understood that ultimately man's freewill rests with the Almighty who does not leave it completely in man's hands. Happy is the person whose strength is in Him (Ps.84:6) who guards the feet of His holy ones. (cf.1.Sam.2:9)

From Prague I travelled by "covered coach" known as a land-coach to Brno, the capital of Morovia. Together with a group of Moravian Jews who were returning home I planned to quickly book the first upper seat of the coach. However, when we came to take our seats in the coach we were joined by two gentiles, an Italian merchant and a Cleric. Though they had delayed their bookings these two scornfully and derisively pushed us out of our seats. Even if we had so wished the coach-driver could not prevent them since he realised that it was illegal for him to take such action. Consequently, we had to remain silent whilst we, the Jewish travellers, had to endure various insults from these two persons who did not give us a moment's peace. In fact, whilst in their company we could not fulfil such religious duties like donning our Tefillin or praying, for they constantly taunted us calling us "filthy Jews". Whenever we came to a

CHAPTER NINE

slight bend (in the road) they would bawl scolding curses and despicable epithets at us saying," get out of the coach and use your feet". They would then push us out on to the road just like baggage.

However, this also proved to be a blessing, since the Almighty observed our troubles. For having tormented us for about ten miles out of Prague we came across a very dangerous part of the road which meant traversing a very narrow valley on one side of which was a cliff which looked like a wall, whilst on the other side there was a very steep incline. Just as we were about to reach this most precarious section (of the road) these two men, as usual, pushed us out and chased us away from the coach. We raised no protest but went on foot whilst they remained seated in the coach. We had moved only a short distance away from the coach when it somersaulted on to the incline I have previously mentioned. The coach was heavily laden with trunks and cases some of which fell onto the Italian merchant so that almost all his bones were broken and falling seriously injured he could not get back to the coach but had to remain on the road and find lodgings in the nearest village. The Cleric sustained no injury but the merchant would not allow him (the cleric) to leave him saying that it was the cleric's duty to do him some service before he died. Moreover, their hearts almost died within them when they realised we rejoiced in the disaster which had befallen them, the Almighty had vindicated our hope in Him before all human beings. Those men left us in this way and we were safely free of them.

We had witnessed the Almighty's vengeance on our enemies so that seated comfortably in the coach we pursued our journey with joy and benevolence in the name of the Almighty. We thanked Him for the kindness He had shown us in this situation for we could now carry out His Precepts on the journey without any evil hindrance or interference. Thus, in the best of health and spirits we reached our destination, Brno, where I saw the Cleric who had left us on the journey. Acknowledging me he observed that he would never again travel in a coach with a Jew.

MEGILAT SEFER

When I made the journey homewards it was in the middle of an ice-cold winter and I travelled with some market-folk in a coach which rested on a sledge so that we moved swiftly on the icy snow since it was very slippery. It was uncomfortable to sit huddled together on the coach for there were many passengers. Hence I and many others had to travel with one foot protruding from the coach. Whilst I was sitting in this position we reached a sharp incline (in the road) which caused the coach to skid so that my foot was caught between two wheels. I felt sure I had fractured (a bone) in the sole of my foot for it was so painful that I couldn't stand on it. So I came home limping like an old man and I had to apply ointments and rigorous massages for several weeks until, with the Almighty's help my leg regained its former strength. After that long and arduous journey I came home empty-handed as well as with an empty purse. My eldest son, Shai, a real treasure, thank the Almighty, was then about seven and was already learning Talmud. My wife, may she rest in peace, had acquired the services of a teacher (for Shai) who stayed in my house and whom I had to feed besides meeting the cost of tuition. My father-in-law the Rabbi, may he rest in peace, also kept a tutor in his house but he (the Rabbi) was envious of his grandson Shai because he was more intelligent and able than his (father-in-law's) sons. Consequently, because of this envy, he would not allow my son to make up a group with his sons. This imposed an extra financial burden on me.

Before I returned home I lost a son, but my wife was soon with child again, so that my financial burden was still further increased. I had made no material gains from the long journey I previously mentioned, but on the contrary, I had wasted time, energy and money. Yet, in spite of everything, I praise my Creator who sustained me when my life was a prey to me (cf.Jer.21:9) throughout the many adventures when my troubles were tied to me like the kneading troughs (of my ancestors) (Ed. a play on words cf. 12:34). However, I did make a slight gain in that I saw the possibility in doing some business with Holland which would bring me a little

CHAPTER NINE

income and enable me to pursue my Torah studies. I tried my hand at exporting Hungarian goats' hair and lambs' wool which were very long and white and which were not available in other countries. I bought these commodities from members of the Broda community who imported them from Hungary and I (in turn) forwarded them to some acquaintances in Amsterdam who were my partners in this venture. In return the latter sent me certain goods which were luxuries in Moravia and Hungary. However, before long the price of goats' hair and lambs' wool sharply depreciated in Amsterdam and a stock of considerable value remained unsold (in Amsterdam), even though it was offered at the new price. This was apart from the cash which I had already given to the Hungarian merchants who would buy the commodities there. For I used to send them cash periodically in place of which they would forward me the commodities on receipt of which I would make a further payment for goods which they would send me in the future. In fact, a few of those merchants appropriated the money I sent them and failed to send me any goods.

Before I conclude my adventures in Moravia I will reiterate some of the wonderful things the Holy One blessed be He performed on my behalf, that is to say, those I can remember, for at present I have forgotten many of them. First, regarding the buying and selling of commodities, a business which at the outset I would term "dispute" ("bad business" for I had to contend with zealots). Thus, a certain person who hailed from Germany and who had bought the right to live in Broda competed with me. This person also paid the local authorities a considerable sum for the marketing of the commodities I previously mentioned with the stipulation that he should have the sole right to deal in these goods. Not only did he come as an outsider to appropriate my business, but he wanted to prevent me forcibly from indulging in it, and therefore planned to inform against me and so ruin me. He had almost succeeded in this plan when he suddenly fell ill, may the Almighty save us from such a situation, and died within a few days, in fact not long after his arrival (in Broda) and his marriage, and all this despite the fact that he was a tall and powerfully built man, may his death be an atonement. Thus, this threat was removed from me. Later his widow having spent all the wealth her husband had left her, went around begging in various cities and also passed through Altona.

On another occasion I experienced a miracle in connection with a certain apostate who, when he was still accepted as a Jew, left some rings and other expensive jewels as a pledge with me. Subsequently, when he apostatised in Broda, we learned that he had arrived in the city with the reputation of being a wealthy Jew, though it was then acknowledged he was a thief and Robber, who, having purchased estates and become powerful, fled to Broda in order to get married and settle in the city. When he had frittered away all his wealth he again apostatised and completely associated with gentiles. He then informed the local authorities against me giving the impression that he had entrusted me with a considerable fortune of his. However, through the Almighty's mercies, I emerged safely from this affair, for though I was summoned before the local court he failed to obtain anything from me illegally, for the court permitted me to retain what I calculated to be my share, having assessed the value of the pledges, and to return the balance to him. This was done, so that, thanks to the Almighty, I did not lose any money.

I experienced yet another unhappy incident in Broda in which I found myself in great physical and financial danger. However, the Almighty brought me out of this strait (cf.Ps.18:20) and delivered me from the snare of the fouler(cf.Ps.91:3). This incident was as follows. Subsequent to the collapse of the business I previously described, I received from Amsterdam the balance of my share in the previously mentioned partnership. This bill of indebtedness was got up in the name of the Rabbi of Amsterdam, R.B--, and he sent the bill through an agent of his viz. Gabriel Wimper of Breslau, where I was to receive payment. I did not want the money to be handed to anyone else for I thought I might to able to make some profit by purchasing certain goods in Breslau. I therefore travelled with some Morovians to Breslau in order to collect the cash. When I went to the above-mentioned Gabriel to collect it he informed that the cash was already

CHAPTER NINE

available but stated, "I would advise you to buy some expensive jewellery from me in lieu of the cash, for you will then be able to make a handsome profit (by selling them) in Moravia". "Moreover", he continued, " I will be kind enough to sell you this jewellery cheaply because of our long-standing friendship." He was referring to the fact that his father had been a lay-leader in Amsterdam when my father, z"l, held the Rabbinate there. He informed me that his advice and assurances sprang from his deep attachment to me. In so doing, he deceived me, particularly since he then appeared to be an affluent person I accepted hid deceitful plan fully relying on him and his assurances that he was acting in my interests. According to his calculation I owed him seventy-seven gold pieces more than the money due to me from the bill of indebtedness in lieu of which I received the above-mentioned goods. I gave him an IOU for the seventy-seven gold pieces which was to be met at a certain time, for I felt sure he would not cheat me. However, as soon as I left my lodgings with those goods and made my way to the city centre I met some merchants who were experts in the business as well as being men of the highest integrity. When I showed them the goods I had purchased, it was as though I had second thoughts about the whole transaction for I was very young and had no business experience, these people who were my friends, reprehended me saying, "what have you done? Your friend cheated you, for the goods aren't worth half the money you paid for them, indeed, it would be all right if they were worth a half! (For example), you have paid an excessive price for the string of pearls he sold you and which are normally sold by weight. So go back quickly, return the goods and retrieve your money". I acted accordingly, and went back to him (G.Wimper) to return the goods and retrieve my money, for I understood from his conversation that it was my prerogative to cancel the deal since I had relied solely on his advice. In fact, it seemed obvious to me that he would be prepared to take his goods and return my money since I had done him no harm nor would he suffer any loss.

But I had miscalculated, for when I approached him and stated these arguments he turned a deaf eye saying that what had been done could not be undone. I cried like a crane (cf. TB. Kid.44a) saying, "Didn't you assure me you were acting in my interests? But now, come what may, I have no need of your favours; take your favours and throw them on thorns." (TB. Beitza 29b) which he had previously seen in my possession since he had now found a buyer. However, he stipulated that I should give him a few days grace since he would have to return to his home-town and enquire of the representative (of the buyer) whether he still wanted to buy the goods. But when this period had elapsed and I was informed by those who knew this person, that he could not be trusted, I put him out of my mind and having waited, to the point of embarrassment I agreed to exchange my goods which were of superior quality for inferior ones. However, the Almighty blessed be He, saw my affliction at the very moment the transaction was to be concluded. For when I aimlessly peered through the window I failed to recognise the person who was looking at me until he raised his voice and spoke to me. I then recognised him as the person who had visited me about eight days ago and who having seen my goods had promised to find a buyer. He had now succeeded and the Almighty had designated this purchaser who was prepared to buy my wares for ready cash. I therefore immediately cancelled the arrangement to exchange the goods and sold them at double the value at which the merchant involved in the exchange had assessed them. So after much worry and loss of time and money I finally brought much contentment to my family. This helped raise my spirit; blessed be He who does good to the undeserving! Yet I still had a considerable quantity of goods which could not be sold either in Pressberg or in Moravia. I therefore had to send a highly reputable merchant as far as Holland where they were finally sold after great difficulties; blessed be the Helper of Israel.

However, this was not the end of that distressing business affair I experienced in Hamburg. For the above-mentioned agent who was the cause of all that distressing business and through whose assurances I had made the hazardous journey through Hungary, caused me further trouble after I had fled that country. For his local

CHAPTER NINE

authority had wanted to buy some of my goods, but because I could not come to any agreement with him we ostensibly parted company peacefully and amicably. However later, when I was safely ensconced in my own home this agent forced me to appear before the Bet Din of Broda. He had appropriated some of my money claiming I had promised him some payment, and he therefore refused to return this money to me since he claimed that because of me he had suffered some loss at the hands of his local authority who demanded that he should at least produce the goods which they had seen when I was in Hungary. This middleman now schemed to obtain from me money which he didn't have the effrontery to claim when I was in business with him and to which he would have been legally entitled. Acting against me with trickery I had to reach a compromise with him and to pay him a sum I did not legally owe him. These are but a few (examples) of the kindness and mercy that the Holy One, blessed be He, performed on my behalf. I should say much more of His merciful acts towards me when I was in Moravia, but I have forgotten so many of them except that presently I cannot concentrate sufficiently to recount those incidents in the order in which they occurred. Moreover such an exercise would involve extending the length of this book. Consequently a few examples will have to suffice for they characterise the many instances (of the Almighty's mercies). For example, the many serious illnesses from which the Almighty, blessed be He, delivered me when I was in Moravia. Likewise, he saved me from many unscrupulous Jews and Gentiles.

Though, in fact, I was much beloved not only in Broda where the majority of the community loved me and blessed themselves in my name because of my general demeanour to which they were endeared. Yet there was no shortage of ambitious individuals nor of those who sought quick gains at my expense, so that I was cheated tenfold. (For example), a person sold me a brass chain at the price of a gold one, but I was not aware of this fraud until I returned here (to Altona). It was then I learned of this fraudulent deal since I had previously shown the chain to several experts all of whom pronounced it to be of pure gold for it was gold-plated.

My repudiation throughout Moravia was equal to that of the most eminent personalities so that the illustrious Rabbi who presided over the Bet Din of Prague viz. R. Gabriel Eshkeles, wanted to appoint me as Rabbi to one of the communities (under his aegis) but I had no desire to incline my shoulder to the yoke of the Rabbinate. However, ultimately the Emperor introduced new prohibitions regarding Jewish marriages in Bohemia and Moravia which were a very heavy imposition on our Jewish brethren. These regulations were in addition to the many existent harsh and cruel disabilities so that I considered my people's misfortunes in that province (Moravia) to be most bitter. I was therefore convinced that I should not settle there and was determined to leave Moravia and return to my own country (Germany) though there was no assurance of gaining a livelihood in Altona. Nevertheless I trusted in my Maker and in the belief that He would not forsake me. Thus, when I felt completely abandoned a remarkable thing happened. Certain prominent Viennese Jews who remained anonymous, provided me with a regular and ample income, approximately twelve Reichthalers per week, and they undertook this obligation for several years. This enabled me to pursue my Torah studies at home for I was free of any economic worries. In fact, I could have mange with half that allowance, for I was young and had only a small family. Moreover, the cost of living (in Altona) was not high, so that I was able to save more than half of the grant which I could retain for the future (when circumstances might change). Though they had never set eyes on me these people were stirred into making this financial arrangement for me because of my great reputation which I enjoyed in far distant a place as Vienna. In fact, the esteemed Rabbi D ? z"l, informed me when I was visiting Vienna that the wealthy and famous R. Samson Wertheim once told him that he knew of me and that he (R. Samson) subsequently stated, "I shan't rest until I have made R. Ya'akov Emden a wealthy man." However, a short time after this R.Wertheim, may he rest in peace, passed away.

The eminent lay-leader Reb M.Feizring, who (at) one time

CHAPTER NINE

wanted me to marry his daughter, promised me, irrespective of this proposal, a grant of one thousand Reichthalers per annum. However, I did not want to depend on other people for my livelihood. Again, when I was visiting Pressberg in connection with the above-mentioned business, certain important admirers of mine urged me to accompany them to Vienna which was less than a days journey away. This would have enabled me to recoup the losses I had sustained in Pressberg, for (these people argued) I had many powerful admirers in Vienna who had always wanted to see me. However, I paid little attention to their arguments since I (have always) found it unacceptable to profit from human beneficence. (Thus,) though I was very keen to visit Vienna whilst the journey would have proved inexpensive and I would have received every deference (there) I refrained from so doing because of my great apprehension of the Catholic priests who were known to carry images of the Cross through the streets of Vienna and that anyone who showed them any disrespect endangered his life. Nevertheless, I had many admirers in that city who had arranged the above-mentioned allowance for me, and though I had not flattered nor sought the favour of any of them either in writing or verbally, they fulfilled their commitment. Quite out of the blue they sent me a tidy sum of gold pieces which I accepted since I was in financial low-water. I then realised that this was the Almighty's way of providing me with sustenance through their good offices. Previously, I had spurned similar offers on several occasions for in my home-town (Broda) there were many who wanted to provide me with a regular income and thus enable me to live comfortably in that community. Rabbi Gabriel (Eshkeles) too, wanted to honour me and deserves praise for acting on my behalf. In fact, on several occasions he indicated his fervent wish to act on my behalf. In his correspondence with me he manifested a deep affection for me. Nevertheless, I paid little attention to all these factors. In truth I left Moravia with considerable sums due to me that arose in particular from my outlay of capital in the business of the woollen hairs that I mentioned above. Moreover, I had bills of indebtedness for all the above-mentioned debts. I had also sunk some of my capital in the wools and skins that I had despatched at my own expense to my partners (in Amsterdam), Reb S.B. and Reb.E.N. These commodities had remained there for some considerable time, just like immovable stones.

Consequently I set out on my travels, initially alone, and made the long journey to Amsterdam without receiving any tangible benefit from any prominent lay-leader, not even a meal. Though, when I happened to be in Dresden the lay-leader Reb Jonah urged me to join him in a meal. I declined his invitation and all who witnessed my refusal were astounded at the humble demeanour Reb Jonah adopted towards me, nevertheless he could not induce me to accept. People said they had never previously known a person to refuse the invitation of so powerful a lay-leader like him. However, I shall not deal at length with the many remarkable events that I experienced on that hazardous journey for they were countless. I also visited Hanover when the presiding Rabbi of the Bet Din of Prague was there for the wedding of the daughter of his son, the Rabbi of Holleschau, to the son of the eminent R. Abraham Aba, the Rabbi of Hildersheim. The latter wanted to honour me with a special gift of a handful of gold pieces but I refused to accept it. He praised me highly and was eager to retain me to study with his son, the bridegroom, but tired and continued my journey (to Amsterdam) and stayed with my previous partner, Reb S.B. . He and his in-laws had greatly prospered since I had last visited Amsterdam and stayed with them. By the time of my second visit to them, during the winter, the object of which was to provide for my family and to deal with my goods which had remained in Amsterdam, (I observed) that the Almighty had renewed His kindness to them so that they had became affluent by virtue of a completely new source.

This was diamond mine that was discovered close to the West Indian side of Brazil; "there are mines for silver and places where men refine gold." (Job 28:1) This mine had an abundance of diamonds about which no one but they (the family of Reb S.B.) knew. For from time immemorial the only source of diamonds obtainable in England and Holland was the East Indies, hence this

173

CHAPTER NINE

new source remained a close secret for several years during which time the Portuguese merchant seamen brought these new precious stones to England in the utmost secrecy in order to see how they would fare with them. These merchant seamen were afraid to publicise the new diamond mine they had discovered for fear that the diamond merchants would not consider the diamonds genuine when they came to buy them. Since they came from a region that was not previously known to be a source for such precious stones. Moreover, they (the new diamonds) were neither as big nor as pure as those deriving from the East Indies from where diamonds had been imported from the earliest times. Consequently the Portuguese merchants who had discovered the mine acted prudently and keeping it a close secret they privately gave a quantity of them (the stones) to the merchant seamen who on their arrival in London revealed the secret to the two sons of the honourable Reb Rosen, may he rest in peace, i.e. to the two brothers Reb Leib(?) and Reb Reuben(?). Previously the latter had been in involved in trading in gold which was imported into London by the Portuguese merchants who were acquainted with the brothers, for they (the brothers) used to buy fragments of gold from these merchants and from this trade the brothers became rich. The merchant seamen regarded them (the brothers) as trustworthy and unobtrusive person and therefore confided the secret of the source of the diamonds to them in the assurance that they (the brothers) would not divulge this information to anyone else. Consequently the brothers bought the diamonds which their friends, the Portuguese merchant seamen brought to them and their business prospered. In this way the Almighty, blessed be He, sent them (the brothers) abundant blessings which the brothers enjoyed for several years. The Portuguese sold them the diamonds cheaply since they (the merchants) obtained them easily and in vast quantities. Again, the merchants were apprehensive whether they would find any purchasers (of their goods) for people might consider the diamonds to be fake or of a very inferior quality. They (the merchants) therefore accepted the price that the brothers offered for they consider them (the brothers) trustworthy.

MEGILAT SEFER

Furthermore, they did not want the brothers to divulge their secret lest it prove to their (the merchants) disadvantage.

Yet a further reason for the brothers' success was that at that period there were many prospective buyers with much available cash, since there were a considerable number of very wealthy people in the West whose wealth had been gained in goods which were subject to excise. These rich people did not know what to do with this available cash for they feared they would lose their capital in the gold-trade that was subject to much fluctuation. Consequently they invested their money in the diamond business, and since they had so much capital they bought a considerable amount of these precious stones at whatever price the Portuguese demanded. Thus the brothers became very wealthy, but this aroused little envy since no one else knew the source (of these diamonds). They (the brothers) made a quick sale of these commodities which purported to come from the East Indies, nor did anyone guess their secret, for the Portuguese kept it to themselves.

Moreover the above-mentioned brothers subsequently came to an arrangement with these merchant seamen whereby they undertook to accept the diamonds at an agreed price with the proviso that the source of these commodities should not be divulged. The brothers kept this secret for several years for they had plenty of cash at hand, moreover they accepted the price which the merchants demanded. Consequently, the family of Reb Rosen, may he rest in peace, became extremely wealthy without anyone knowing the source of this wealth. In fact, though they were regarded as so very rich that no one was able to assess half, quarter or third of the wealth the Rosen family attained. They continued to maintain this degree of prosperity (for some considerable time), and it was only after several years had elapsed that people began to ask how they had gained such unusual wealth. The Rosen family indulged in much charitable activity, a fact which aroused further curiosity. As a result other merchants who came to envy them did not rest until they had instituted a careful investigation of the Rosen's wealth and discovered their secret, "they searched out their secret, and they hunted out their

CHAPTER NINE

secret wealth." (cf.Ob.6) Hence they too, took advantage of this new business venture. Thus this trade was so extensive that eventually all (wealthy) merchants had a hand in it with the inevitable result that the price of these diamonds appreciated. Nevertheless priority rested with the Rosen brothers who had initially introduced this trade, who had maintained this advantage for several years and consequently profited to the tune of many thousands of Reichthalers , in other words to countless wealth. Indeed, all the other diamond merchants failed to achieve a fraction of the brothers' success, for they gained such an abundance of wealth that their table was plentiful, richly flavoured and full of the blessings of the Lord (cf.Deut.33:23)

All this happened in the interval between my first and second visit to them. In contra-distinction my business reached such a low ebb that hardly anything remained of the capital from which I could have eked out a living. As for my goods and skins which had remained in an attic over a long period, some were moth-ridden whilst the remainder were sold at a heavy loss. However, the Almighty prompted these good men (the Rosen brothers) to act generously towards me so that for several years they supported me with the gift of an annual grant for my maintenance. In fact, initially they exceeded their original commitment to me. Were I to venture recording my further ills and the cruel incidents which befell me in the period I had to stay in Amsterdam because of excessive melancholia (may the Almighty spare us such ills) (you) the reader would be astounded, for you would consider it hardly plausible. Indeed, a physically strong person could barely have endured such ills, how much less a person as frail as I who in addition was plagued and smitten and afflicted by the Almighty. The main cause of my misfortunes arose from the fearful losses I had sustained in the above-mentioned business which affected me deeply and caused me such great anguish which no amount of wine or whiskey could dispel. Any solace I could find came from drinking hot tea to which I had become addicted from the period of my first major journey. I had read a book by a Dutch doctor which highly praised this drink and henceforth I drank it regularly. In fact, it was the only thing which quenched my thirst. From then on I behaved like a Nazarite in respect of wine or any other alcohol, apart from a cup of wine which I had during a meal. For many years I found tea of great physical benefit, but on this occasion I drank an excessive amount since it gave me some respite from my pain and anguish for it helped relieve my low and thus afforded me some comfort. However, it became my tormentor and enemy for my blood turned to water so that my urine spouted forth like a fountain so that I had to urinate virtually every minute and this caused me severe and bitter pains in my private parts. On several occasions I could hardly take a step without wishing to relieve myself and on other occasions I fainted and almost breathed my last were it not for the Almighty's tender mercies.

    Were I to describe everything that happened to me in Amsterdam the mind would boggle, the eyes stare in astonishment, the ears would writhe in pain at listening to it, the heart would cease to beat and the spirit would constantly tremble. I will therefore state the brief essentials and merely touch on the Almighty's kindness to me even when I was ill all day. Throughout all these terrible adversities the Almighty did not suffer my foot to slip (cf. Ps.121:3); May His name be praised to everlasting, may it be known to eternity, for all this was caused by Him. For I had to prolong my stay in Amsterdam through half the summer and a complete winter in the hope that I would obtain a favourable purchaser of my merchandise which still remained in that city just like an immovable stone. This was why I was overcome with worry and could find no peace of mind neither by day nor by night (particularly) because of the need to spend so much time in a foreign land. I was like a traveller who had pitched his tent some six hundred from his home and young family for whom his heart yearned. (cf.Jer.31:19) I could find no tranquillity but was engulfed on melancholy. Tears were my meal both day and night as I asked myself when will I (be able) to provide for my family (which passes by like a shadow) and find a more permanent abode in the shadow of the Almighty; this had been my hope from when the spirit of wisdom first made its impact on me.

    I mention my shortcomings to place on record how excessive

CHAPTER NINE

pain and worry almost destroyed me. But for the tender mercies of the Almighty I would have perished in my affliction (cf.Ps.119:92) which assumed a variety of suffering unlike anything I have ever heard. This brought me into contact with a foreign medical book written by Dr. Buntekel, a Dutchman, to which I was attracted during my travels in that long exile , which I experienced for the first time. Indeed, I was eager to learn and understand the essentials of the German language which my father, z"l, had never taught me. Nor had I been taught to write German so that I had to learn it on my own. However, I was completely ignorant of non-Jewish literature though I was always interested in studying worldly affairs, about other nations, their religious beliefs, their ethics, character and history, all facts on which our religious Literature did not provide any information. There were several reasons for my interest in non-Jewish Literature e.g. it would help me in responding to the challenge of sceptics, to be more sociable. I would achieve these aims if I acquired a knowledge of the customs of different countries, their geography, and the character of their inhabitants, as well as the discovery and examination of their secrets. I longed to learn this by studying their literature but I couldn't find a way of attaining this goal since I wouldn't permit myself the luxury of paying a teacher of foreign languages for I was afraid I would waste too much precious time, apart from which I hated the idea of spending money for this purpose. Moreover, (I felt) such a course of action would cause me public embarrassment.

However, I became acquainted with one of the young servants who was learning to read and write German and quietly taking him aside I asked him to show me the format of the German alphabet which he had begun to study with the assistance of a gentile teacher. This servant hardly knew the format of the ordinary letters let alone the capital letters. He could not read German script nor did he understand the way the letters were formed into words. This lad showed me the letters no more than a couple of times, i.e. he pointed out to me an A, B, C etc. nothing more, but with the help the Almighty who grants man knowledge, I quickly mastered the ability to recognise the letters of the German alphabet. Subsequently, unassisted I applied myself to a study of the composition of (German) words so that I was able to make sense of a particular subject without the assistance of any teacher or guide. Hence in a short time I was able to read a (German) book fairly proficiently just as if I had studied under a teacher for several years. However, I only succeeded in reading German print, but in respect of German script I was still unable to make sense of it due to a lack of practice. In fact, even in writing Gothic print (letters) there were certain shapes and markings as well as variations in the formation of letters which I cannot understand to this very day. For all this (skill) was gained surreptitiously (cf. Job 4:12) and hurriedly and (even) the young servant who guided me had an imperfect knowledge of the basic reading and writing of German. Moreover, subsequently I was too embarrassed to seek assistance in filling the gaps in my knowledge of the language.

Yet, notwithstanding these facts I quickly applied myself to reading as many non-Jewish books as I could lay my hands on and ultimately I attained fluency in even reading Dutch and other foreign newspapers. I also came to understand a fair amount of Latin and was able to read many books on various aspects of European culture. This enabled me to understand the wisdom of many nations, as well as their religious customs, and to discover their ideas of us (the Jews) and our holy faith. I was also very eager to understand how our Earth came into existence which, according to their literature, was caused by the motion of the planets. For though some mention is made of this in our texts the description is very brief. Again I was keen to learn about the world of Nature, the character of minerals, and the specific qualities of plants and herbs. Above all, I was eager to learn something about Medicine, the politics of monarchs and their important wars apart from other important historical events. I wanted to know something about the new geographical discoveries, the oceans, rivers, deserts and any traces of their origin, the craftsmanship (of other nations), their stratagems, frauds, their shrewdness and their fictitious literature. I read all this in their

CHAPTER NINE

literature and became fully acquainted with them (Gentiles), their activities and all their ideologies, both false and genuine. I acquired all this so that I would not be bereft of worldly knowledge. However, I took care not to study these topics in any depth and only read about them when I was in a situation in which Torah study was proscribed. Yet on several I occasions I extracted sweetness from the strong (c.f.Jud.14:14) and the honey which I found in them I scraped into my hand (c.f.ibid.14:9) so as to make use of it for a religious purpose when I was confronted with questions which seemed shut up and concealed (c.f.Dan.12:9). Above all, because of this activity I was able to acquire the (relevant) facts with which to deal with the queries of sceptics and heretics, so that such people would not consider me ignorant. However, I devoted much of my leisure in reading books on medicine and the preservation of health on which human life depends. Moreover, I studied Natural history to the degree I considered essential for the preservation of the human species.

I now come to the real purpose of recording my study of all those books. For on one occasion I came across the medical book that I previously mentioned (by the Dutchman Dr. Bantekel) in which I read how he praised the heath benefits that accrued from drinking hot tea. This book encouragingly prescribed regular drinking of this drink assuring the reader of its over-all healing properties. I took this advice seriously and tried it for several years, viz. from 1724 when I returned from my first long journey until 1792 when I was involved in my second exile to Germany. Throughout this period I used to drink tea both morning and evening. It was in fact, my staple liquid and I found it most beneficial to my health. Indeed, apart from tea I hardly drank anything else. It was my first drink in the morning and I quenched my thirst with it soon after I had digested my lunch. Henceforth I completely renounced beer which never again touched my lips except on very unusual and rare occasions. Even when I was visiting Moravia I did not drink wine, which was cheap and plentiful there, except on festivals or at a meal connected with a religious ceremony. Apart from these occasions I rejected it, only tea afforded me pleasure and peace of mind making me feel as though I had drunk spiced wine. Throughout these years, both when I was at home or on my first or second long journeys (of exile) this drink did me a great of good. But when, for my sins, I succumbed to melancholia whilst in Amsterdam I thought I would obtain some relief from my low spirits by drinking large quantities of tea which I thought would prove pleasurable and afford me some respite from my distress and grief. For many occasions in the past whenever I was in low spirits I would not touch any alcoholic drink which I found harmful, but endeavoured to raise my spirits by drinking large quantities of tea. I now thought this procedure would help me avoid the worst excesses of harmful melancholia. However, on this occasion it proved to be my undoing for on drinking, a large amount (of tea) my blood turned to water, so that I suffered spells of fainting and also had to make constant visits to the toilet with the result that my suffering was doubled and I experienced overwhelming pain.

Not realising the cause of my illness I endured excruciating pain and suffering for about six months and this despite the fact that I studied medical treatises. Moreover, I felt such a burning sensation in my entrails that on several occasions I was on the point of expiring. Nor for a long was I able to get any sleep, at night I used to wish that it were morning. In fact, several times people were compelled to profane the Shabbat on my account, or in the middle of the night they had to arouse people who were asleep so that they could get me a drink of hot water or a remedy for loosening my bowels. I tried many remedies and gradually gained some respite. However, the problem of urinating which compelled me to be constantly excused did not cease. I had to tolerate it for more than twenty years, although I had long abandoned drinking tea but had opted for coffee. For I found it impossible to become used to alcoholic drinks except for three or four small cups of wine which I drank at one meal, but I could not drink any more. Nevertheless, the previous ills I mentioned were slightly reduced, though I seemed to be permanently affected by that scourge (problem of urinating). However, once I returned home and enjoyed the security of family

CHAPTER NINE

life, this scourge gradually disappeared. In fact, with the Almighty's help, the most important step towards effecting cure of melancholia when several years later, as I have already said, my bile duct was opened. Yet I was not able to get rid of the problem of urination and return to normality until I made my third long journey to Amsterdam in 1751. It was during this journey that, with the Almighty's mercies, I was completely cured of this illness, so that in the very same place where I had first contracted this illness (for my illness came about through an excessive amount of hot water), the Almighty, blessed be He, now sent me a cure through the drinking of cold water, though the latter caused me severe pains.

However, in 1753 thank God, I returned home physically sound, feeling quite a different person. I never again suffered from the excessive urine from which I was completely cured after its effects for about twenty-four years in which I was weary of life (c.f. Gen.27:46) and had despaired of being cured quite believing it would accompany me to the grave. Thank God I was now cured after suffering a bout of other pains besides the distress of the difficulties of constant travelling that I have previously described. Indeed, this urinary disease had taken its full toll of me. May He who heals the sick, who is the Helper and Saviour of the needy in whom I have always trusted, redeem me from all my ills and may He grant me the consolation of witnessing the return of His redeemed ones to Zion, may this be His will, Amen,

Subsequently I left Amsterdam with the intention of going to Altona without any delay and settling in my birthplace and my family's home city. As I passed through Emden the community wanted me to be their Rabbi, an idea that had never crossed my mind. For as I have previously stated I opted for obscurity and hated the Rabbinate, I therefore rejected the invitation and stayed with the lay-leader Reb Jonathan Levy. In Emden at that time was an eminent and intelligent lady who was the daughter of the Torah scholar Reb L---, may he rest in peace, and the daughter-in-law of the above-mentioned Reb Jonathan. She insisted that I eat and lodge in her house and, with her considerable intelligence, she aroused the interest

MEGILAT SEFER

of her father-in-law, her husband and the lay-leaders of the community and in general made every effort to retain me in Emden. I however, had not been informed of any of this. These people quickly went into action and, convening all the community they unanimously agreed to the proposition (of giving me a call to the local Rabbinate). Hence on Chol HaMoed Pesach (I had originally come to Emden for Pesach and had intended to remain there until after the festival and then to leave for home) I was elected as Principal Rabbi and decisor of the community. Immediately following this meeting representatives of the community visited me to inform me of the community's decision and begged me to accede to their request which I did though, as I have already stated, it was not in accord with my true feelings. However, I realised that it was ordained by Heaven, for I had never previously considered such a possibility and had not therefore attempted to win the support of anyone yet the Almighty had effected complete accord in the community's decision to appoint me. Moreover, the community was in sore need of a Rabbinic decisor since they were like sheep without a shepherd, consequently, I felt my objections (to the Rabbinate) weren't so important (cf. Gen.19:20) since I would now be able to pursue my Torah-studies to my heart's delight free from any impediment. Yet a further consideration was that with the Almighty's help I would enable the community to behave as Jews should. I therefore wrote to my wife, may she rest in peace, (requesting her) to come to Emden with the rest of my family and all my impediments. At the beginning of the summer of 1729 the Almighty brought them viz. my wife and my two sons, Meir and Zalman, may the Almighty preserve them, to Emden in good health and spirits as swiftly as if they had been carried on the wings of eagles. Meir was then about twelve and the younger Zalman about six, whilst my daughter, may the Almighty preserve her, was a little girl. My family came with all my moveable possessions and books, Praise and thanksgiving are due to He who dispenses mercy and wonderful acts; may He who performs great and inscrutable deeds be blessed.

    In Emden the pains from the urinary complaint I previously

CHAPTER NINE

mentioned, though somewhat reduced, continued to plague me so that I could not sleep was very shaken (cf. Ps.6:4). My wife, may she rest in peace, was most distressed for me for I could barely breathe, so that my zest for married seemed to have disappeared, God forbid, for we had no more children during our stay in Emden. A further reason for this may have been the illness of my wife, may she rest in peace. However, just before we left Emden the Almighty blessed her with conception and she gave birth to a son in Altona. Despite all this I zealously pursued my Torah-studies in Bible, Mishnah, Gemara (with Rashi and Tosefot) as well works which covered religious topics of a non-mystical nature and classical mysticism. So that with the Almighty's help even the darkness of night was not too dark for me. (cf. Ps.139:12) I studied these topics with local students and with my sons, may the Almighty preserve them. Moreover, I dedicated my hand to the Almighty by writing aids to Torah-studies several works of which I had already begun when I still in Broda. During my stay in Emden I completed the first part of my work, Lechem Shomayim on two sections of the Mishnah (Zeraim and Moed) and succeeded in writing almost half of my Mor Uke'ziah, a commentary on the Tur Orach Chayyim which I had begun in my youth and am presently involved in preparing a second edition. In Emden too, I completed a considerable part of my She'elot Ya'avetz besides various articles on Talmudic topics and other basic works, the texts of which I corrected and annotated. I also got up a compendium of homiletic and literal texts.

Thank God, I gave the community a religious lead. I also introduced many new important regulations (designed) to remove the difficulties which had previously confronted the community. I mentioned a few of the latter in my reply to a letter I received from all R.Moses Hagiz in which he expressed his deep anger at the extreme stringency of my measures. I made every effort to act justly and righteously towards all those who sought my services and I was able to do so without receiving any tangible reward. I also studied with the sons of the very wealthy but refused any payment for this tuition. I even refused payment for teaching the son of the honourable lay-leader Jonathan Levy Senior, whose wealth was assessed at many hundreds of thousands of Reichthalers and who had sent me a munificent gift for accepting his son as my student. Nor would I accept a penny for the Talmudic discourse which I delivered on Shabbat HaGadol and Shabbat Shuvah though it had previously been the custom (for the community) to grant an honorarium of twenty-five Reichthalers for each discourse. Indeed, the intellectuals (in the community) including those who had studied at the Prague Yeshivah averred they had never heard Derashot more pleasant than those which they heard from me. However, I deeply resented having to waste so much time in studying homiletics in which, except when I had to, I had never been interested. For I gained spiritual satisfaction solely from the study of Gemara and the Codes of the Decisors; and from comprehending a Biblical text or Midrash that would enable to fully appreciate our holy Torah and consequently observe it properly. My intention was not, God forbid, to show any arrogance, how much less to laud it over others, but my sole purpose always was to express my love for Torah by being constantly involved in the study of it for the perfection of my soul. Yet with the Almighty's assistance I made good progress in my studies including homiletics and original interpretations of Aggadic texts. Consequently, whenever I required them, the Almighty, blessed be He, designated the most pleasing ideas which were pleasant and sweet to the ears yet which corresponded to the essential meaning of the texts. I have no doubt that the Almighty, may He be praised, favoured me in the ability to bedeck several strange Aggadot, after only a first glance, with decorative attire and with ornaments more precious than fine gold. Let me therefore sing to the Lord because He has been so kind to me (cf.Ps.13:6) Let me thank the Lord, blessed be He, for the portion He has allotted me.

I will mention yet one other aspect of my (spiritual) leadership of Emden viz. that I showed no favouritism to the eminent nor feared any individual, but I showed equal regard for the prominent and less prominent, the poor and the rich. Thus, within a short time I gained the reputation of being one of the eminent

CHAPTER NINE

Rabbis of Germany and my fame continued to grow in all regions. Nor do I need to stress that I was beloved by the whole community from the lower strata to the upper strata. Indeed, I was like a veritable angel of God to them. No one gainsaid my pronouncements nor objected to any of my gestures. (In fact) only one person manifested some opposition to me at the beginning of my Rabbinate and proved to be a thorn in my side. This was the above-mentioned Iay-leader, Jonathan Levy Senior, for though he initially agreed to my being accepted as the presiding Rabbi of the Bet Din (of Emden) he thought I would be subservient to him in certain matters since he was so very affluent. However, he soon realised I had no greater regard for him than for any other member of the community. In fact before my arrival he was accustomed to issue orders concerning commercial business and since he enjoyed a powerful status he did as he pleased not only regarding mundane affairs of the community but also in spiritual matters for which he had never shown any deference to Rabbinic authority. Indeed, (before my arrival in Emden) the only one to give Rabbinic decisions in Emden was the teacher whom Reb Jonathan employed in his home for his sons. It was this teacher who had seen to the problems of both an individual and communal nature. But he (the teacher) was compelled to act as Reb Jonathan desired and who (always) endeavoured to please the latter. In fact, the teacher often behaved in the same way towards Reb Jonathan's son, my friend and disciple, Reb E--. When I therefore began to give the community (of Emden) proper spiritual guidance similar to that which my father, z"l, had given, and to impose stringent rules on them I showed them considerable affection both rich and poor. The exception was this Reb Jonathan who was set in his ways and who at first because of his customary attitude did not know what to think. The teacher too, who lived in his house was displeased at my having assumed the leadership of the community thinking that he had deprived of something which was rightly his. Reb Jonathan therefore planned to harm me and denigrated me among his family, though I trusted him. I was confidentially informed of this by an emissary of Hebron who was then visiting Emden (who told me) that Reb

MEGILAT SEFER

Jonathan endeavoured to carry out his nefarious scheme by denigrating me in his (the emissary's) presence. However, I paid no attention to all this but retained my integrity whilst trusting in the Almighty.

On one occasion a visiting Cohen who was blind stayed with Reb Jonathan. On the holy Shabbat when the visitor by virtue of being a Cohen had the right to be called first to the Reading of the Torah, Reb Jonathan presumably to annoy me, sent a message to the teacher who was present with me in the synagogue, asking (the teacher) whether it was right to consider a blind Cohen one of the quorum to be called to the Reading of the Torah. The teacher permitted it, but since the question was not put to me I was extremely angry and entered into a heated discussion with Jonathan the Elder, though eventually we were reconciled. Regarding the decision whether it was permissible to call a blind Cohen to the Reading of the Torah, with God's help I wrote a long Responsum (on this question) in which I set out the various aspects for prohibiting this practice. The reader will find it in my Responsa (She'elot Ya'avetz No.41). It was because of this incident that the scholar R.Moses Hagiz, may he rest in peace, then wrote to inform me that Reb Jonathan was making slanderous statements about me stating what he had previously stated in a letter to Hamburg. In my reply to R.Moses Hagiz I defended myself against Reb Jonathan's slanderous accusations. The following is a copy of the letter which I addressed to the above-mentioned scholar in which I prove my innocence. (The letter is missing from the MS. and was probably destroyed)

I finally decided to abandon the Rabbinate and leave the community (of Emden) where I had gained so much respect. For truthfully I originally accepted this yoke (of the Rabbinate) against my will. Now however, I had found an excuse to leave the Rabbinate for I sought neither the community nor the salary. But the community's attachment to me was so strong that they would not allow me to have my way but urged me to change my mind by offering many gifts. For every section of the community was

CHAPTER NINE

prepared to make any sacrifice on my behalf and therefore made every possible effort to retain me. Shortly after this the daughter of the above-mentioned Reb Jonathan Senior died. He had married her off shortly before my arrival (in Emden) but she died in child-birth. Reb Jonathan therefore lost his daughter and his money viz. a considerable fortune which he had given her as a dowry. For since she was the first daughter of his first wife he had incurred a considerable outlay, whilst she (his daughter) left a baby son who lived for short time so that the child's father inherited the dowry. Moreover, the teacher who lived in Reb Jonathan's house and who acted as a Rabbi, as I mentioned previously, caused discord between the community and me, died during the same period. Seeing he was only a young man his passing caused me considerable distress.

Subsequently, however, the accord between Reb Jonathan and me was completely revived so that the whole of the community was deeply attached to me. Moreover, Reb Jonathan's cherished son, a distinguished young man was one of my students as were the sons of several affluent men of Emden. However, I would not accept payment for my teaching a policy I had adopted when I lived in Broda. For, thank God, my deeds drew me near to Him and I was privileged to see the realisation of the Biblical text, "when a man's ways please the Lord, he makes even his enemies live at peace with him." (Prov.16:7) In particular my whole approach to financial matters silenced my enemy so that he became a changed character and enabled him to sing my praises. Hence, I never again had an enemy in Emden, nor suffered any mishap to which person is prone. Yet I was not happy in Emden; "behold for my peace I had great bitterness," (Is.38:17) especially in respect of physical health. For throughout our stay there my family and I were affected by fever caused by the air, water and food, which did not agree with us. Hence we suffered throughout our residence in Emden and did not enjoy a full life because we were so racked with pain. For a long time before my arrival in that city no freshwater fish was available, for the soil of that whole region was hard having been ruined by flood water which had remained in the region for the past seventeen years, for the river had burst its banks and flooded the whole area. Consequently the soil now contained deposits of salt, whereas previously it was a region of rich pasture and fertile soil. Henceforth the soil deteriorated and lost all its fertility. Moreover, because of the injurious sea water the fish in the rivers were destroyed. (cf. Hos.4:3) Thus, the water was unhealthy and the soil barren, virtually destroying its inhabitants. However, during the summer in which I settled in Emden we were suddenly blessed with an abundance of fish. For the waters of the river began to sweeten and effected the return of fresh-water fish which were so plentiful that they could be bought cheaply. Consequently the community commented, "the Rabbi has brought us the good fortune of fresh-water fish" for they had never before tasted fish of such quality but only sea-fish that had always been available.

Whilst in Emden I indulged in much business and made some profit without too much trouble. I merely wrote to my acquaintances in Amsterdam who sent me some commodities which I knew would sell quickly in Emden. I then handed them to a reputable merchant who shared the profit of their sale with me. Thank God, I did not lose any money but, on the contrary, I made a profit without too much bother. Nevertheless none of us i.e. my wife, sons and daughter had any peace of mind during our stay in Emden. For as I have already stated all of us endured ill-health because of our frail constitutions since the climate proved unhealthy to us. Indeed, has I been able to abandon the community all of whom were on the best of terms with me and constantly urged us to remain in Emden, there were many occasions I would have left that community though my stay there would have been short. However, whenever I thought of so doing and when the opportunity arose when I resolved to leave for my native community of Altona the community made me change my resolve by winning and appeasing arguments. Nevertheless, I constantly waited for the right opportunity and moment to leave Emden peacefully. My wife, the Rabbanit, may she rest in peace, was very ill with the fever of which she was a constant victim. In fact, throughout our stay in Emden she

CHAPTER NINE

was dangerously ill from the bleeding of the womb which was often heavy. I therefore sent her to Amsterdam and from there to Leyden where she received some treatment from an eminent professor. However, when she returned to Emden the same degree of bleeding recurred. But on the eve of our departure from Emden she was again with child.

Yet another reason for my desire to leave Emden was that I could see little future for my sons, long may they live, in the community. My eldest son reached the age of Barmitzvah during my first year's residence there. I taught him for about three years and subsequently sent him to Hamburg. From there he went to his grandfather in Poland i.e. to my father-in-law, the Rabbi of Broda, may he rest in peace, who arranged a most suitable marriage for his grandson with the daughter of a very wealthy man who hailed from Lissa. It was because of this connection with the latter gentleman that my father-in-law, may he rest in peace, obtained the Rabbinate of Posen for my son's father-in-law enjoyed considerable prestige in that region. I sent my wife to my son's wedding whilst I remained in Emden, for I found it too difficult to make the journey and my wife was most eager to see her father. Then, as I have stated, she made the journey to join me in Altona. Three years after my son's wedding, years which I spent in Emden as a hireling, further trouble occurred between the above-mentioned elder (Reb Jonathan Levy) and me. It all began on Rosh Hashanah when his younger son who had not yet grown a beard, wanted to blow Shofar. But I could not allow such a dull young man enable the congregation to fulfil this religious duty on this Holy Day. As a result, enmity between us again intensified and he planned to take vengeance on me by refusing to pay my salary, but I remained silent. Subsequently Reb Jonathan did a foolish thing and virtually put himself in an invidious position with the local (Gentile) authorities. This occurred when he gave instructions for an announcement to be made in the Synagogue to the effect that I was not enamoured of the local authorities. Relying on his power in the community Reb Jonathan felt that no one would dare disclose this announcement to the local authorities. However, one of his local enemies did dare to speak up and immediately disclosed his action to them (the authorities). Consequently all the representatives of the community were summoned to appear before the authorities so that each one would declare what they knew or heard about the announcement. I too, was summoned to appear before them to declare what I had heard.

Now I enjoyed a high reputation with these people particularly because of my correct behaviour in financial matters. For apart from the fact I evinced little interest in the latter which was unlike most other people. I was very liberal with my money. In fact, whenever I had to deal with a case involving a Gentile and a Jew that came before the local judicial authorities, they would invite me to join the court for which I received a fee. On one occasion I suggested a compromise on behalf of a Jewish defendant who had been summoned by a Gentile plaintiff to appear before the local court. I then declared that if my suggestion did not meet with the approval of the plaintiff I would pay the sum I had suggested the defendant should pay so as to exonerate the latter from taking an oath before the court. In this instance the plaintiff would not accept my compromise so I kept my promise and paid the money on behalf of the defendant and I thus became the latter's surety. In short, I did this in many similar incidents and the local authorities got to know about it. Thus I gained a very high reputation both among our co-religionists as well as among the Gentiles.

Consequently, when the local authorities learned of the announcement in the Synagogue from the enemy of Reb Jonathan the latter thought I would now avenge myself for all the enmity Reb Jonathan had evinced towards me from the moment I had arrived in Emden, for now the Almighty had delivered him (R. Jonathan) into my power. Reb Jonathan's enemy had helped trap him so that I could now demand what Reb Jonathan owed me. This seemed quite obvious to this enemy who happened to be a faithful adherent of mine. It was he (the enemy) who had therefore advised the authorities to question me so that I would state exactly what had occurred so that Reb Jonathan's enemy's statement before them

CHAPTER NINE

would be confirmed. For everyone knew I was a truthful person who feared no one and that even if I were offered all the wealth in the world I would not be compromised. Hence, one they (the authorities) had questioned me to ascertain the facts I would not hide anything from them. This behaviour was unlike that of the major part of the community who were subservient to that wealthy man (Reb Jonathan) and were afraid of him so that since he wielded such power they would suppress their evidence.

Before I went to the authorities Reb Jonathan's enemy invited me to his home to supply me with a correctly worded and reasoned statement (which I should make before the court). For he was convinced he had afforded me the opportunity of demanding compensation for everything Reb Jonathan had done to me. As Job observes, "though evil tastes sweet in his mouth, rolling it around his tongue." (20:12) So he, (Reb Jonathan's enemy) observed, "now you will see what I will do to my enemy whom the Almighty has caused to fall into my hands." I encouraged him in this thought so that he should get the authorities to summon me, though my real intention was to spoil the plan of completing ruining Reb Jonathan. When I was finally summoned to appear before the authorities they requested me to state what I knew about the incident and not to suppress any fact. Now although all my co-religionists who were summoned had to swear they would speak the truth, I apologised to the authorities and requested I be excused from taking this oath for I had never previously taken an oath in court even one which enjoined me to speak truthfully.

My request was granted and I was exempted from the oath since they realised that even without the oath I would not conceal any fact regarding my enemy. When they (the authorities) asked me whether I had heard the announcement in the Synagogue I replied did not hear it, nor do I know anything about it." They then asked whether I wasn't in Synagogue on the day the announcement was made to which I replied, "even though I was present in the Synagogue and the beadle made some announcement, which was one of his regular duties, I paid no attention to them for invariably they weren't concerned with my position nor with any of my functions. For I usually stand in the synagogue clad in a Tallit and face the wall (of the Synagogue) so that I can concentrate on my prayers. Hence I pay little attention to anything else nor to any communal announcements which usually touch upon business appertaining to the community." The authorities thoroughly cross-examined me on this matter to extract a statement which would incriminate Reb Jonathan but they did not succeed. In fact the result was contrary to their plan for I did not permit myself to be guilty in this respect but "kept watch at the door of my lips." (Ps.141:3) since my thoughts were not the same as the slanderer's.

    My statement to the authorities swayed (the verdict) in favour of Reb Jonathan so that what appeared to be a disaster for him proved to be to his advantages. Eventually the anger of the authorities died down (cf.Jud 8:3) for all the other people who had made their declarations with the object of harming Reb Jonathan were not so acceptable to the authorities since they (the authorities) rejected them because those witnesses were Reb Jonathan's enemies. Hence they (the authorities) argued that Reb Jonathan's enemies had libelled him. Consequently they (the authorities) completely acquitted him (Reb Jonathan). Had they made a reverse decision then all Reb Jonathan's wealth would have proved of no avail and he would probably have lost his whole estate because of this incident. When he (Reb Jonathan) saw me going to the authorities he regarded me as a murderer who intended to behead him and as a debtor who had found an opportunity to exact all his debt. However when he was given a copy of my deposition before the authorities regarding his conduct, he began to sing my praises saying that he now realised the true nature and character of a genuine Talmid Chacham and the difference between an altercation with an ordinary person and a real Talmudic scholar. Consequently he plied me with blessings since (he realised) it was through me that he escaped a great misfortune which was in store for him and that it was through my agency that he was saved from the snare of the fowler, and which was unlike his behaviour towards me.

CHAPTER NINE

Subsequently Reb Jonathan became a true friend of mine until the very day I left Emden, for "when a man's ways please the Lord, He makes even his enemies to live at peace with him." (Prov.16:7) Indeed, Reb Jonathan constantly evinced the greatest affection towards me, and when I had finally decided to leave Emden he warned me not to settle in Altona claiming that he was old and experienced and therefore knew that community better than I, for I was a young man when I had left Altona and therefore did not really know the community. He was worried lest I regret my decision to move there. In this vein he warned me not to leave Emden. However, I declined his advice for my heart seemed entwined with my birthplace particularly because of the general ill-health which my family suffered in Emden. Moreover, I realised that my temperament and that of the local lay-leaders was incompatible for they wanted as to be subservient and beholden to them so that I would virtually be their slave. This was their customary attitude in their relations with their Rabbi but I had never been a slave to any human being and consequently I hated the idea of such a Rabbinate.

In the summer of 1722, about six months before my departure from Emden another incident occurred which further aggravated my hatred of the Rabbinate and which confirmed my decision to move from there. Some visitors to the community arrived, some purchasers of sins, a mission of pestiferous angels, who let it be known that they had come as emissaries of the community of Minsk in Lithuania, who were suffering a terrible persecution because of some libel of which the community was accused. The latter had been fabricated by these emissaries to defraud and despoil various charities and to obtain sacks of money with the object of rusing the above-mentioned community which was in fact existing quite peacefully, though according to those emissaries was in dire distress. They had brought with them counterfeit letters which purported to have been written by the leaders of the above-mentioned community to other communities and which informed the readers of their terrible misfortune and begged them for their (financial) assistance. These letters also stated that they had appointed these emissaries whom they named, to travel throughout Europe to collect funds which they would take back to Minsk to save those who would otherwise die.

The whole of German Jewry learned of the activities of these robbers and cunning swindlers who emptied the charity boxes designated for all the poverty-stricken, who deceived a number or German (Jewish) communities as well as those of the Sephardi community of London and Amsterdam. For, under the threat of Cherem, the latter were forbidden to donate any of their charities to Ashkenazi poor whomsoever the latter might be. In fact I recollect a certain incident which occurred when my father, z"l, had first settled in Amsterdam. Certain authentic emissaries of the community of Lublin arrived in that city, who were personalities enjoying the complete trust of the community they represented. My father therefore, made every effort to help them and interceded on their behalf with the Sephardi community, requesting that the latter should help those people in their distress. As a result of my father's earnest entreaties and because they (the Sephardim) couldn't turn my father away empty handed since they regarded him as virtually a divine angel, they acceded to his request and handed him a donation to give to those emissaries of Lublin though they regarded it as a gift to my father whom they considered to be a Sephardi. In this way they avoided an infringement of the ruling which prohibited them from donating to Ashkenazi charities. They (the Sephardim) strictly adhered to this ruling yet these swindlers (purporting to represent the community of Minsk) seduced them (the Sephardim) into making considerable donations just as though the original ruling did not appertain to these emissaries. Hence, on this occasion they did not adhere to it. (the ruling) From this whole incident it seemed that in the conduct of the Sephardim and that of many lay-leaders of German Jewry we saw the realisation of the prophecies of Jeremiah in that their downfall was caused by wicked men.

Finally, when these false emissaries visited me in Emden I felt their mission was a completely false one. Yet initially I befriended them particularly since I was related to one of them through my

CHAPTER NINE

father though ultimately this person proved to be a son of R. Hertz Vilna (Jacob b. Benjamin Wolf) who was associated with the Bet HaMidrash of Nathan Nata Mannheim (in Jerusalem), a member of the circle of Judah Hasid (Segal). But I had no reason to be proud of this relative though he was important in that he had been involved in a struggle which split that generation (into Sabbataeans and Anti-Sabbataeans). He was of handsome appearance and somewhat of a Talmudic scholar, so that I was very attached to him until it became clear that he was involved in this fraudulent mission. The other member (of the mission) was an expert in practical Kabbalah and skilled in the manipulation of the secret names of God (a Baal Shem). I examined him closely and found him to be a virtual chamber-pot, a bloodthirsty and deceitful person as well as being a boorish ignoramus. Thus I was certain that they (the above-mentioned two men) were Sabbataeans. With them they had brought a third person who hailed from Minsk who was young, intelligent and scholarly, and who was well-versed in the Talmud including the relevant commentaries of Rashi and Tosefot. He was the scion of an eminent Lithuanian family and was separated from his wife to whom his family had married him off when he was very young. Several years had now passed since he had deserted the wife of his youth and had gone to live in Germany. This was the person these two men took with them to confirm their integrity. For in Germany this young man had the reputation of being a talmudic scholar of some significance. Moreover, he was of unblemished character, apart from the fact that he was separated from his wife. Perhaps the latter did not adversely reflect his character for he had no intention of leaving his wife a grass widow, God forbid, since he was prepared to release her with a get (divorce) and to settle the debt for which the Ketubah (marriage document) obligated him.

However, his wife was preventing this since she did not want to be divorced. I befriended and became very attached to him for I could see he had all the characteristics of a scholar and though he was only young I predicted that this young man would one day be an eminent Talmudic scholar. When these false emissaries had stayed

MEGILAT SEFER

with us in Emden for only a few days, my uncle Leib Benjamin, who was my mother's step-brother and hailed from Grodno (Lithuania), paid me a visit. I had not anticipated his arrival, yet even if he had lived at the other and of the world (it seemed) the Almighty had brought him to us. When he sat down to a meal with us we came to speak about the emissaries who were then staying with us and whose visit to Emden concerned the cruel persecution which had befallen the community of Minsk. On hearing this my uncle who was a simplistic person, arose in astonishment and wouldn't accept this news saying, if there is a persecution of Jews in Minsk, I am not aware of it, for I arrived in Emden only a short time ago and Mink in very close to my home-town, yet I know nothing of such a persecution. In fact there is neither a major nor minor persecution of Jews in any part of Lithuania. Yet according to those swindlers the persecution (in Minsk) was supposed to have occurred a year ago!

Consequently I came to the definite conclusion that this mission was fictitious and completely false. I then put the members of the mission to the test and taking the letter which reported the persecution and to which the signatures of the lay-leaders of Mink were appended and said to them, " If you are honest men I will give you every possible help, for I too wish to share in the Mitzvah of redeeming captives, which is the main purpose of your visit. However, to obviate any perverse talk (cf.Prov.4:24) or slander your integrity must be put to the test. (I suggest) we make a donation to your cause whilst you commit into our keeping the money you have collected in Germany, Holland and England which we will send to Breslau. We will then arrange for these funds to reach your community through a prominent lay-leader of your choice. We will give you a legal receipt for the money (you will commit into our hands). By acting in this proper manner you will obviate any local slander or evil reports. Moreover, any personal gifts you may have received will remain with you, in fact, we will add to them. But we want to ensure the safety of the funds specifically donated for the poor of your community. (All) this will prove to your advantage whilst the mitzvah (of Pidyon Shevuyim) will be enhanced (if we

CHAPTER NINE

consider) the responsibilities (you assumed) with all your journeys. In fact, this was the usual procedure adopted by all honest emissaries so that they should be guiltless before God and Israel. (cf. Neh.32:22) In this way you will gain honour from God and mankind. (cf. Pirkei Avot 2:1)

However, notwithstanding my ability to express appropriate statements to people of integrity who are prepared to listen (to me), I could not penetrate their deaf ears to thwart their fraudulent scheme. Indeed, however much as I tried to persuade them not to reject my most suitable proposition, whether I spoke softly or harshly, I was completely unsuccessful. In fact, those two spies who had been sent out secretly (cf. Josh.2:1) were as cunning as snakes in beguiling everyone with their persuasive tongues that they even caught my closest friend with their deceitful net. For one of these devilish emissaries was staying with my friend whilst the other (emissary) stayed with my friend's elderly father. From the beginning to the end of my residence in Emden this friend was more attached to me than a brother and would have given his life for me. In fact, because of this friendship he was constantly opposed to his father. However, on this occasion he opposed me in that he encouraged these wicked emissaries by swearing near the holy ark in the local synagogue that these emissaries were good and trust-worthy men and that I had libelled them. I then came to realise that "an ignorant man cannot be pious (Pirkei Avot 2:6.) and that one shouldn't befriend such a person, for as a result of the lies and flattery of people who were morally suspect he had taken a false oath. Hence, "they that are godless in heart lay up anger". (Job 36:13)

But, above all the majority of contemporary German Jewish lay-leaders proved to be simplistic men by trusting those flattering impostors. They succumbed to unworthy people who took advantage of their (the lay-leaders) hospitality by the most profane mockeries of backbiting (cf. 35:16) and who deceived them by tricking them out of their money. Consequently, these lay-leaders caused us to fall into the trap through the rhetorical letters which they (the lay-leaders) gave those swindlers and so proved to be accomplices of sinners. They (the lay-leaders) ruined themselves and others by bearing witness on behalf of men whom they really did not know, and seeking the latters' best interests they abetted all their (the false emissaries) chicanery. I was most distressed (over the fate) of my above-mentioned friend who, for our many sins, suffered a bitter fate in losing his wealth disastrously. To crown it all he lost the intelligent wife of his early youth shortly after I left Emden. He then married his second wife who squandered all his wealth. Shortly after he too died and his second wife took all she could get from the estate and remarried. All the dowry she brought went to waste and she died leaving the children of the first marriage as impoverished orphans. I was most upset when I remembered the integrity of their (the orphans') mother but who can say whether it was their fathers false oath did not prove a curse which finally destroyed himself and his family? Let the lay-leaders take this lesson to heart, for it will be sufficient if they learn (from this incident) not to put all their trust in their wealth.

    I have now completed recounting incident of the above-mentioned false emissaries who were most adept in hitting fools with the fist of flattery (cf. TB. Sotah 48a.) and in seducing people with their captivating talk. It was because of this that they escaped my grasp in Emden so that I failed to got anything from them. Quite the reverse, they received a considerable number of donations in Emden. I was amused by the behaviour of those fools (who made these donations) for they squandered their money on such unseemly people. Nevertheless, I said and did all that had to be said and done to get at the truth (of this) business. What did I do? I got hold of the letters patent which were in their possession which they purported to have brought from Minsk and which authorised them to act as emissaries and to collect funds on behalf of those Jews who had been condemned to death and help abrogate the fatal threat which hung over the community of Minsk. Appended to this document were the signatures of the leaders of the community and sent it to a true friend of mine in Altona viz. the scholar R. Hagiz, may he rest in

CHAPTER NINE

peace, requesting him to make enquiries regarding the authenticity of the letter. In an accompanying note, I observed that no task was beyond him (cf.Job 42:2) and that he should find some natives of Minsk who happened to be visiting Altona who would confirm the authenticity of the signatories (to the document) and who would know if the community of Minsk had suffered the above-mentioned persecution. Now something quite remarkable occurred for R.Hagiz chanced to meet a lay-leader of Minsk who happened to be visiting Altona and whose signature was appended to the letters patent. This person had visited Germany many years ago and was now forced through economic circumstances to resume his travelling which brought him to Altona in the very same week in which the false letters patent carried by those deceitful emissaries had reached Altona. R. Hagiz invited this lay-leader to his house and showed him the document to which his (the lay-leader's) signature was appended saying, "please tell me whose signature this is?" The man was most dismayed and replied "Who is the man and where is he who committed this deed to falsify signatures and to invent this harsh persecution which, in fact never occurred."

When I received Hagiz's reply with the news of this remarkable incident of how the Almighty had arranged for him (R. Hagiz) to meet one of the signatories to the document which had been carried by those lying emissaries and how the Almighty had brought this lay-leader from distant lands at that precise time and so confirm the complete falsehood of that mission and thus verify my opinion I showed it (R. Hagiz's reply) to my associates. However, not only were they little impressed by the fact that they had been deprived of funds destined for the poor in general who had been robbed of what was rightfully theirs, but they continued to ply those false emissaries with splendid gifts when they (the emissaries) departed from their community. Nevertheless I warned those emissaries who travelled through various communities to empty the boxes of charity and advised them not to visit Altona for they would be caught in a trap there. However, they did not listen to me but relying on their previous success and their previous deceptions they thought they would obtain the same support in Altona as they had achieved in Emden by blinding and deceiving people with flattery. Hence they continued to Altona full of confidence. However though nobody paid heed to me in Emden, my net was spread throughout the community of Altona, so that everything I had predicted actually occurred. For when they arrived there the trap was spread at their feet to catch them in the form of a decree of the lay-leaders of the community. Hence these emissaries were thrown into prison and made to meet the expenses incurred in their arrest and incarceration. However, the lay-leaders could not recover the charitable funds which the false emissaries had procured nor the funds they had illegally appropriated. They (the emissaries) were banished from Altona with great scorn and derision (cf. Ps.44:14) and hounded to destruction (cf. Ps.140:12) thus becoming an example of abhorrence of all swindlers and their ilk.

As for Reb Wolfe whom these emissaries brought with them to act as a false witness, he detached himself from their company and repented or his wrong with a full confession of his guilt. I have described the latter in my responsum (She'elot Ya'avetz) in which R. Wolfe addresses a question to me regarding a Talmudic dissertation he had written. Before I conclude my adventures in Emden I will briefly record another incident in which the Holy One, blessed be He enabled me to perform an important mitzvah. For the Almighty put in my way (cf. Gen.27:20) a certain person who sought my assistance in his efforts to become a penitent. He had long despaired of marrying since he was rather old, but while directing his return to Judaism I insisted that he marry within a year. He followed my advice and married successfully so that he was privileged to become a father before he died. However, I declined any of the considerable financial rewards which this man offered me. He informed me of the birth of his son when I had already returned to Altona and on reading his letter I remembered the whole incident.

To revert to the main narrative. The incident of the false emissaries further strengthened my resolve to leave Emden, for I

CHAPTER NINE

observed that even my closest friend in Emden could no longer be trusted. Moreover, I felt a change in this friend's attitude when he had spent a few days on business affairs in Hamburg. For on his return he thought I would visit him to see how he was faring. I did nothing of the sort, for I never saw my father, z"l, behave in this way, and I therefore regarded such behaviour as a profanation of the honour of the Torah. But this man was very angry with me stating that when he paid a short visit to Hamburg the elderly Rabbi of the Three communities had personally paid his respects to him, whereas I, a comparative youngster and the Rabbi of a small community considered myself to be more important than that eminent Rabbi who was the most respected person of his community. Consequently, this friend became a different person and the warm affection which had hitherto existed between us became considerably cooler. When I learned of this I made a firm resolution to leave Emden as soon as possible and opted to live as a free layperson in my native city (Altona) rather than a slave to the community of Emden. For I preferred obscurity to fame and to be accepted for the person I was and not to be imposed on by other people. In particular, I could not tolerate the arrogance of the German lay-leaders, especially in smaller communities where they were considered tin gods. The idea of being imposed upon by other people was something I had never hitherto experienced and I was therefore resolved that I would rather live in the corner of a roof than to suffer this servitude which, however elevated, made me bear other people's responsibilities and all the errors they made in their ignorance. I preferred a meal of herbs which I could enjoy in tranquillity, as Scripture has it "better a dry crust with concord with it, than a house full of feasting and strife" (cf. Prov.17:1)

I was accorded the greatest respect in Emden and the whole community revered me. I also enjoyed an ample income, though it barely sustained my family for I didn't pursue wealth nor any extraneous income which was above boards, I wasn't involved in any business transactions with any members of the community nor did I act as a marriage-broker as did other contemporary Rabbis, how much less did I hasten to the wealthy to procure their many gifts, for (I knew) that was precisely what they wanted me to do! I did not accept any payment for teaching, in fact I returned whatever fee was sent to me in this respect. Moreover, during the whole period of my Rabbinate (in Emden) I would not accept any additional fee for my Derashot although the community found them very pleasant and opined that they had never heard such Derashot. Indeed, former students of the Prague Yeshivah who had sat at the feet of the eminent Rabbinic authority, R. Abraham Broda stated they had never before heard such Derashot which displayed such acumen, erudition and delicate thoughts, not even from the most eminent Rabbis of Germany.

I was equally popular in communities near Emden who craved "to shelter under my wings" and who addressed to me any problems they had in the sphere of Rabbinic learning or Halakhic decisions; in all such matters they would write requesting my opinion. Above all, I never sought social advancement which, had I so wished, I could have attained to the highest degree. In brief, I fulfilled my resolve with the Almighty's help and towards the close of 1732 I arranged the renting of a house in Altona subsequent to informing the local authorities who replied that I would be most welcome in my native city. I sent all my impedimenta to Altona by sea, whilst my family and I travelled by road. My wife, the Rabbanit, may she rest in peace, had already left Emden several months previously to attend the wedding of our eldest son Shai, and when I left Emden she was staying with her father the Rabbi of Posen, may he rest in peace. The community (of Emden) made every effort though unsuccessfully, to make me change my mind, especially the elderly lay-leader R. Jonah whom I have already mentioned, and his respected son R. Abraham, who were persistent in their efforts to make me change my decision. Even the important Gentiles (of Emden) censored the local Jews when they learned of my departure, and caused the latter much embarrassment by stating: "what have you done, where now is your wisdom and understandings, where will you ever find another person like your former Rabbi, who will be able be your spiritual leader?"

CHAPTER NINE

Neither these sentiments nor any other form of flattery had any effect on me, but I left Emden in the best of spirits and the community gave me an impressive farewell. Yet despite the latter they thought my departure was only temporary and that I would ultimately return to Emden. I learned this from personal experience, for when I wrote to Emden (some time after my departure) on behalf of a local Rabbi who sought my former position they replied they were not looking for another Rabbi but for me, and that this had had been their intention for quite some time. Hence, they indicated they were not interested in any other Rabbi irrespective of his discernment and knowledge, be it who it may, since they were deeply attached to me. They therefore waited and hoped I would return to Emden and resume my Rabbinate there promising me increased privileges as well as salary. However, I replied politely that since I had left (Emden) I would not return and that when prospects were uncertain one stayed put. Furthermore (I stated) that had I not had cogent reasons for leaving (Emden) which I have already stated I would not have left that community. For everyone there was dear to me, as the Book of Proverbs states, "as in water face answers to face, so the heart of man to man"(Chap. 27:19) (I continued), the Almighty knows that even if I were able to obtain the most important Rabbinate in Germany, which was apparently the general opinion, for the community of Frankfurt-on-Main, the largest in Germany, was full of my praises and wanted me to accept the Rabbinate there, I would not have exchanged Emden for Frankfurt-on-Main. For I was deeply attached to the former community since I was able to concentrate on my Torah-studies in Emden and had no desire for important Rabbinic positions or to look for social prestige by lording it over any major community where I would obtain much material benefit besides social status. However, sheer necessity led me to hate the Rabbinate, essentially for the reasons I have previously stated.

Nevertheless, (despite the sentiments that I had expressed in my letter) they still hoped they could persuade me to return though this hope was like the hope of the travelling merchants of Sgeba. (cf.Job 6:19) But seven or eight years after I had left Emden they again wrote begging me to return and indicating that if I were consent they would more than double my previous salary, for (the letter continued) every member of the community was prepared to make a voluntary contribution towards my annual salary and that this assessed contribution should be regarded obligatory. Moreover, they promised I would be the Rabbi of the whole region over which) would have complete religious control, for all these communities longed for my acceptance (of their offer). They therefore sent a letter the honourable lay-leader David Leverden, a wise and intelligent person, requesting him to do all he could in gaining my consent to their proposals and that he should agree to any demands I would make and thus ensure my acceptance. This letter was in addition to those which my particular admirer wrote to me in which he begged me not to disappoint them. However I was not seriously impressed by any of this correspondence.

The community of Emden awaited my consent for some ten years during which time they evinced no desire to appoint another Rabbi (and would not have appointed one) were it not for the earnest requests of my brother-in-law on behalf of his father-in-law. Previously they proposed to grant me far better privileges than I had enjoyed during my first Rabbinate (in that community), and I was sorely tempted to accept them for I had come to realise that the future in Altona did not hold much in store for me. My capital which I had invested in jewellery and precious stones and in which I was helped by the lay-leader Gurdashi had depreciated, although my capital did not amount to much. However, I could not change my decision (to remain in Altona) for although I was depressed I did not feel too low since I had bought a home in Altona and had spent a great deal of money in renovating it. Moreover health wise things augured well in Altona for the fever to which all my family had been prone in Emden ceased when we settled in Altona and though I myself was prone to a form of cystitis, the attacks were now less frequent. My wife, the Rabbanit, may she rest in peace, also experienced some relief fro her former ailment although she was already with child before she left Emden and had gone as I have

CHAPTER NINE

already said, to our son wedding before returning to Altona with the family two days after my arrival there. During her pregnancy she suffered a recurrence of such a serious haemorrhage that we despaired of her life. However, the Almighty spared her though she suffered a few other haemorrhages during this pregnancy. On the first attack she was treated by the doctor Reb Simchah and I showed him the tablets which the specialist in Leyden had prescribed for her. When he saw them he was astonished stating that the specialist had endangered her life and that he was very surprised my wife could tolerate a regimen, the overall effect of which cancelled any benefit. However, Reb Simcha's treatment did not help my wife for after a short time she had another haemorrhage and almost despaired of recovery were it not for the kindness of the Almighty who heard our fervent prayers which ascended to heaven so that she recovered her health. Subsequently she gave birth to a perfect baby-boy but, because of our sins the child did not survive, beyond his seventh year as I have previously stated. Two years later gave birth to my daughter Esther, long may she live, and then she had two other daughters who died very young. Of all her children I was left with two sons, may the Almighty spare them, who became Rabbis, and two daughters. However I lost two sons in Moravia and two daughters in Altona during my wife's lifetime, whilst a son and daughter died after my wife's demise. Hence only a few of my children are alive, may the Almighty grant them life!

MEGILAT SEFER

CHAPTER TEN

I will now revert to an account of my initial re-settlement in Altona. When I arrived all the community came to welcome me with every deference and affections and asked me to ask for anything I wished and they would do their best to fulfil my request. My answer was to acclaim (cf. Zech.4:7) the good will and spirit of generosity (cf. Ps.51:14) they had shown me which I regarded as having been fulfilled and accepted by me. I had but one wish and that was to live tranquilly in the house of God and to serve Him upon whom I cast the burden of sustenance (cf.Ps.55:23). As for you (the community of Altona) please allow me to have a minyan (quorum) in my house so that my home will become a permanent centre for evening and morning prayers since because of my illness which was the basic cause of my abandoning the Rabbinate of Emden, I will find it difficult to attend the large communal synagogue and it would not be right for me to pray o my own. Therefore, (I continued) kindly grant we this one request for my spiritual welfare, for apart from this I have no desire to burden you with my material requirements. They replied that they gladly (acceded to my requests and that in fact there was no

207

CHAPTER TEN

need for me to talk about it since they had not refused a similar request which had been made by a person who was not even a native of Altona. Thus I was permitted (to hold a private minyan) just as they had permitted the scholar R.Moses Hagiz even though he was not an Ashkenazi. However, besides this they were ready to grant any other (reasonable) request I might make. So the general trend of their friendly conversation with me was that I could make any request of them and thus test their goodwill towards me. However I wanted nothing but the religious matter I have already mentioned. Since the community had permitted me to hold regular minyanim in my house I initially spoke with R. Hagiz, may he rest in peace, since he lived close by and was very friendly with me since my Rabbinate in Emden. In fact, we were deeply attached by a special relationship as was apparent from our correspondence in Torah-studies, part of which is included in my Responsa "She'elot Ya'avetz" and in his "Shtei Ha-Lechem". It was he who obtained a house for me at an exorbitant rent prior to my arrival in Altona, for he had little experience of such matters.

So shortly after I arrived in Altona, it was just before Rosh Hashanah 1733, I went to pray in the synagogue in his home (the minyan comprised Ashkenazim and followed the Ashkenazi prayer rite) throughout the whole of Yom Tov. I begged him to maintain this minyan for regular morning and evening services throughout the year and if he were to do that I would be a regular attendant. For (I observed) we got on well together and our friendship would continue. However, (at the same time) I pointed out that the local community had granted me permission to hold my own private minyan. But (argued) if he wouldn't agree (to a regular minyan in his house) I would have to establish my own for I would have no alternative, since it was very inconvenient for me to attend services in the large communal synagogue whilst, at the same time, I couldn't tolerate the idea of praying without a minyan. Previously other friends of his who attended his synagogue on Shabbat and Yom Tov had earnestly requested him to agree to hold regular services in his home throughout the year so that they would not have to go searching for a minyan during the rest of the week; their endeavours proved unsuccessful. Hence, I was saved from an embarrassing situation, though all my talking had proved quite useless. (cf.Job.24:25) Consequently I had to arrange a regular minyan in my own home. This caused some friction between us for R. Hagiz regarded my action as a thorn in his flesh and, as I later learned, he began to harbour some animosity towards me though I did not consider it a reason for dampening our warm friendship. For I had made a reasonable request of him and in any case, he was duty bound to pursue my proposal for to pray without a regular minyan would surely be a profanation of God in the eyes of the wider community. Moreover, when I visited his synagogue I noticed a fire burning in his stove which was certainly lit on Shabbat for heating water. In fact, I had heard some talk of this when, I was still in Emden but I would not believe it until I came to Altona and saw it with my own eyes. Nevertheless, I did not make a single comment. Apart from this I saw him do certain things which, in my opinion, were unbecoming for such an eminent person. Likewise, I made no comment on his behaviour for he was a very irascible person; hence I thought I would let the matter rest. Yet in spite of all this, my attachment to him both in my behaviour and conversation remained unimpaired, but he thought my action (regarding my own private minyan) was wrong and later he wrote denigrating things about me who had every trust in him.

In addition to the above-mentioned incidents (there was a further incident) when I published my book, Lechem Shomayim, I did not ask for his approbation. In fact, I avoided such a procedure since I did not approve of the highly exaggerated praises that he would undoubtedly have employed. For this was characteristic of him whenever I requested his approbation of my publications. This was not in any way surprising, for he would laud a person for whom he had no regard whatsoever in such exaggerated terms that they would appear untrue. I was very annoyed with him over such behaviour for he did not really believe what he said, a fact which I clearly learned in

CHAPTER TEN

his letters to me when I lived in Emden. In one of these letters he ridiculed the scholarly Rabbi who presided over the Bet Din of the Three Communities viz. R.H.Y. whom I have previously mentioned. In fact he spoke to me about this Rabbi in the most insulting terms whenever we met in Altona. Indeed he never ceased to speak disparagingly of him, to pour scorn on him, his scholarship, his Halakhic rulings or legal decisions. In short, he regarded this Rabbi as a figure of contempt and derision.(cf. Esther 1:18) Yet when he met this Rabbi face to face he (R. Hagiz) showed him (the Rabbi) the greatest affection. In one of his publications he introduced the Talmudic Novellae of the Av Bet Din and praised him in such exaggerated terms that he exhausted all the epithets that really belonged to prophetic personalities! I however, regarded such behaviour as most objectionable as well as misleading.

Nevertheless from the very outset his affection for me was genuine, for I heard him speak about me in the most glowing terms, and this apart from what he wrote about me, a fact which I mention in my Responsa (She'elot Ya'avetz) where I allude to some of his correspondence with me and shower him with praises. This state of affairs continued until, as I have previously noted, our mutual affection was modified. However I am unaware that he ever spoke disparagingly of me though he did make some quiet complaints about my betraying him, though this was further from my mind. Thus when he left Altona to return to the Holy land I thought we parted in great affection, for he was most eloquent (in my praises) in the presence of a large crowd who had come to see him off. Again in reading his book, "Shtei HaLechem", I noted that he included my responsum as to whether an eminent Sephardi Cohen who was under a cherem could pronounce the priestly blessing. In fact R. Hagiz previously showed me that particular page which also contained most laudatory notes about me, which I did not like. I therefore made him swear he would not describe me as a "Gaon" for I hate such exaggerated epithets particularly when they are expressed by a hypocrite. For these reasons I refrained from accepting his approbation of my Lechem Shomayim. This further cooled the ardent affection which had (hitherto) existed between us when I was Rabbi of Emden, when we regularly corresponded and when he showed me the greatest affection both in writing and conversation. Furthermore, when I had first settled in Emden he wrote to me enquiring whether all was well with me and gave me his blessing and at the same time informed me of the criticisms levelled against him by people because he used the full freedom of his pen to publish biting criticisms of eminent Rabbinic authorities who had published certain works. This was apart from the fact that he felt no compunction in pouring much scorn and humiliating criticisms on eminent contemporary Rabbi who dwarfed him in scholarship. He incorporated these criticisms in his collected works, yet his derision brought these scholars little dishonour because he himself lacked genuine erudition. I personally reproved him for this behaviour in a lengthy responsum which was in fact a public reprimand. The latter is includes in my She'elot Ya'avetz (No. 33). R. Hagiz conceded the point without humiliation and accepted the criticisms of his friend (myself) gracefully, nor did he lose his temper which was his usual reaction to criticisms of his conduct.

Consequently, my bond of friendship with him was reaffirmed and fastened with cords of affection particularly since he knew me from those early days when he lived in Amsterdam, though I was a youngster at the time. Moreover, I was aware of all the hardships he had suffered in his campaign against that snake Hayyun with whom he had fought "for the sake of Heaven" and had suffered much. I was therefore mindful of our earlier friendship (particularly) between him and my father, z"l. This was in addition to the fact of my realising he had humbled himself in accepting my criticism of his conduct when he said he regarded it (the criticism) as a compliment to him. Again, he was full of my praises when in my absence he spoke of me in the Three Communities and demonstrated his true friendship for me in a practical way by doing whatever he could to please me, though (at the time) I was a comparative child and he was quite too old. Nevertheless, the incidents I previously mentioned caused a rift between us when I came to re-settle in Altona.

CHAPTER TEN

Then there was another factor (which helped reduce the warm friendship that had existed between us). Certain foolish and amoral people had libelled me in stating that I had gloried over him (R. Hagiz) and taken advantage of his disgrace in speaking disparagingly of him not only in conversation (with other) but, (they had alleged) I had actually published statements discrediting him. I know nothing of this for I never discredited him publicly nor did I ever entertain such ideas. For though his publications contained some unpleasant and even slanderous statements apart from superfluities, all of which were beneath his dignity, (I refrained from criticising him publicly). Moreover, when returned to Altona I saw certain thing in R. Hagiz's house which I did not expect of a traditional Jew e.g. there was a constant fire in his stove throughout the Shabbat which provided him with hot fresh coffee though he was of sound health. Again, his excessive prattling in synagogue also annoyed me for this amounted to a profanation of God in the presence of the general congregation. Much worse was his neglect of praying with a minyan on six days of the week and, this despite the pressing requests of his Shabbat and Yom Tov minyan to meet (for prayer) during the rest of the week. This could have been easily accomplished had he given his consent, but he refused, despite those urgent requests so that the members of his minyan failed in their endeavours. But above all, (I was antagonised) by his attitude towards the presiding Rabbi of the Three Communities, R.Y.H. who was an eminent personality, yet R. Hagiz's behaviour towards him was hypocritical both in conversation and in general. For he (R. Hagiz) would excessively praise this Rabbi in his (R. Hagiz's) publications which were printed in Altona, whereas behind the rabbi's back he would mock and deride him. In fact, even in those published articles some sharp criticisms of the Rabbi were implied, though R. Hagiz took care to make such criticisms unobtrusively.

Indeed, there were other activities of R. Hagiz which I considered wrong but I have no desire to disparage him more than necessary for "his love, hatred and envy are things of the past (cf. Eccles.9:6). However, I will not conceal facts which I consider necessary to protect my reputation so that my children will know how to rebuff any criticism of my conduct. For in fact I witnessed many unusual and overt deeds of his the purpose of which I cannot fathom. For why should he have behaved in a way which shocked people? (cf. Job 21:5) Nevertheless, Heaven forbid I should criticise such a scholar who acted for the public good in several fields and who sometimes justly reproved his fellow Jew. This was particularly true of the Hayyun affair in which he gave his all in defence of true Judaism. Nor did he refrain from informing the latter as to the proper way to behave so that in his writings he reprimands contemporary lay-leaders for whom he had no respect and whose favours he did not curry. Yet another example was when he gave full force to his pen in reminding wicked people of their defects. For all this I hold him in great affection so that even if I saw him behave in a way which I considered improper I turned a blind eye and protected and defended him, whether it was correct of me or not, in order to quell the slanderous murmuring and suppress public criticism of him. This will be obvious to anyone who cares to look at the respectful and affectionate tone of my correspondence with R. Hagiz, for I contend that the love of the Almighty covers all sins. For the majority of people considered him a God-fearing person and although he occasionally erred who can discern errors? (Ps.19:13) Consequently, I concealed his sins and did all in my power to behave beneficently towards the man from when I was Rabbi in Emden. But he did not reciprocate this attitude towards me. For from when I returned here (to Altona) he dissolved the bonds of friendship with me for no substantial reason, not because of what I did, but because of some slanderous talk which he thought had emanated from me but which, in fact, came from those who spread the profanest mockeries of backbiting (cf. Ps.35:16). Thus the bonds of love and affection that had existed between us and which were publicly acknowledged were torn asunder and as I learned later, he blamed and hated me for a sin of which I was not aware. For though he had tried to hide his true feelings towards me he could not conceal them insofar as I could sense that the affection he had had for me had lost

CHAPTER TEN

its former warmth, for there had been a deep affection between us.

He (R. Hagiz) spoke about me to my visitors who later informed me that he had a serious complaint against me but he failed to give any details. However, I as usual behaved with the utmost integrity. I showed no anger nor, far be it from my father's son, did I act hypocritically, in fact my conduct towards him (R. Hagiz) remained unchanged. Thus, when we met at a local hostelry for the purpose of Hachnasat Kalah and, as usual, he conversed with me but I could not constrain myself from adopting his attitude of hypocritical conversation which was contrary to my nature. However, I addressed him as follows: "I find it necessary to question your honours behaviour and beg you not to conceal any facts from me. For I learn you have a complaint against me, whereas I am unaware of any wrong I have done you. I feel there must be some truth in this allegation since the previous accord that existed between us no longer prevails. Consequently I am surprised why your honour converses with me so insincerely, for it is quite obvious his sincerity is questionable. Why should a situation exist between us which can only lead to trouble and induce sin?" I asked why he was overtly friendly to me but inwardly he bore enmity. If I had wronged him why doesn't he reprimand me to my face which is the duty of a person of his status. "Tell me of any sin I have committed against you, let me know the nature of your complaint, and do not exonerate me of my sin." If I have been amiss in any way in my behaviour towards him of which I am unaware, perhaps it was through error, but then who can discern errors? (cf. Ps.19:14 Should thus be so then I will do everything possible to make amends for this error. If I have behaved badly towards him in any way I will cease this type of behaviour.

In this way I pressed him (R. Hagiz) against the wall and so touched his heart that he revealed his innermost thoughts and replied, "I have been informed that you wanted to take advantage of my ignominy though you had already accomplished this in the book you recently published." When I heard this false rumour I stood aghast saying, how could you suspect me of a characteristic which I do not possess and accept the gossip of slander-mongers who employer the products of their imagination to destroy the amity which existed between us"? I continued to defend myself so as to rid him of these preconceptions and asserted, "scorners as well as informers have spread lies about me, evil people whose greatest pleasure is to arouse jealousy and strife between close friends and cause contention between brothers (Prov. 16:28). For "a talebearer breaks up friendship and with his mouth the godless person destroys his neighbour"(Prov. 11:9) Why therefore, should his honour make such an accusation which nobody who knows me would believe? For was it ever my intention, God forbid, to cause him harm from which I would benefit? May the Almighty spare my father's children. Indeed every one knows that I did not burden a single member of the Three Communities to my advantage. Quite the reverse, thank the Almighty, many people benefited through me; would they did not requite evil for the good that I did. Why therefore, would I not be content to leave him alone and not disparage him publicly and so cause him the (alleged) harm I previously mentioned. I would never behave in such a way, blessed be the Almighty, so why should I change my favourable attitude towards other people and particularly towards him (R. Hagiz), an attitude which I have always manifested. (I continued) How much less would I wish to provoke him just now when we are such close neighbours? In fact why should l behave in the way he alleges for no apparent reason? Therefore, (I argued) he should have severely reprimanded those people who made such slanderous statements about my behaviour. This (I asserted) has never been my response. For though there has been no lack of such people who have informed me that your honour spoke disparagingly about me I did not accept their statements. (In fact) it was not until I received abundant confirmation of their statements that I began to feel that there was some basis to their reports. Consequently, I have now taken the opportunity of informing him of all this for I had no wish to keep it to myself but rather to show him that my feelings towards him were perfectly sincere. Moreover, I swore that none of the stories about me have any substance and therefore beg him not to pay any attention to false rumour-mongers. Such behaviour is

CHAPTER TEN

characteristic of the foolish idlers (cf. Ps.49:14) who have acquired wickedness, a band of slanderers, hypocrites and liars. Furthermore I begged him to inform me who these people were, those who disseminated such stories and accused me of such wrong so that I would learn the identity of such impostors.

Then we would see if they had the effrontery to repeat their accusations in my presence and we would be able to ascertain whether their statements were true. Then he (R. Hagiz) would realise that they were spies who had come to observe the impression their poisonous talk would make. (a play on the words "nakedness of the land" Gen.42:12) I then requested him to inform me what he had discovered in my "Lechem Shamayim" which so discredited him that he was rightly indignant. However he did not want to disclose anything. The upshot of this (meeting with R. Hagiz) was that at I did my level best to defend myself in his presence and exonerate myself from the alleged wrongs I was supposed to have committed against him. (At the same time) I pacified him with the object of ridding his mind of any wrong he thought I had done him. Moreover, I made it quite clear that the baseless hatred he bore me was due to slanderers of which King David wrote in his divinely inspired Psalms. Furthermore, (I argued) it was not right for a personality such as he to believe such slanderous statements regarding a true and trusted friend whose relations with him were most amicable. For what harm had he done me that I should be annoyed with him? I therefore urged him not to make an issue of this business, and thereby destroy a close friendship but he should calm down. In reply R. Hagiz assured me he would not mention the matter again but would behave as if nothing had ever been said. Furthermore, he assured me that his amity towards me was as true and complete as it had been in former times. I, in all innocence, accepted his assurances believing that his bitter feelings towards me had ended. Indeed, it did not occur to me that all his talk was insincere. For in practice his discreditable behaviour in public proved the reverse (of all his talk), since a few years later he manifested all his ill-will (towards me) in notes to his commentary to the Mishnayot of Zeraim which was published in Altona by the agency of Elisha of Grodno. It seemed divinely ordained that the latter approached me begging me to write an approbation of the above-mentioned work. Although I was reluctant to undertake this task just as I had previously not been prepared to do this for anyone else; but I couldn't ignore this elderly person's urgent pleading, so much against my will, I acceded to his request and accepted R. Hagiz's book in order to read it for it was already published. Having perused a few pages it seemed that I had been struck by a plague, for I discovered that it contained statements which I had never expected nor considered possible. For R. Hagiz had made comments to the tractate Bikkurim which hurt my feelings; he had planned to wound me unobtrusively with his scourging tongue. I then understood why he had previously been so angry with me, for he had now loosened his bridle and revealed his true colours, indeed, Moses had removed his mask (cf. Ex.34:34) I then stretched out my hand against this harmful comment in order to repay him in his own coinage.

My reply came in my approbation of his book. My defence was implied in the contents of my approbation (of his work) whilst I covered up the sin (cf. Ps.32:1) which he had cunningly devised against his friend who had trusted him. I had no desire to write a lengthy approbation, in the course of which I would delineate the essential error of the criticism which he had levelled against me precipitately and the libellous comments he made on my book ("Lechem Shomayim") whereby he virtually slung mud at it after praising it profusely. However in the Asarah haLechem which I set forth at the end of my "She'elot Ya'avetz". I took him to task and replied to all his delusions and babbling in his scheme to criticism me between the lines without a full investigation of the real significance of my comments. This was his approach in many of his previous articles in which he criticised eminent scholars who, even if they were puny, were far greater than he. For he cupped the wind in the hollow of his hands (Prov.30:4) I illustrated this characteristic of his by adducing some examples in my "She'elot Ya'avetz" quite apart from instances which I did not reveal. However, in the latter work I

CHAPTER TEN

repelled his complaint against me and defended myself against "the strife of tongues" (Prov.31:21) For he had punished me for a sin which I never acknowledged. Still, whatever it was, it is now gone and forgotten.

Then there was that particular occasion when we parted and he was about to return to the Holy Land. He then visited me in Emden in order to bid farewell and in the course of our conversation he lost his temper with me because (he alleged) I had written something against him and R. Shimshom Hasid regarding the problem of a person from whom a testicle had been removed by surgery and about which I had already published my "Iggeret Bokeret". During the above-mentioned conversation R. Hagiz asserted that I had opposed his ruling on that question. I replied that the solution to that Halakhic problem did not depend on the age (of the decisor), but logical and reasoned argument of our Sages, yet it seemed he had not adduced the slighted reason for his decision, nor the sources on which he had based it. On the contrary, (I continued) his monograph (on this topic) was full of scorn and derision. It was for this reason (I said) I was loath to mention his ruling (on the question) in my above-mentioned article, but had indirectly rejected his decision since his statements were inane they were invalid ab initio. In fact it was on this occasion that I observed his criticism of the presiding Rabbi of the (local) Bet Din, R. Ezekiel Katzenellenbogen just because I had wanted to publish the latter's opinion (on this question). Apart from this particular occasion R. Hagiz was subservient to R. Ezekiel and flattered him both in his presence and in his (R. Hagiz's) articles. In fact, whenever R. Ezekiel published any article on whatever topic he (R. Hagiz) accorded it the highest approbation and employed highly exaggerated laudatory epithets whilst applying that even such epithets did not do full justice to the real value of the article. Nevertheless, behind R. Ezekiel's back he (R. Hagiz) poured scorn and derision on him, (R. Ezekiel) his Talmudic erudition and his conduct of affairs. I cannot find any excuse for such conduct unless it was because he (R. Hagiz) was poor and living in a county (like Germany) of whose language he was

MEGILAT SEFER

ignorant and that consequent he fount it necessary to be subservient to the Presiding Rabbi of the Bet Din whose extraordinary good fortune is something which defies description. Yet he was not so dependent on that Rabbi that he (R. Hagiz) had to indulge in lies. Despite this, German Jews accorded him (R. Hagiz) great respect and sent him gifts though in some ways his behaviour towards them was unbecoming. For example, the occasion when he behaved abominably towards the publisher Reb Zalman. Yet the community tolerated such conduct so that he obtained a considerable amount of money from then during his stay in Altona and particularly when he left to return to the Holy Land. They then plied him with various kinds of gifts, both young and old brought him an abundance of them, so that he left Altona in much splendour. His departure from me was friendly and peaceful for I had expressly promised to behave in this was (at least) publicly.

I will now revert to the main subject of this account. I have already mentioned that as soon as I arrived back in Altona all the local scholars and eminent personalities were eager to greet me and stated, "Come in peace." They welcomed me most respectfully but gladly, in fact with the joy of one who had found a great treasure.(cf. Ps.119:162) But the aged Presiding Rabbi of the (local), Bet Din, R. Ezekiel (Katzenellenbogen) was abashed when he learned the news concerning Jacob (me) and that I had set up house in Altona. However, he could do nothing to prevent it, though given the opportunity he would certainly have treated me as he did my eminent father, z"l. For when he,(R. Ezekiel) learned that a certain group were planning some form of livelihood for my father so that he would be encouraged to return to Altona he did everything in his power, through the agency of Reb Behr Cohen, to frustrate this plan. However, this had little significance since he (my father) was destined for a higher (Rabbinic) position viz. the Rabbinate of Lvov, all of which I have described previously. In the same way I now learned that R. Ezekiel was most perturbed at the news that I had set up house in Altona. Nevertheless, I accorded the respect of visiting his

CHAPTER TEN

home at the earliest opportunity to greet him and enquire of his welfare. However, the majority of the community were indignant because (they felt) that despite his age he should have first visited me and welcomed me since this was the custom when an (important) visitor arrived in the community. He (R. Ezekiel) was indeed fortunate to be the guide of such a large community which then could boast of several Rabbinic scholars of far greater eminence than he, men who virtually dwarfed him (in scholarship). However, his lucky star gibed at him in an extraordinary way for people could not understand him when he spoke, whilst his appreciation and knowledge of Torah was indicated by his only (major) publication. His general demeanour and ethical standards were identified with self-interest and his only concern was his advancement. In all things he acted at the behest of Reb Behr Cohen whose advice he would always seek or, he would ask others as to Reb Behr's opinion in any particular matter. Were I to detail all that Rabbi's activities I would need a separate volume particularly since, thank God, I am the scion of eminent men, z"l, over many years established communities and were God-fearing and beneficent leaders.

Moreover, my own reputation, thank God, was no smaller than his even though I was then a young man. For it is not the place which graces a person, but quite the reverse. (TB. Taanit 21b) This applies particularly to a rabbi like R. Ezekiel who paid little attention to his own self-respect or to the reputation of his community but who would show deference to all lay-leaders, even to those who were young and virtually unknown. An example of the latter was the way he (R. Ezekiel) behaved towards Reb.A.Emden whom he rushed to welcome though this really demeaned the Rabbinate of the Three Communities. Yet his sole purpose in behaving in this way was in order to receive a suitable gift. Yet how much more should he have respected me and so accorded respect to the Torah, and to my deceased forebears? It was for this reason that people made excuses for him saying it was not right for an elderly person who was also the Rabbi of the Three Communities to visit me first. I therefore hurried to his home, as I have already stated. People thought that he would subsequently reciprocate by visiting me. However, when I did pay him a visit he did not receive me gladly. In fact, my conversation with him was hardly friendly, for I did not hear him return my greetings nor did he show any good manners by offering me something to eat. In short, he did not accord me any friendliness or respects. I therefore immediately sensed that I was a thorn in his eyes and that he had no thought to honour me with the customary visit since he realised he would not receive any gifts from me, unlike his visits to lay-leaders who plied him with gifts because it appeared to be etiquette.

Furthermore, he was worried lest I deprived him of some of the perquisites he presently received from local members (of the community) and that consequently I would be instrumental in reducing the gifts he and his family had hitherto received. However, when he came to realise that I wouldn't accept any tangible benefits from local members but, on the contrary, I, thank God, was always ready to help those in need and that I would even help him and his family, (as I have already stated) he befriended me and sang my praises when I was not present. But when I first returned to Altona he was perturbed by the thought that I might cause him harm. It was for this reason that on my first visit to him his face went different colours and he was struck dumb so that he could not reciprocate my greetings that I extended to him in his home. However, before I continue my story I must comment on the Rabbi of the Three Communities for I cannot dismiss him lightly though I have serious misgivings in stating these few comments. At this particular time (1733) he had held the Rabbinate of the Three Communities for thirty-five years without any major opposition. His name appeared in approbations of contemporary Rabbinic works in which he received exceptional praise. Similar praise was accorded to his own work though the reader might consider that even if he did not really deserve such laudations, or even half of them, at any rate some praise was justified. Consequently I will adopt my usual approach to such topics and not hide the truth nor abandon my moral standards,

CHAPTER TEN

but will truthfully state his merits and demerits and so maintain my integrity. In this way future generations will appreciate that the attainment of such an eminent rabbinic position does not depend on the person's merits or genuine virtues but by dint of good fortune. Of course he certainly possessed some virtues as did his family who was not eminent, for he was the son of a poor teacher. Yet occasionally one can find a pearl in a poor man's purse, and as our Sages inform us "do not disregard the children of the poor, for Torah shall come from them" (TB. Nedarim 81a). On the other hand, perhaps it was from his mother's line or from his forebears in general by whose merits he attained such eminence). Hence, even petty men enjoy advancement. Indeed, "my heart trembles and is moved out of its place", (cf. Job.37:1) when I contemplate this fact especially when I remember the holy and saintly personalities who possessed Torah-learning and genuine wisdom and who attained the highest virtues, men who were the progenitors of Israel yet, because of our many sins did not enjoy a moment of happiness, nor a single day of real tranquillity, rest, peace, or repose (cf. Lam.Rab.Intro). All of which this Rabbi (R. Ezekiel) enjoyed for many years, in all, about thirty-five years in the Three Communities. Yet this would have been remarkable even if a Quorum of inferior Jews could have put up with him!

But, as I saw it, he (R. Ezekiel) was the strap of chastisement (cf. Macc.3.12.22b) for the Three Communities because they failed to acknowledge the material and spiritual benefits in which they basked during all that period in which my father, z"l stayed, in the Three communities. At that time those who would destroy the community stubbornly opposed him, as I have already described. Consequently, they (the Three Communities) saw the realisation of that Scriptural verse, "because the people have contemned the waters of Shiloah that move softly!" (Is.8:6) This sentiment is reiterated by the Sefer Hasidim (Par.694) which quoted the Talmudic adage "when the shepherd becomes angry with his flock he appoints for a leader one who is blind."(TB. Bava Kama 52a) This was the general feeling when my father left Altona for Amsterdam for in that same year they came under the aegis of those four evil lay-leaders whom I have already mentioned, so that with my father's departure the community acknowledged that the glory and splendour of the community left them (Gen.Rab.)

Regarding the appointment of R. Ezekiel, he came from a distant country, although it was Lithuania, and from a people of a barbarous language (cf. Is.28:11) with which the inhabitants of Germany were unacquainted. Moreover the new Rabbi's was most unintelligible as well as hesitant. Nor was he acquainted with anyone in the community except for Issachar Cohen who had business connections with Lithuania. And firstly his Rabbinate (of the Three Communities) was obtained by purchase. For lssachar Cohen, who was very wealthy, had an ugly daughter whom he could not marry off to a wealthy individual nor, in fact, to one who was not wealthy. Since he could not succeed in Germany Issachar Cohen opted to arrange his daughter's marriage to a respected and suitable Rabbinic scholar of Poland. He succeeded in this endeavour though most deceitfully. He found a marriage-broker who undertook for a proper fee to arrange a marriage for Issachar' s daughter with Rabbi Herschel, may he rest in peace, the son of the presiding Rabbi of the Bet Din of Broda (Uhersky Brod) who was related to our family and was a fine man. He (R. Herschel) had previously been the Rabbi of a small Lithuanian community and had lost his wife. It was then that the marriage-broker proposed his marriage to the daughter of Issachar Cohen promising to assist him (R. Herschel) in obtaining an important Rabbinic post. However, that the girl was very ugly was concealed from him. When the arrangements for the marriage had been finalised and the day of the ceremony had arrived R. Herschel saw his intended bride (for the first time and refused to marry her; he would rather have been choked than attached himself to her. Nevertheless, his well-wishers virtually tricked him into marrying her arguing that once the marriage had been arranged he could do nothing (about it) and if he didn't consent to marry her (now) in the end he would be compelled to marry her, for Issachar Cohen would sacrifice all his wealth to avoid any humiliation to his daughter who

CHAPTER TEN

had not done him (R. Herschel) any harm. They maintained that since he (R. Herschel) had not made proper enquiries about the young lady at the outset it was his loss, (as the Rabbis put it) "your field has been flooded" (TB. Ketubot 12b). Consequently, (they argued) it would be to his advantage not to be involved in any litigation before a Bet Din from which he would not gain anything, for the verdict would go against him. Therefore, he should take the wife designated for him. He (R. Herschel) fell for these deceptive arguments and agreed to the marriage. As a result he received a considerable sum of money (lit. a Tarkovful of golden dinars) which was to pay for the Rabbinate of Kedainiai (Lithuania). In other words Issachar (Cohen) arranged an exchange (of Rabbinic positions) with R. Ezekiel who was then the presiding Rabbi of the Bet Din of Kedainiai by promising R. Ezekiel that he would do everything possible to obtain the Rabbinate of the Three Communities for R. Ezekiel whilst the latter, in turn, would arrange for R. Herschel to obtain the Rabbinate of Kedainiai which then owed R. Ezekiel a considerable amount of money. Moreover, Issachar Cohen promised to pay R. Ezekiel all the money that the community of Kedainiai owed him (R. Ezekiel) and that the latter would reciprocate this kindness by obtaining the Rabbinate of Kedainiai for Issachar's son-in-law as soon as possible. In this way the community (Kedainiai) would avoid paying their debt to R. Ezekiel. (On the other hand) if this were not possible then Issachar would lend the community (Kedainiai) the money which was owing to R. Ezekiel. It was in this way that the exchange of the Rabbinates was effected.

R. Ezekiel's position was bolstered by the action of Issachar Cohen who attested that the former was renowned throughout Lithuania as being one of the most eminent Rabbinic scholars. For since Issachar did business with Lithuania he knew something about that community. Moreover, the Three communities were completely ignorant of the arrangement to exchange the Rabbinates, which I previously described. In addition, Issachar was regarded as a trustworthy person so that the members of the Three Communities took him at his word viz. that R. Ezekiel was as eminent a scholar as

MEGILAT SEFER

Issachar had portrayed for they had no reason to suspect his (Issachar's) integrity nor did they think he had any other motive but a genuine religious one i.e. the benefit which would accrue to the Three Communities in obtaining such a great personality (like R. Ezekiel) whose virtues, according to Issachar, surpassed those of anyone else. However, Issachar was acting in his own interests and those of his family. R. Ezekiel also played his part in this affair by publicising his reputation in the Three Communities who know nothing about him. These are the facts as related by those who knew what really happened. Thus R. Ezekiel sent a special envoy was either a Rabbinic scholar or teacher in Lithuania and who was a close friend of his (R. Ezekiel). Who knows how much R. Ezekiel paid this man for the service of disseminating his (R. Ezekiel's) reputation among the Rabbinic scholars of the Three Communities. This envoy particularly directed his attention to the outstanding local scholars who hailed from Poland or Lithuania who dealt with all litigation and halakhic problems. For whenever German-Jewish communities were involved in the appointment of a Rabbi they particularly looked for one who came from abroad, a person whom they never know, for generally they had little regard for rabbis who came from Germany. Another difficulty was that those who were selected to appoint a Rabbi were not scholars nor were they capable of a true assessment of a Rabbi. Hence they could not distinguish between a favourable or unfavourable candidate so they were compelled to seek other peoples' advice (in this matter) viz. those people who came from Poland or Lithuania, or they enquired of local Rabbinic scholars since they (the selection committee) felt they could rely on those people who were themselves dependent on the Three communities.

But the majority of teachers in German Jewry would praise any Rabbi since they would gain materially. For he (the Rabbi) would encourage them to think and speak highly of him by greasing their palms and so ensure they would do him service (cf. Num.3:3) . Consequently they (the teachers) would generally advise the lay-leaders who sought their opinion (regarding the most eminent and praiseworthy Rabbis of their native lands. Hence the committee

CHAPTER TEN

selected to appoint a Rabbi would turn their attention to those Rabbis whom the teachers recommended. Thus when the occasion arose for the appointment of a Rabbi for the Three Communities the above-mentioned person was ready to hurry here (to Altona) to buy supporters for R. Ezekiel with pieces of gold. He acquired this support by paying through the nose (the full price cf. Gen.23:9) particularly the assistance of the local teachers who had no previous knowledge of R. Ezekiel. This emissary persuaded them (the teachers) to declaim his (R. Ezekiel's) Rabbinic novellae in the manner in which they were skilled as well as other Rabbinic bon mot which they had assimilated but which originated from other Rabbinic scholars. Furthermore, he "persuaded" these people (teachers) to teach their pupils various topics (purporting to emanate from R. Ezekiel) which they (the pupils) would repeat at home every Shabbat, a custom which was widespread throughout Germany. But the teachers, having accepted gifts of money indulged in lies and sacrificed the truth by teaching their pupils a fine interpretation of some Scriptural or Rabbinic sentiment which they (the teachers) knew originated from a great Rabbinic authority of past generations but which the pupil was to repeat in the name of R. Ezekiel. Such was the latter's conduct. Hence when the boy came to repeat what he had assimilated from his teacher and delivered some Rabbinic novella he had learned the previous week, he would loudly announce: "this is the interpretation of Rabbi Ezekiel Katzenellenbogen, the Rav of Kadainai."

Many of the teachers behaved in this despicable manner, but money helps spread a good reputation (a pun on the text "for money answers all things" Eccles.10:19) Eventually therefore R.Ezekiel's a reputation grew within the Three Communities for people would repeat with highly exaggerated praise some fine ingenious sentiment which purported to come from this Rabbi. In this way the community was deceived, for when the teachers were (eventually) asked whether they knew this particular Rabbi and whether he enjoyed a high reputation and was therefore a suitable candidate for the rabbinate of the Three Communities they replied, "Certainly, he (R.Ezekiel) is an exceptional person who has no peer in Torah, in erudition, in general wisdom or in piety." Moreover, (they continued) he has no equal in oratory nor in all the characteristics which our Sages laud. Indeed, in respect of his intellect no one can fully appreciate it were it not for the fact that he (R.Ezekiel) has to observe a weekly fast so as to weaken his intellectual prowess and so refrain from profound statements, whilst the person who hears these sentiment must also fast to be physically weak and by reducing his fat and blood refine his physical frame and so enable his brain to fully appreciate the thoughts of R.Ezekiel. So great (they asserted) his intellectual capacity. This was the gist of the reply which the teachers gave to those who sought their advice, people who were acting sincerely and relying on these men (teachers) as blind men follow their guides. Yet the teachers had never seen nor had any genuine knowledge of R.Ezekiel. However money helped proclaim his reputation. In short, iniquitous behaviour effected the arrival of this man (R.Ezekiel) and the religious leadership of the Three Communities. Just as when a shepherd is annoyed with his flock and so appoints a blind ram to lead them so it is with the (religious) guide of a community. At the beginning of his Rabbinate he (R.Ezekiel) found Altona a garden of Eden, but ultimately it had become a wild desert. Thus when the leaders of the community joyfully came to greet him (on his arrival) and gazed for the first time on the personality of their new leader from whose light they hoped to benefit just as the teachers had attested, as a reward they listened to some Rabbinic discourse from him. But they could not understand a word since he spoke with stammering lips and in a foreign language. (cf.Is.28:11) I say, without exaggeration that his stuttering was incomprehensible, and I should know for he spoke to me on several occasions during the thirty years he lived in this community, yet I could barely understand what he said. His speech must therefore have been even more incomprehensible when he first arrived in Altona. For he had come from Lithuania where people spoke an unintelligible language. Hence, on that occasion (following his arrival)

CHAPTER TEN

his audience asked him to write out his short Rabbinic dissertation so that they would have the opportunity to read and comprehend it, but they failed in this endeavour since the contents of the dissertation were like a sealed book.(cf.Dan.12:4) Moreover, the writing was so bad that it was virtually illegible. In fact, just like his chirping and unintelligible speech. To cap it all, people could not understand the language in which it was written. This even applied to those who had some experience of these three facets of knowledge viz. writing, speech and language. He was indeed a unique, personality. This was true, apart from his great virtues which I have previously mentioned.

These more educated people realised they could not understand R.Ezekiel's bon mot which he had expressed and which they were eager to assimilate. For they were eager to appreciate the essential qualities (of the new Rabbi) in the context of the highly exaggerated laudations of him by the local teachers who had produced testimonials (or calamities) on his behalf (see TB.Avoda Zarah 2b). They (the more educated people) therefore asked the teachers who were standing near the Rabbi to explain to them what the Rabbi had written since the teachers were slightly more eloquent than the Rabbi seeing that their speech was intelligible and being educated they could understand the language in which the Rabbi had written (his bon mot). The teachers attempted to read it but could not make, sense of it (cf.Lam.2:9) nor did those who heard it understand anything of it. Yet this incident merely confirmed the need for these people to have taken the precautions I previously mentioned concerning the Rabbi's great intellect. Again, perhaps on this occasion had not yet fasted or had fasted excessively. In short, it was because his audience had not fasted that they did not deserve to appreciate his wisdom. In fact however, even if these people had beaten their heads they would not have understood the Rabbi, for he was not possessed of understanding. Indeed, the topic on which he spoke was incomprehensible to human intelligence.

But what is done is done! Yet one cannot avoid the divine decree (which states) that there is no punishment without cause (cf.TB. Berakhot 5b). For as I have previously stated this was the divine decree issued against the Three Communities since they contemned the waters of Shiloah (a reference to the Chacham Tzvi). Thus it was their sins which caused this situation viz. that the Almighty should appoint a shepherd over them who was motivated by self-interest, who failed to feed his flock with knowledge and intellect but who scorned Torah learning and poured scorn on its scholars. For our many sins henceforth anarchy prevailed (in this community) and his sword made orphans in the street (cf.Deut.32:25). However, that powerful personality and lay leader Reb Behr Cohen, whom I have already mentioned was very pleased with this type of Rabbi for he (the Rabbi) obeyed him (Reb Behr) and did everything which he (the Rabbi) understood to be the wish of Reb Behr whom he addressed as "Zeide" i.e. (my) grandfather "Zeide" being the Polish for grandfather. Whenever the Rabbi was consulted about communal affairs or problems concerning particular individuals he (the Rabbi) would first enquire as to what was Reb Behr's opinion in the particular issue and would then act in accordance with Reb Behr's expressed feelings paying no consideration (whatsoever) as to whether such action was to the good or detriment of the people concerned. He (the Rabbi's) main concern was that his actions had the approval of that rich and powerful personality (Reb Behr). Thus R.Ezekiel did everything possible to win the approval of Reb Behr and his family, sons-in-law and close friends, all of whom enjoyed considerable power and prestige in the contemporary community. Consequently the Rabbi showed them the greatest deference as well, as much affection particularly since he enjoyed much material benefit from the great affluence of Reb Behr and his children and friends.

Apart from this, he (the Rabbi) did not lose out in respect of other wealthy man in the community for because of his (the Rabbi's) subservience to Reb Behr they (the other wealthy men) plied the Rabbi and his family with an abundance of gifts and largesse. For the Rabbi of the Three Communities enjoyed considerable authority over individual members (of the community) particularly regarding

CHAPTER TEN

communal business appointments, legal matters including civil law in all of which he (the Rabbi) held decisive power. Therefore, people went in great fear of him since he could virtually put paid to their life. In fact he did this to a number of important people in the community and was consequently the cause of their becoming completely impoverished. He effected this state of affairs by either postponing judicial decisions or perverting justice in the litigation in which these particular people were involved, he especially caused great hardship to some of the most eminent and honourable families of the Three Communities e.g. the family of Reb Moses ben Leibisch, and the extremely learned lay- leader, a person I have already mentioned, and the family of the prominent Reb Mendel b. R. Nathan who were related to me by marriage and who were the founders of the community of Altona. All these were eminent and affluent people, erudite in Torah and God-fearing. Yet because of his (R. Ezekiel's) conduct they were virtually destroyed and become impoverished; may the Almighty have mercy on them. Indeed, whenever I remember these facts I feel terribly cut up.

We too suffered similar treatment (at the hands of R. Ezekiel) and, as I have already stated lost a considerable amount of money. However for our many sins, the two families I previously mentioned ended their lives in poverty and those who survived can be regarded as dead may the Almighty have mercy on them! If R. Ezekiel achieved nothing else but this throughout his Rabbinate in the Three Communities, it deserves publicising in order for posterity to take note and to pray to the Almighty, blessed be He to save them from such a communal leader. (Indeed) they should pray that He deliver them from such a character. But in fact, he caused more harm to the Three Communities than just that. For he almost destroyed the community and turned it upside down just like a dish. How can I (fully) describe some of the terrible things for which R. Ezekiel bears responsibility? Then there were some aspects of the behaviour of his family; who can do justice in describing any of these? One should not be astonished if such misdemeanours are committed by families of communal leaders since such families had bad examples to emulate, but surely one would not expect such conduct from R. Ezekiel's family? I have said enough. However, I must mention one incident which concerned an alleged dissolute woman whose unsavoury behaviour had been attested by one witness. R. Ezekiel wanted her to accept a get (divorce) from her husband which, as I saw it, was contrary to the Halakhah. I had no wish to have anything to do with this case nor was I in any way obliged to look into the details of it. However, R. Moses Hagiz, z"l, sent me some of the details since he was implicated in this affair which involved a woman being compelled to accept a get in circumstances which made such a procedure contrary to Jewish law.

From the evidence in the case I could not see how it was sufficient to compel the wife to accept a get, I therefore could not concur with the decision of the (local) Bet Din. I informed R. Moses Hagiz of my opinion when I was in Emden when he sent me the details of the case asking me to look into them. I also expressed my honest opinion to the Dayanim of Altona viz. that I did not know on what basis they had come to a decision in this case and (pointed out) that the Talmud and the majority of decisors record far more complex cases than this one yet the Rabbinic authorities didn't forbid a wife to live with her husband in circumstances which were essentially the same as this particular case. When Dayan R. Nathan learned my opinion he remarked to his associate R. Baruch Akiva, "I told you our ruling in this case was incorrect." Nevertheless R. Ezekiel compelled this husband and wife to live apart for more than twenty years. However, R. Ezekiel failed to mete out equal justice to the (alleged) paramour for the latter's brother and father-in-law were important lay-leaders. Thus justice and morality demanded that he (the paramour) should have been punished. For it was unjust to separate husband and wife whilst the (other) guilty party (the paramour) was completely exonerated. Moreover, the enforced separation of the couple was worse than death for the wife. Consequently the latter wrote to me on several occasions requesting me to see her and discuss the possibility of my investigation of her case. But I did not want to be

CHAPTER TEN

involved in any decision as to her guilt or innocence. Ultimately, R. Ezekiel exonerated her after receiving a sum of money from her.

Then there was the case of the daughter of Gumpricht who was married to Reb Zalman from whom she had several children. On a particular occasion when she was annoyed with her husband she informed R. Ezekiel that she had committed adultery. Consequent to this admission R. Ezekiel wanted to publicise her guilt and to state that she was forbidden to live with her husband. Ultimately however he (R. Ezekiel) was compelled to revoke this decision. Yet despite all this I defended his (R. Ezekiel's) reputation and for many years refrained from speaking disparagingly of him or to him in any altercation. Hence, when he realised I meant him or his family no harm he showed me particular affection. In fact however, I was instrumental in bringing him tangible gains. He therefore sang my praises in public and visited me on every festival. For my part I respected him and believed he was a scholarly person who deserved his eminent position, and that the sins of the contemporary generation were the main reason for the inability of rabbinical authorities to conform with the demands of the Halakhah. I therefore did everything to defend his reputation although he did not deserve it. On another occasion, he was also completely in the wrong regarding R. Shimshon Hasid and R. Moses Hagiz though ultimately his decision concerning them proved correct. It was for this reason I continued to defend the truth for which I spent a considerable amount of my capital; nor did I gain any material benefit from all my exertions in this endeavour in this endeavour.

Then there was the case of the woman who was involved in a situation of Levitate marriage. R. Ezekiel wanted me to be concerned with the latter and consequently sent me his views on the topic, through one of his officials and requested me to look into them. I posted my reply for him and his Bet Din to consider whether they readily concurred with my opinions viz. that there was no evidence or any other valid proof which could release this woman from her legal tie with her brother-in-law. Therefore this woman named Chayah remained in this prohibitive state for several weeks. However, the man whom she wanted to marry who was a relative of the deceased husband sought to prevent the perpetuation of his relative's (the decreased husband's) memory (c.f. Deut.25:6) He, (the relative) therefore made a regular morning visit to R. Ezekiel and finally persuaded the latter to agree to his request. Thus according to the prominent agent, Reb Zalman, the Rabbi unobtrusively but arrogantly released that woman from all the legal prohibitions which had hitherto prevented her from marrying the man of her own choice. True he (R. Ezekiel) had not asked me, his junior, to join the Bet Din which granted this permit, but I had been a member of that Bet Din which had originally confirmed her prohibitive status, and it would therefore have been etiquette to inform me of the reasons for granting that release. Moreover, at the time I was involved in there publication of my responsa (She'elot Ya'avetz) and was dealing with this very topic of Levitate marriage which, I believe, I had set out in writing (print) and sent a copy of it together with my own views to R. Ezekiel. Consequently I included this particular case in my work.

    The publisher was an admirer of R. Ezekiel and informed the latter (that I had included that particular incident in my work). Subsequently R. Ezekiel complained of my conduct to the communal lay leaders who used to comply with all his requests since he, in turn, had shown preference to them in all communal affairs. For though he (R. Ezekiel) had been invested with great power and authority by the Crown and according to the rules of the community was its principal authority he allowed the governing body of the community complete freedom in imposing their will on individual members and to intimidate them as they saw fit and acceding to their caprice. This situation caused considerable out cry (in the community) but there seemed no way out of the dilemma. Hence, he (R. Ezekiel) obtained the consent of the governing body to all his requests or they made no effort to investigate matters but simply implicated themselves in iniquity. Thus, they acted precipitately and ordered an official announcement to be made in the main synagogue condemning my publisher, Aaron Zetger and prohibiting any of his publications. The

CHAPTER TEN

latter was mainly dependent on me (with the Almighty's assistance) for his livelihood for I used to pay him handsomely for his work (on my behalf) and treated him kindly not only by paying him in advance but also lending him money gratis and never insisting on a pledge or a bill of debt. However, because of the aforementioned (behaviour of the Communal Council) his source of livelihood was destroyed, so that the loan I had made him to the tune of a hundred Reichthalers was forfeit and now constituted a gift (from me). In fact, R. Aaron sought assistance but it was not forthcoming, and even R. Ezekiel turned a deaf ear to his (Reb Aaron's pleas). I too cried like a crane on Reb Aaron's behalf but was equally unsuccessful.

I went to the Communal Council with the document announcing the public sale (of Reb Aaron's property). The Council then comprised all the Communal lay leaders together with R. Ezekiel. I made no secret of my accusations against them for the wrongs they had perpetrated against that poor man (Reb Aaron), wrongs for which in fact they blamed me. I also complained of the loss they had caused me by their untoward action which they had taken they had taken without prior investigation of the case, but simply at the request of R. Ezekiel. I addressed them as follows: "Please hear what I have to say. The Presiding Rabbi of your Bet Din sits opposite me, let any honest person say whether since the time I settled here I have behaved presumptuously in respect of decisions in Halakhic matters, or whether I voluntarily involved myself in Communal affairs or in matters concerning an individual (in his relations with the community) unless I was asked by either you or your Rabbi. On several occasions I was most reluctant to accede to your invitation to investigate a particular case or ruling so that it should be regarded as a decision in which more than one Rabbinic authority was involved. However I could not refuse your Rabbi's or your own request. Gentlemen, on one occasion I exerted every effort to plead and contend on your Rabbi's behalf after he had sought my assistance. In the same vein I wrote lengthy responsa to defend him against his critics and offered them (the responsa) on the altar of the printing-press to win the favour of the Almighty by strenuously defending his truthful Torah. In so doing I expended my own money and received no assistance. This you can tell by this document (announcing the public sale) which I now place before you. In all these matters my statements were apposite and were favourably received by your Rabbi. However, in this present affair in which I have been compelled by your Rabbi to examine its legal composition, I did not consider the summons all too kindly, for I belong to that group (of Rabbis) who are apprehensive at giving a Halakhic ruling. Nevertheless I could not avoid acceding to his request. But on this occasion I could not agree with his decision for there is no partiality in Torah matters. Indeed the (local) Bet din appreciated my opinion and freely admitted that the lady (involved) in this particular case was not free to marry whomsoever she wished. Suddenly a new stage has arisen now one in which I had no fore-knowledge. True I am young and he (the Rabbi) is advanced in years, nevertheless since I had acceded to his request to examine the case and to express my opinion in writing, it is unjust that he should have acted in the way he did and not informed me of his reasons for retracting his original assent to my responsum and for his sudden change of mind. Moreover, this particular case is concerned with a woman forbidden in marriage so that we are all in the same boat (so to speak), and one cannot bore a hole in his seat (with impunity) for all Jews are sureties for each other.

Moreover, R. Ezekiel wants to be considered a wise person by his silence. Therefore, I too am allowed to be silent and will ignore your ruling for since it emanates from you, it is not your prerogative to give rulings on Torah matters. As for me I will write to the most eminent Rabbinic authorities beyond Altona and seek their opinions then we will see whose opinion is correct. Let us accept their ruling and not your decree which you promulgate without stating your reasons". I then left the (Council) in great indignation. Subsequently they sent their deputy, the Chazan, to me warning me not to publish this case nor to include it in any of my publications during the lifetime of R. Ezekiel. But I remained adamant and replied insolently that I would act as my Maker directed. Nevertheless I controlled my feelings and obeyed their ruling for I felt I was not obliged to

CHAPTER TEN

sacrifice myself over this affair. It was enough, I thought, that I had rescued my soul and that the Lord would punish the sinner according to the magnitude of his sin. Let the responsibility I felt, rest squarely on the shoulders of the person who could have protested but not on me, for those lay-leaders were more obstinate than I. Consequently I refrained from writing to any Rabbinic authority beyond Altona. However, I learned (later) that R. Eliezer Rokeah of Broda, may his memory be blessed, who was then the Presiding Rabbi of the Bet Din of Amsterdam, had been approached by R. Ezekiel for his opinion (on this particular case) and had disagreed with R. Ezekiel's ruling, and in fact forbade that woman to marry. I also leaned that when R. Eliezer heard that the woman in question had married (without receiving Chalitzah) he was very indignant as well as distressed. Incidentally, before I left the Council chamber where I had gone to complain about the Council's ruling, I severely reprimanded R. Zenvel Cohen for being a spokesman for R. Ezekiel as well as a staunch supporter of his. I addressed him as follows: "Please listen to me R. Zenvel. I realise you are not sincere of R. Ezekiel for such behaviour is contrary to the Torah. So how much more so is this obligation of the person who has been invited to participate and join the Bet Din (in order to help reach a just decision) for "the owner of the beam must examine the joists which hold the beam" (TB. Berachot 64a) in order to avoid a fatal accident. At any rate, I would like to know the reasons behind the Rabbi's legal permit (for the woman to marry) for though I originally excluded myself from given a decision and did not insist on my opinion being accepted yet, (Rabbi Ezekiel) I am your disciple who desires to drink of your water (=Torah)(cf.Jer.15:18) and if the waters are steadfast I will not regard them as waters that fail. Now therefore speak up and justify your decision "for I will not remove the speech of men of trust." (cf.Job 12:20) R. Ezekiel was struck dumb and said absolutely nothing. However, the lay-leaders spoke on his behalf and said to me, "the Rabbi is not required to give any reason or proof of his decisions, what has been has been and there can be no retraction. "But I disagreed stating the Rabbi is obliged (to give his reasons) not only to be free from any suspicious conduct and prove he is guiltless before God and His people Israel, but because this is a Torah matter and we must learn to establish a Halakhic ruling, for "he who withholds corn will not be exempt from punishment." (cf. TB.Sanhedrin 91b) (an interpretation of Proverbs 11:26)

However, though I made a long and well-reasoned speech to which I tried to put the Rabbi in a good light provided he gave reasons for his second ruling; I was unsuccessful. In fact, it seemed I was addressing stones and wood. However, the lay leaders said they understood the situation and they declared that I should not be involved in this matter nor publish anything about it. In my reply I said, "I don't accept your ruling which is harsher than Pharaoh for he didn't forbid the Study of Torah nor did he proscribe our religion in any way. You behave slyly towards me, whereas I speak reasonably though no one seems to understand me for not one of you speaks with any knowledge or intelligence. But I realise you are afraid of Popros (he was Reb Zenvel's uncle and as it eventually happened R. Zenvel was very much under his (Popros') thumb) and for this reason you did not behave so well towards me". For our many sins, only a few weeks later Reb Zenvil was declared a complete bankrupt and remained heavily in debt to Popros. When the latter summoned him to appear before the Bet Din, Reb Zenvil, may he rest in peace, lost his sanity because of his dire situation. This was the beginning of the realisation of the warning of my father, z"l, regarding the family of Reb Behr Cohen. Henceforth the economic situation of all the friends and relations of the latter declined inexorably until they were left virtually without a morsel of bread, may the Almighty have mercy on us.

Regarding my book which was half-finished until the passing of R. Ezekiel, with the Almighty's help I completed it and it was then published just as the lay-leaders had previously requested. Some time after this we learned that the man (involved in the case) and had married the woman (who was tied by Levirate marriage) was still alive. I obtained this fact from certain people who had this information from bona fide witnesses. Hence my suspicions

CHAPTER TEN

concerning this illegal marriage proved to be well founded. Moreover, a remarkable fact emerged about that (illegal) marriage viz. that the woman (in question) could not attain a ritual state of purity to enable her to cohabit with her husband whom she should not have married since she was definitely subject to the status of Levirate marriage. Thus Heaven prevented them from sin. Subsequently, they both died, the woman having remained childless, although she was quite young and had had children from her first husband though, they (the children) had died during his lifetime. In fact, the man with whom she had contracted the forbidden marriage had had children from both his first and second wives. However R. Ezekiel had denied these facts, a fact which I have stated in my book (She'elot Ya'avetz Pt.1chap.51.)

There was still a further incident in which I was involved. A certain married woman informed R. Ezekiel that she was involved in an affair with another man. Her husband, Reb Z---,a member of a respected family of Altona was then in Danzig. They had had several children, but she had proved to be so cantankerous that her husband had left home some time ago and had gone abroad. Apparently the wife was wildly extravagant having little consideration for her husband's financial status. Moreover (it seemed) she paid little attention to her home. It because of these factors that the husband had come to hate his wife and eventually abandoned her. Thus, having been left with her children she found it difficult to make ends meet. Apparently her alleged adulterous behaviour was prompted by revenge for her husband's behaviour. The wife, in fact, was the daughter of a reputable person viz. Gumpricht, who at one time had been a prominent lay-leader but, at the time of this incident, had fallen on hard times. It was because of the latter reason that R. Ezekiel no longer considered him important. For he (R. Ezekiel) used to curry favour with the affluent members of his community even when, as I have stated earlier there was no apparent need for such behaviour. Consequently, the Rabbi publicly denounced her as licentious and an adulteress. Her father, whom I have a previously mentioned, then visited me complained bitterly about the treatment meted out to his daughter and that no one seemed to object. I replied that if the facts (which he had stated) were correct then R. Ezekiel had not acted correctly. Hence, it would be incorrect for him (the father) to passively accept R. Ezekiel's decision, for it wasn't merely a question of affecting the father's reputation, but the decision (of R. Ezekiel) was contrary to the Halakhah, for a wife's statement whereby she forbade her husband to associate with her no validity. Moreover, such a decision could ultimately lead to an increase of illegitimate children, apart from the fact that the husband would be compelled to divorce his wife which, in this instance would be illegal. Again, R. Ezekiel's decision would raise doubts regarding the legitimacy of his children and would bring discredit to the wife and her family; this was not the way Jews should behave.

Consequently I advised him (Gumpricht) to approach the communal lay-leaders and inform them of the irreligious way his daughter had been treated. He followed my advice and, thank God, was successful, for the Communal Council abrogated R. Ezekiel's ruling and the woman was released from her prohibitive status. Furthermore, they (the Council) compelled R. Ezekiel to publicly proclaim the woman's innocence. (Thus) we note that at that time the lay-leaders controlled the Presiding Rabbi of the local Bet Din even though his authority prevailed over the poor and recalcitrant. The latter authority emanated from the Crown i.e. the power to adjudicate, to make Halakhic rulings, to impose fines and other punishments, nor did anyone challenge this authority. In fact, a Rabbi controlled by the lay-leaders who had to be completely subservient to him. However R. Ezekiel behaved subserviently towards them and willingly obeyed them, fulfilling their rulings and decrees. In this way he gained the approval of the powerful members of the community who praised him for his humility. Woe to such a defective humility which is nothing else but hypocrisy. For, (in reality) he supported the authority of the affluent and powerful in treating individuals according to their caprice, so that he would gain more prompt material rewards. They (the affluent and powerful) for their part

CHAPTER TEN

constantly benefited him by their friendship and affection. Thus, they recompensed each other; he by supporting every wrong which they perpetrated against individual (members of the community) who were powerless against them and whom they disliked, and they by supporting the Rabbi when he dealt unjustly towards those whom he disliked and whose protests at such injustice went unheeded. Thus, "between the midwife and the travailing woman the child of the poor woman dies."(Gen.Rab.60) As for those from whom he could not gain any material benefits he adopted a stone-like posture and in this alone he behaved "like a Talmudic scholar who took vengeance and harboured ill-will like a snake" (TB. Yoma 23a). If he bore a grudge against anyone he (the Rabbi) would wait for the opportunity and would not rest until he had his revenge. Regarding his perversion of justice, "the couch is too narrow for two lovers to be joined together."(cf.Lev.Rab.17) In other words a large volume could not comprehend (the numerous instances). He would give a legal decision before noon yet by the afternoon he assumed a completely different attitude. In the same vein he and his Bet Din were, in particular, suspected of accepting bribes, and there were numerous grounds for this suspicion. In fact, one bona fide person told me that he had a case which was brought before R. Ezekiel's Bet Din where one Dayan asked him what was he prepared to pay so that the decision (of the tribunal) would go in his favour. Thus there was incessant talk that the Bet Din asked for their slice. "Woe to the ears which heard such words; woe to the generation which experienced such behaviour!"

With respect to legacies, he (R. Ezekiel) took whatever he pleased usually a vast amount. In fact, I heard that his share of the legacy of Shlomo Yoffin amounted to four hundred ounces of silver, and this was only one of numerous examples (of his share in settling legacies). It was from such sources that he became wealthy and was therefore able to give considerable dowries to his daughters. However, this wealth vanished as quickly as it came for the daughters whom he married off died during his lifetime, in fact, only a few years after their marriage. Hence he lost his daughters as well as the considerable wealth he had made over to them. Moreover, much of the wealth he had gained illegally also went to waste; all of if it was lost in disastrous circumstances and through the depravity which he witnessed in his own family, as I have already described. This apart from other factors which I will not mention here. Because of our many sins this community declined during his Rabbinate, because of the sin of Robbery and false oaths which were abundant in this period and were regarded as a joke and as quite permissible. But because of (this behaviour) the community of Hamburg lost the right of adjudication by its own courts, a right which in former times it had enjoyed to the full, just as the community of Altona. For it was on this very basis that the Three Communities had originally been established i.e. the Three Communities enjoyed jurisdiction in civil-law which was effected through the agency of the Rabbi who was the presiding authority of the Bet Din. However, the secular authorities of Hamburg grew weary of hearing the complaints of members of the community regarding their Rabbi's jurisdiction and his judicial decisions so they deprived the Communities of this privilege, and declared that from henceforth a Jew must not appear before the Court of the Presiding Rabbi of the Three Communities. (Later R. Eibeschuetz was deprived of those (same) judicial powers in Altona as I will later describe, with the Almighty's assistance). All these events were the realisation of those Scriptural verses "it came to pass in the days of the Judges who turned aside into their crooked ways" (Ps.125: 5)

What can one say about R. Ezekiel's novellae, his interpretation of texts and his sermons? (Except) that they were objects of derision. Even if one were told about them one would hardly believe the foolish statements, the inane observations and ideas that provoked excessive laughter from all who listened to them. Regarding his judicial and Halakhic rulings which I possess in print, anyone who appreciated this field of learning would be astonished (after perusing then), yet those (published) constitute only a small proportion of them. Moreover, regarding his (magnum opus) which

CHAPTER TEN

he constantly had reprinted and part of which I incorporated in my Teshuvot Ya'avetz merely to serve as an example of his scholarship, certain bona fide people told me that the eminent Presiding Rabbi of the Bet Din of Frankfurt-on-Main, R. Judah Katz as well as other Rabbinic scholars that this work "Knesset Yechezkel", should be burnt. For illustration I will mention a few of his errors when he deals with straight forward Talmudic and Halakhic ideas. On one occasion in Altona he (R. Ezekiel) heard the Chazan R. Yokel, may he rest in peace, reading Parashat Shemot and vocalising the word "ho'ovnoyim" (in the sentence you shall look upon the birth stones Exodus1:16) with a Kametz under the alef i.e. ho'ovnoyim. Thereupon the Rabbi reprimanded the Chazan saying, "You have made a mistake, the word should be vocalised like ho'avonoyim with a kametz under the bet. (Perhaps he thought this was Rashi's interpretation of the word!) Such was his expertise in the text of the Bible!

He (R. Ezekiel) evinced similar expertise in his knowledge of the Oral Torah i.e. Talmud. Thus, on one occasion when he was delivering an exposition on the tractate Megillah and had come to deal with the question raised by the Rabbis in folio 15b viz. "what was the reason behind Esther's invitation to Haman?" To which R. Eliezer said she had concealed traps for him." (Based on Psalms 69:23) R. Ezekiel believing that "pachim" (traps) was "pachim" (tins) consequently stated R. Eliezer's answer that she had concealed small jars (krueglich being the German for a small jar). On another occasion he was dealing with the statement in TB. tractate Rosh Hashanah (18a.) that "all creatures pass before Him like sheep" which the Talmud observes means "all creatures are reviewed with one glance."(from the Almighty) but he (R. Ezekiel) explained the latter phrase to mean "they are all marked with red paint which was the procedure adopted in the tithing of sheep"! He gave many similar erroneous explanations so that any one hearing them burst into laughter; I will say no more. However, I would not mention any if his (R. Ezekiel's) actions unless they were committed overtly and therefore cannot be denied. Presently there are still a number of people who are aware of such actions.

When he first assumed the Rabbinate of the Three Communities the pious and eminent Torah scholar R. Gershon Shneper, z"l, observed, "had R. Ezekiel approached me when I was one of the Governors of the Talmud Torah in order to be licensed to teach in the Three Communities I would never have granted it." Yet despite (these shortcomings) he (R. Ezekiel) ruled the community with much presumption and immeasurable power, yet he gained the reputation of being most modest and tolerant though indeed, he was malevolent and did as he pleased. He scoffed at people whom he oppressed, people who were most indignant with him because of his character and his misdeeds and who occasionally, because of their dire situation and bitterness of heart, spoke defiantly and harshly in his presence. He would listen in silence and then reply, "Go to the Almighty, let him sue me!" Such was his humility! Nevertheless he wielded a rod and strap to forcibly chastise the community, nor could anyone protest against this behaviour. In this sense he showed intelligence in that he was not quick-tempered but controlled his anger; so he did as he pleased nonchalantly avenging himself on his enemies and knowing only full well that they would fall into his power.

Consequently there was never any need for him to be distressed in any way. Indeed he loved himself and preserved his health and strength constantly refreshing himself with drink. In fact he always had a large stock of wine, mead, whisky and liqueurs that were kept in a special part of the house. Moreover, he had special containers (for those drinks) and employees to produce them by the best possible methods. This was something that no other communal-leader possessed. Thus, apart from the dainty foods which were as plentiful as dust in his home, he lacked nothing which would disturb his peace and quiet and consequently, he saw no reason to temper his joy and physical pleasures with fits of anger or remonstrance. Yet he avenged himself on his enemies at the opportune moment. He showed no concern for poverty in the community nor did he pay any attention to the poor peoples' cry for help. For Reb Behr Cohen had

CHAPTER TEN

managed to obtain a royal licence for him (R. Ezekiel) which gave him excessive authority to control the poor by coercive measures which included, inter alia, their arrest and desolation through imprisonment simply because of his command.

No one could question his authority. In fact the local gentile judiciary and their officials implemented his rulings and fulfilled his behest just as if they emanated from the Emperor himself. As I have previously stated whilst Reb Behr Cohen was alive R. Ezekiel followed his behest just as the foreigner dances to the tune of the bear. He possessed yet one other fine characteristic viz. when he noticed people laughing at any of his inane interpretations of various texts he was very pleased for he imagined their joy was the effect of the great pleasure they derived from his novel interpretations which, he thought, were sweeter than honey to his audience. However, in reality they were being disrespectful and mocking him for they regarded him as a jester. Yet he was not intelligent enough to realise that they were really laughing at his dreams and his expositions. Thus he left his audience in good humour and always boasted that his reputation was enhanced by every one of his discourses. In addition to the many pleasures he gained from constant imbibing of wines, whiskey other drinks he was a gormandizer all his life. Moreover, because by temperament he had as stone his life was replete with pleasure for all that he did and learned in this world appeared good and pleasant to him, since he had never realised his own shortcomings. On the contrary, his heart found pleasure in his own folly as well as in all his repulsive behaviour. However, it was only when he became wealthy that he was overjoyed and believed that he was unique, for he believed that the planet (under which he was born) was assisting him in the success of every step he took. It was only in family matters that he experienced unhappiness, though he did gain some joy from a few of his children. It is an astonishing fact that all his life he succeeded in everything even though some of his actions were most reprehensible. But at the same time his community suffered such a serious decline that it reached its lowest ebb. Nevertheless, he remained sound in mind and body (cf.Ps.73:4) so that he could sit drinking day and night until he became intoxicated. For he would gormandize everywhere and with every one, particularly at a Brit or wedding, when he would keep company with uncultivated and frivolous folk. Hence he eventually became a source of amusement to the wider community whilst the more respectable elements in his community were embarrassed because he so denigrated and profaned the honour of the Torah in public.

It was for this reason that the lay-leaders of the Communal Council ordered him not to attend every festive meal except those of the eminent members (of the community) or where he actually participated in the preceding religious ceremony. Furthermore, no other Rabbi was so actively engaged in so many inane activities as he was. For in his own home he constantly enjoyed the company of boors and idlers who would inform him of all the gossip and activities that were going on in the community and in the Jewish world in general, whilst they were entertained by him (with food and drink). Above all, he had spies who investigated the status of every member of the Three Communities. Consequently, he was fully acquainted with the position of these members and with their activities, knowing everything that went on in their homes, who was rich or poor, who needed credit, whose star was on the rise and was therefore prospering or the converse. Furthermore, he got to know which member required his assistance in some judicial matter. Moreover, he was consequently able to arrange suitable marriages and to exploit every method of increasing his wealth and power. In addition, he was consequently able to wreak vengeance on those whom he realised were not friendly disposed towards him since these spies revealed the deepest secrets of every member. Those of the latter whom he favoured he would elevate, whilst those who did not win his favour he would humiliate. If, in his (R. Ezekiel's) opinion a certain member had not fulfilled his duty to him in respect of gifts for Purim or Rosh Hashanah to the degree which he had been assessed (by the Rabbi) he would exact vengeance judicially i.e. when that donor appeared before the Bet Din. Alternatively, he would exact vengeance in the assessment of that donor's chances to obtain some

CHAPTER TEN

communal honour i.e. in the appointment of lay-leaders, or lay-Judges or Court officials, or Dayanim. Otherwise, he would do this person a disservice in the arrangement of a marriage or he would let it be known that the particular person was not a man of means and thus reduce the latter's credibility and jeopardise his livelihood. He had a register for Purim and Rosh Hashanah (gifts) during which periods all members of the Three Communities passed before him like sheep, which enabled him to keep a strict eye (on the proceedings) and to observe if anyone accustomed to bring him gifts on those occasions was absent, or which one increased or decreased his usual donation. Indeed, the success or failure of a person who required the Rabbi's services in matters of adjudication depended on what was recorded in that register. In fact a well-known personality who was a Rabbinic scholar told me about a highly reputable person of Altona who was not one of the Rabbi's admirers and was therefore unaccustomed to send him (the Rabbi) gifts. It so happened that this person summoned a debtor to appear before R .Ezekiel since this debtor owed this individual several hundred Reichthalers. But, the plaintiff was unable to get the defendant to meet his debt because R. Ezekiel caused the plaintiff all kinds of difficulties by either delaying judgement or perverting the course of justice by various forms of trickery he (R. Ezekiel) could invent to exonerate the defendant. Ultimately the plaintiff lost his money. R. Ezekiel had behaved in this way to wreak vengeance on the plaintiff because the latter was not included in the list of those who gave gifts to the Rabbi on Purim and Rosh Hashanah. When the plaintiff realised that situation and having a number of debtors to whom he had given goods on credit he reconsidered his position. For, he argued, why should I behave in a way that causes me heavy losses by refraining from conferring gifts on the Rabbi on Purim and Rosh Hashanah. Surely, even if such gifts would cost me about four hundred Reichthalers it would be a mere trifle if thereby I win the friendship of the Rabbi who would help me when I required his assistance in any adjudication with my debtors. Consequently he behaved in this way (towards the Rabbi) and henceforth became a changed personality. For having thereby become an admirer of the Rabbi he succeeded in has law-suits (with his debtors). In this matter the Rabbi of the Three Communities compelled its members to conform to his demands and to confer many gifts on him. (Woe to the ears which hear such terrible things about a person who occupies the seat of justice and pronounces Halakhic decisions. We can imagine the opinion of the illiterate concerning those who administer Jewish law and Torah scholars in general.) In fact, many of them uttered the curse, "May they perish!" Thus, the illiterate scoffed at the representatives of the Almighty as though all Rabbinic scholars were suspected of bribery.

Hence the members of the Three Communities stood in great fear of the Rabbi (Ezekiel) for he struck unobtrusively. Thus he imposed an inordinate fear of him on the whole community, though, as I have already described his behaviour caused them to have a low opinion of him. In fact, he really did not have one admirer, the exception being a few powerful men in the community who showed him real affection because he favoured them and fulfilled their wishes when they wanted to avenge themselves against certain individuals or to impose their authority on them. In this activity he gave them his full support and always made himself available to them (the powerful). Indeed without his assistance they would not have succeeded in carrying out their plans. For according to the recitations upon which the community was founded the Presiding Rabbi of the Bet Din had authority over the lay-leaders whilst any ruling to which they consented was invalid unless it was passed by the full membership of the community. However R. Ezekiel removed all these restrictions on the power of the lay-leaders giving them complete authority whether for just or unjust purposes. (This was why they (the lay-leaders) were (later) deprived of their social-status to which they had aspired during the Rabbinate of R. Ezekiel. For they ruled the community with a strong arm and showed no more care for the rich than for the poor (c.34:19) Subsequently these lay-leaders supported a serious decline in their power and authority "as from the highest roof to the lowest valley". (cf. TB. Hagigah 5b)

CHAPTER TEN

Indeed, they were deprived of whatever powers they possessed. Then with the appearance of R.Eibeschuetz came contempt so that "it was the same for the priest and the people" (cf.Is.24:22) as I shall later describe, with the Almighty's help. Moreover, this was the essential reason for the controversy and divisiveness that was soon followed by the dissolution of the Kehillot. For certain individuals found pretexts to avenge themselves on the lay-leaders and to deprive them of their authority simply because they (the lay-leaders) where divided in their opinions, whilst those who sought their destruction depended on R.Eibeschuetz to support them in down-grading the lay-leadership. They (the former) gave R. Ezekiel their full support in his efforts to obtain complete authority. He, therefore, implemented their plans to reduce the status of the lay-leadership to a nonentity, whilst they, in the same vein, assisted him (R. Ezekiel) in the injustice that he perpetrated against certain individuals who occasionally appeared before him (R. Ezekiel) for some adjudication. Thus they took the Rabbi under their wing since he and they were acting in each others' interest.

A further reason for people regarding the Rabbi as an object of ridicule and taunt (cf. 1 Kings 9:7) was the fact that though he was defective both in speech and voice, unless it was the call of cash, so that his singing and chirping were so unusual that they induced laughter and scorn in anyone who heard them, yet he regarded himself as a Chazan and a wonderful singer. Thus, when he prayed in the main synagogue on Festivals and the High-Holydays when he lead the congregation in prayer and he stood by the Reader's desk it produced laughter and derision in the synagogue. Indeed, one who had not experienced his intonations or the sound of his chirping has never experienced anything so funny! This made him a target of much scoffing and derision to such an extent that when jesters who performed in banqueting halls wanted to provoke more laughter so as to enhance the joyous atmosphere of the occasion and put the guests into a jovial mood they, would begin to chant the tunes of the Presiding Rabbi of the Bet Din and completely imitate his characteristics and gestures. Then all the audience would burst into such laughter that the noise split the very ground. They, (the guests) were used to the merriment and extraordinary gestures of these jesters, but by this particular imitation they aroused more uproarious laughter than would be provoked by the gestures of complete imbeciles or by the imitations of performers who seemed to alter their features when they pranced and danced. When R. Ezekiel heard of such activities he showed no concern; on the contrary, he was as overjoyed as one who had been a public benefactor since he was the source of all that public mirth. However, occasionally there were important communal personalities present at these merry-making events who were most concerned and disconcerted at hearing the scornful and irreverent observations which were directed at the Presiding Rabbi of the Three Communities for they regarded such behaviour as a profanation of the Divine Name and insulting to a Rabbinic scholar in the presence of the illiterate. Consequently they tried to prohibit those singing jesters from appearing at weddings or on other joyful occasions. Moreover, they protested at such behaviour stating that such jesting denigrated the respect for the Torah as well as for the community. Yet, what was R. Ezekiel's reaction? He invited a young fellow who was adept at whistling and who publicly imitated the Rabbi's tunes and chirping in order to gain a livelihood and said to him privately, "come and I'll teach you one of my songs which you cannot intone correctly. Sit down and I'll teach you the song which will be pleasurable to the public and, at the same time, will help to increase your earnings." To such an extent was this Rabbi convinced of the success of all whims that even such folly and foolishness as this gave him great pleasure! Not that he was so foolish; for in anything which was to his financial advantage he proved to be both wise and most shrewd, but his power of imagination led him astray. Indeed in achieving fame and fortune he was without par.

    As for his communal workers and the Members of his Bet Din their behaviour was the realisation of the scriptural verse, "just as a ruler listens to falsehood,(so) all his servants will be wicked."(Prov.29:12). (Thus) they took money from people whenever

CHAPTER TEN

they could, whether in the capacity of official tax-collectors or not. Hence when I married my second wife I had to give them (the officials) a number of Shock Heller (coins) without asking the reason for such payments for I was then very preoccupied. Then when I married my third wife who was my niece, though these officials were unaware whether I had received a considerable dowry they made demands of me which were far more than what the beadle sought for himself. In fact, the latter would not erect the Chuppah until I had first met the demands of the community i.e. the Presiding Rabbi of the Bet Din, Rabbi Ezekiel.

However, I will not go in to further details as to the latter's activities.

MEGILAT SEFER

CHAPTER ELEVEN

When, as I have described earlier, I visited Hamburg for several weeks the lay-leader Reb Joel Shaw who had been a genuine admirer of my father, z"l, became my enemy because I was compelled to stay with Reb Behr Cohen. It was then that a bitter enmity developed between these two people (Joel Shaw and Behr Cohen) because of the controversy over my father's removal from the local Rabbinate. As a result Joel Shaw had been in Herem (ostracised) for some years and was disqualified from any communal office in Altona during Reb Behr Cohen's lifetime. However, a few years before I came to live in Altona Reb Behr Cohen died and Joel Shaw was restored to his previous status by being appointed as a lay-leader to that community. This was the situation when I first returned to live in Altona. However, I immediately sensed that he (Joel Shaw) was not friendly disposed towards me. For all the community came out to welcome me (including those who were unfriendly to my father, z"l) and received me joyfully assuring me they would fulfil my every request. I made no specific request of them with one exception, and that was that I should be permitted to have a minyan

CHAPTER ELEVEN

in my house for regular prayers since it was most inconvenient for me to attend services in the Great Synagogue. This was in fact the main reason for my leaving Emden. All the community of Altona were agreeable (to this request) except Joel Shaw who had not joined those who welcomed me to the community. However I had been tolerant enough to visit him (Joel Shaw) at his home on the advice of R.Moses Hagiz whom I then always heeded since he was very much my senior. Consequently, I adopted a favourable attitude towards him (Joel Shaw) believing that perhaps it was because of his old age and physical incapacity that he had not come to welcome me. I therefore visited his home to pay my respects (to him) fully believing that he would be a true friend to me (as he had been to my father) for I could not conceive that he would bear me any baseless hatred. However, he proved to be a constant impediment to me, for he did everything to prevent a Minyan from meeting in my house. Yet the community had raised no objection to R.Moses Hagiz, may he rest in peace, who enjoyed this privilege (of a quorum in his home) despite the fact that he was a Sephardi and not a member of the community whilst I came from a line of Rabbis and was a native of the community. Moreover, I had not proved to be a burden to the community in any way.

However, as long as Joel Shaw remained in the community I had no respite from his opposition. Every week he would send the communal beadle to me to protest over this matter (the Minyan in my house) and though during the month he was not on active duty I enjoyed some respite, when he resumed his monthly office he renewed his protests. Hence, on a number of occasions my regular Minyan was disrupted. I found this insufferable and not only I, but so did the people who were members of that Minyan who were equally aggrieved. For they found it pleasurable to pray without the chatting that was prevalent in the Great Synagogue. On one occasion they suspended my Minyan during the High Holydays, the Day of Atonement and Succot so I attended the Sephardi Synagogue whilst the people who were members of the Minyan were compelled to attend services in the Great Synagogue. Among the latter there was a genuinely religion person, Ephraim, may he rest in peace, who was a descendant of righteous proselytes. On the eve of these particular High Holidays he stood at the entrance of my house bewailing the fact that he was unable to participate in my Minyan since he did not feel inclined to attend the Services in the Great Synagogue where he would have to associate with unbecoming and disrespectful people. But a terrible fate awaited him for because of our many sins the honourable Ephraim was murdered in the Gt. Synagogue. (This was the result of the following incident).

He (Ephraim) happened to notice a worthless visitor publicly smoking a pipe on the Synagogue premises, which considerably upset that fine religious individual. He therefore protested at this person's misbehaviour telling him that he had no right to behave in this way on the Synagogue premises. When the miscreant ignored Ephraim's protest he (Ephraim) hit the man's pipe which fell out of his mouth onto the ground. This so provoked the visitor that he grasped a knife and thrust it into Ephraim's body piercing either his entrails or his heart and fatally wounding him (Ephraim) for he died about a week later. But (remember this) such a person still lives, he will not see the grave." (Ps.49:10)

I was most distressed at the fate of such a fine person like Ephraim who met his end because of his religiosity and his keenness to pray in my home; may his memory endure for ever! However, for our many sins, the guilt lay with the communal leadership which was directly responsible for this tragedy. Though Ephraim forgave the murderer the latter was brought to trial in the state court which sought to avenge the crime, but because witnesses were reluctant to come forward and the victim (before his death) had denied that murder was intended, the court ruled that the accused should swear he hadn't intended to strike a fatal blow and he would be exonerated. This was effected and the accused was freed in accordance with human justice. All this was the effect of the suspension of the Minyan which used to gather to pray in my house.

Now let me tell you what favours I did on behalf of Joel Shaw's son-in-law though this was in no way to help dispel his (Joel

CHAPTER ELEVEN

Shaw's) enmity towards me. It so happened that just before I came to live in Altona the lay-leader Norden enquired of me regarding the character of Reb Zalman Stern, Joel Shaw's son-in-law. The Nordens had learned that Zalman wanted to arrange a marriage between his daughter and their brother, the honourable Reb Zender, and they (the Nordens) would accept only my recommendation. They accepted my advice and consequently I agreed to become a Shadchan (Marriage-broker), a function which, unlike other Rabbis in Germany, I had hitherto avoided even when I held the Rabbinate of Emden. There were two main reasons for my disinterest in that activity. First, I could not possibly become fully cognisant of all the relevant facts about the lay-leaders and their sons and daughters without involving myself in a thorough investigation of the particular families and I was afraid that such involvement might prove harmful and would provoke ill-feeling towards me. The second, and more important reason, was that marriage-broking would prove too time-consuming and in composing introductory letters as well as having to concentrate on different aspects of this activity that might mean, God forbid, neglecting my main interest viz. the advancement of Torah-learning, though in this regard I had to face other impediments. Thus, I had hitherto refrained from being involved in such activities but, as I have indicated on several occasions, I could not refuse to help these people (the Nordens) and consequently I implicated myself in this particular affair from which I didn't desist until, with the Almighty's assistance, I had effected this betrothal with the agreement of both families. (Actually) in assessing the situation I felt I would gain very little in arranging this marriage. For previously the Nordens used to send me precious stones for the sale of which I received a commission. But now I had provided the Nordens with a relative (by marriage) who had also begun to pursue the same line of business he would acquire a great deal of my agency (in precious stones) so that my livelihood would obviously suffer. Nevertheless I did not withhold my good offices on behalf of Reb Zalman. Indeed when I was arranging the marriage I explicitly stated in a letter to him (Reb Zalman) that he shouldn't consider me simply a marriage-broker who was acting on behalf of his daughter, but rather as a person who was helping to considerably advance his status through a marriage alliance with a family who were then held in the highest repute throughout German Jewry because of their wealth, renown and munificent charitable endeavours which were without equal. Moreover,(I continued) all the highest strata in German Jewry were most eager to be attached to this family because of their great wealth and business activities in precious stones, as well as for their integrity which was of the highest order. Hence, (I concluded) any person who had dealings with them was blessed with wealth.

Reb Zalman seemed to me to be a fine person and I therefore thought that because of my activities on his behalf he would always be my true friend. For (I argued) I had no ulterior motive nor did I seek self aggrandisement in this matter. Indeed, I could easily have found some excuse to abandon my role as marriage-broker and to have occupied myself with some other business. In fact there were many people who earnestly desired a marriage alliance with the Nordens in particular Reb A. Eli who also had a comely daughter and wanted to arrange a marriage between her and the brother of the Nordens. Reb Eli was a highly respected elder (of the community) who had been a reputable lay-leader for several years besides the fact that he was far richer than Reb Zalman Stern. Moreover, he (Reb Eli) was in no way involved in the business of precious stones quite apart from the fact that he was related to me by marriage and had proved to be an old and trusted friend of mine. In fact, it was because of my involvement in arranging this marriage that he too, turned against me exclaiming, as an irate enemy, "Am I not as important as Reb Zalman, why then have you abandoned me?" Even so, I considered Reb Zalman Stern even a finer person than Reb Eli and therefore successfully concluded the marriage alliance, although it was to my disadvantage. For not only did I not receive the usual marriage-broker's fee from both families, but Reb Zalman gave me less. Nevertheless, I was prepared to tolerate this since I thought that he (Reb Zalman) would assist me whenever I required his help, either in proffering me good advice in any business that would come my way,

CHAPTER ELEVEN

or in getting his father-in-law to become more friendly disposed towards me, as indeed Reb Zalman had promised me.

Consequently, soon after the marriage alliance had been concluded I visited him (Reb Zalman) to show him some precious stones I had received to sell and to enquire as to their quality and price, for I had little experience in that business. For I believed that in him I had a good friend and a fine and well-disposed person whose advice I could trust. But though outwardly he gave the impression of being a fine person his essential character was quite the reverse. For he planned to make a complete take-over of the Nordens business, and even envied me because of the few business dealings I had with them (the Nordens). Indeed, Reb Joseph Benedet, who depended me for a livelihood, informed confidentially that Reb Zalman and his wife complained bitterly over the fact that I was involved in business which was rightly his (Reb Zalman's). Yet it was I who had introduced him to considerable business with the Nordens in which precious stones to the value of more than one hundred thousand gold pieces were involved annually, but he (Reb Zalman) did not give me a penny as a broker's fee. In contradistinction over the years I did business with the Nordens (in precious stones) I did not earn half the annual income of R. Zalman. Thus he wronged me on two counts. For not only did he and his father-in-law (Joel Shaw) fail to show me any kindness, but the latter's envy towards me increased twofold, because of my business dealings with the Nordens, for which both of them envied me. This lay at the root of Joel Shaw's enmity towards me, though he tried to attribute it to some other factor. (His hatred was such) that he persecuted and opposed me at every turn, and not only regarding the private Minyan that I mentioned previously.

Yet I had to act in the way I did though I suffered for it. In short, Joel Shaw was my constant foe, and had he been able to expel me from Altona he would have done so. This was clearly confirmed by Reb J. Buchbinder who was related to Joel Shaw. For when I asked him (J.Buchbinder) whether it way because of my desire for a private Minyan that Joel Shaw had behaved so badly towards me, he replied, "God forbid." Then he confidentially informed me that his (Joel

Shaw's) hatred for me was rooted in envy. Because of his many provocations I was most indignant with Joel Shaw and remarked to his son-in-law (Zalman Stern) whom I had invited to a dinner (in my home) in honour of his son-in-law (Sh.Norden) that I was certain his father-in-law wouldn't die of old-age before he had witnesses the disgrace of his family. This is exactly what happened. For a short time after this Reb Joel Shaw's son-in-law Menachem Steuckhart who had been a money-lender in Frankfurt-on-Main had to flee to Altona together with his wife, Joel's daughter. Then a few years later, Reb Zalman Stern, whom I did not consider to be as bad as his father-in-law, died during the latter's life-time, leaving many children to be cared for by Joel Shaw, but little money. For in his passion to acquire wealth Reb Zalman had obtained a great deal or credit from business acquaintances. So though he had acquired considerable wealth and was blessed with success in the years he had done business with the Nordens, in his latter years he had acted too hastily and consequently lost a great deal of money. I have now informed you of the opposition I found when I first re-settled in Altona. On the contrary, all the community including the people who opposed my father, z"l, were deeply attached to me and particularly the family of Behr Cohen and his sons-in-law. Indeed even the elderly Presiding Rabbi of the Bet Din, Rabbi Ezekiel, as well as his family praised me, though not in my presence. The local Communal Council showed me particular affection and every Succoth they would send me a gift of a beautiful Etrog. This remained an annual gift until 1751 when Eibeschuetz arrived, for with his arrival came disdain (of me.)

  Thus I met with friendliness on all sides since my deeds endeared me to the community. For not only did I offer my assistance to all and sundry in terms of money or any of my worldly possessions but, as I will describe later, I almost became a serf (in my services) on behalf of certain people. First let me mention a few facts about the favours I performed for the family of Abraham Wiener who were slightly related to me, though I regarded them as close relatives. Yet all of them repaid my good deeds on their behalf with evil. At the outset I was most distressed about the impoverished

CHAPTER ELEVEN

Benedet, the son-in-law of Abraham Wiener, whose adverse economic status placed him in the grip of poverty. I was overcome with pity for him and was determined to do everything I could to help him, as our Sages put it, "great is learning which is conducive to action." Hence when I observed that everyone in the community was friendly disposed to me and because so many were genuinely fond of me that they were prepared to express this attachment to me tangibly, though I was reluctant to accept anything from them, I though had the opportunity of finding favour with the Almighty by touching the hearts of certain generous people in the community so that they would ensure a livelihood for Benedet. Consequently I did the following; I drew up a document in which the under-signed obligated themselves to make a voluntary donation for the maintenance of Benedet. (In this document) I extensively praised the latter in the most exaggerated terms and stirred the emotions of those who perused it with such lucid and figurative language that even his brother-in-law, Z---, may he rest in peace, felt that my praise of Benedet was excessive. However, I felt most distressed about him. Moreover, my attachment to the poor but learned people made me disregard the rules imposed on one by his exalted position in life, so that this procedure (of excessive praise) was really contrary to my natural conduct. For I detested those people who indulged in exaggerated praise of other people, but on this occasion I threw all restraint to the wind because of my close friendship with Benedet coupled with my attachment to Torah-learning. Therefore I personally knocked at the doors of generous families and paid early visits to the lay-leaders of Hamburg whom I addressed as follows: "Since I have noted your beneficent and just characters and that on several occasions you indicated you would help him (Benedet) I have presumed on your goodwill which suggested that anything I requested would be no imposition for you, well now the Almighty has chanced to set before me a most important Mitzvah and my visit is to enable you to enjoy the privilege of fulfilling it. This Mitzvah is to come to the assistance of a fine but impoverished man who is a Talmid Chacham." These people immediately expressed their gratification. Then Reb Seligman asked me, "who composed the wording of this document?" To which I replied, "a Polish Jew who happens to be making a private visit to this region." He then remarked, "I cannot believe that!"

Even so, the contents of the document together with my pleas on his behalf helped Benedet to the tune of several hundred Shock Heller over the period of years which each of the undersigned had obligated himself, in fact, I still have that document. Yet despite all the strenuous efforts I made to stir the hearts of generous people so that they would show kindness towards the impoverished Benedet, they in fact displayed their generosity because I personally had requested it. Indeed, they stated quite categorically that they were not supporting Reb Benedet because of the unfortunate situation in which he found himself. In fact, they spoke disparagingly of him. (They stated that) were it not for the respect in which they held me, they would have had little regard for him. In this respect I must especially mention Meir Cohen, Behr Cohen's son, who was related by marriage to Benedet. Initially I felt sure his prompt support of Benedet was motivated by a sense of obligation (because of his relationship to Benedet). However, he (Meir Cohen) told me quite explicitly that he had not intended to expend anything on Benedet for the latter did not deserve it, but that he (Meir) didn't want to dismiss me empty-handed so that if I wanted a donation from him he would gladly make it. I replied, "so let it seem that I am receiving the donation for myself." However, Meir (Cohen) emphasised that he would accede to my request (for a donation) on the assurance that I personally would be the beneficiary of his generosity. I therefore had to say to him (again), "It will be regarded as if I personally had received your donation (for my own benefit)". He then promised a generous donation of fifty Shock Heller per annum for several years. His brother Judah Seligman and his brother-in-law Elijah Oppenheim and a number of others reacted similarly, each one making their donation on the understanding that they were doing me a kindness, otherwise they would have dismissed me empty-handed.

However, there were two important lay-leaders whose

CHAPTER ELEVEN

donations I assumed would exceed the other benefactors, but they summarily dismissed me. They were Joel Shaw, who was related to the impoverished Benedet, and the respected Elijah Sher, both of whom were distinguished lay-leaders. Yet I had no success with them, for despite all my strenuous oratorical efforts to provoke their pity, they refused to make any donation. Joel Shaw explained why he refused and spoke most disparagingly about Benedet for example "people have spoken to me about his (Benedet's) misdemeanours, that he has been suspected of receiving stolen property and of accepting bribes to pervert the course of justice." These were my particular activities on behalf of Benedet quite apart from the gifts I made him from what people sent for my own use. On one occasion his brother-in-law, Tuvyah, may he rest in peace, asked me to buy an iron chest from Benedet which was still in his possession and was now empty (of cash). I immediately paid him the price he requested viz. fifteen Reichthalers, though it was not worth half that amount. I was also liberal with my money towards Tuvyah's father-in-law, Joseph Bressler. For he often used to borrow money from me, to the tune of about fifty Reichthalers, more or less, and I never ceased to oblige him by lending him the sum he requested without asking for any kind of security, whilst he, profited from the loans I made him. He used the money to his own advantage and used to repay me whenever it pleased him, whilst I, God forbid, derived no benefit whatsoever from these loans. On one occasion I lent him fifty Reichthalers which Reb Tuvyah counted out as he placed the money into the hands of Joseph Bressler's agent. He (Bressler) delayed repayment for some considerable time, and when he did repay he sent me only forty-nine Reich Thaler that is one Reich Thaler less than was due. When I informed his agent of this fact Reb Tuvyah, who was the uncle of Seligman's wife was most indignant with me arguing, I definitely counted out the money into the hands of the agent (when the loan was being repaid), then why didn't the agent say something?" At any rate, Joseph Bressler failed to repay the one Reich Thaler he owed me, yet on several subsequent occasions he borrowed money from me whenever he needed it. Yet these two men, Benedet and Tuvyah, became my enemies in my controversy with R.Eibeschuetz. Benedet aided and abetted the destruction of the community by bringing Eibeschuetz to Altona but subsequently, as I shall later describe, the latter caused him (Benedet) much harm.

    Regarding the remaining members of the Elijah Oppenheim's family I did all I could to help them, particularly Nathan, may he rest in peace, and Tuvyah, Elijah's sons, to whom I acted as a father and patron in all their requests of me. Moreover, I readily lent a considerable sum of money to the father-in-law of Nathan which involved me in a tidy mortgage. In fact I had almost despaired of regaining that money, but after some considerable time and with much difficulty I managed to save my property. Those two brothers, Nathan and Tuvyah, remained my constant friends for they acknowledged the favours I did them. Their brother-in-law, Wolf Helli also received favours from me. I entrusted him with money I had earned by selling jewellery and when I received a promissory note I would hand it to him in exchange for a promissory note he had received from Amsterdam and for which he charged me whatever he considered to be the correct fee, though the latter proved to be incorrect according to those who were experts in this business. For I had little experience of the system of money-exchange and therefore relied on his integrity. Subsequently I learned that he had not dealt honestly with me, as I will later describe. However, as I do not want to interrupt the main theme of this narrative I will drop this subject until I reach the time when these events actually occurred. In fact I only mentioned it to inform the reader that Elijah Elia and his family turned their backs on me when the controversy I shall later describe began. They were the source of the of the disaster that befell this community and the source of hypocrisy which affected the wider community. For they believed the lying statements were made concerning me viz. that I was spreading lies about R.Eibeschuetz out of jealousy of his elevated status (in the community). For people argued that this man Elijah Elia, was my trusted friend particularly because of his wife's relationship to me, and that I was the crown of all his family who initially showed me a

CHAPTER ELEVEN

special affection. Moreover, (people said) Elijah himself had gained the reputation of being a fine person, as in fact I regarded him, though he was a fool, yet (people said) he and his in-laws had acted treacherously towards me. Consequently, people trusted Elijah so that he was the cause of constant trouble (to me), though ultimately he acknowledged the wrong he did. However his repentance and confession came after "the waters were threatening his very life," (Ps.69:2) for, because of our many sins, he paid in full (for the wrong he did), as shall describe later. May his death be an atonement for his sins! Then his wife and family admitted that they had behaved irreligiously.

 Apart from the fact that all my resources were readily available for all who sought the assistance of Jacob, I did another thing. Soon after I resettled in Altona I chanced to see my friend Nordon of London who had previously helped me and whom I had not expected to see (in Altona). I then informed him that I would no longer require his assistance since I would manage to live on what I had. However, I made one request of him viz. that I should receive the money he was obligated to give me on behalf of the local poor. If he agreed (I said) all well and good. He gladly accepted my suggestion and continued to send me a regular sum of money to donate to any charity I thought fit; this practice continued for some years. May he be remembered for good because of another favour (to me) viz. he used to send me certain English merchandise the sale of which with the Almighty's assistance, helped increase my meagre income. However, in this endeavour I found things difficult and not quite as I had hoped. For I was compelled to pursue this form of livelihood which, in reality, I preferred above all other gifts, and I would probably have succeeded in obtaining a livelihood quite easily had I been fortunate in obtaining the appropriate goods at the right time. Then indeed, all would have been well. But Norden wasn't able to fulfil his good intentions to the extent he deserved even though he was closely attached to me and a man who was true to his word who was always ready to help me and to accede to any request I made of him, a fact to which I have already referred. However, because of considerable sluggishness on my part I did not take to that type of business with any real enthusiasm. In fact, my true desire was to earn a living solely by my own efforts and with the assistance of He who creates and sustains all living things, from the horns of the bull, t he eggs of birds, rather than from any human benefactors, by whose favours I managed to gain a livelihood though it involved me in considerable trouble and subsequently ceased altogether.

Now let me describe my experiences in some chronological order, for I must now mention the other lay-leaders viz. the Nordens and their brother-in-law who established a type of Yeshivah for me in Emden and promised to maintain it. They were faithful to this promise from when I first settled in Emden until 1740, but subsequently their support ended. However, when I first re-settled in Altona they extended their commitment to me for a few years. But I considered the next act of kindness a far greater favour than all their earlier kindness. For they now gave me jewellery on credit to enable me to make a profit. This also continued for some years and I achieved some measure of success (in this endeavour). Nevertheless when I first re-settled in Altona, thank God I gained a comfortable livelihood, though I left little to chance and tried to economise even though I could have been extravagant. However, during that phase of my life I paid little attention to the value of money and was in no way concerned as to what I would eat on the morrow; for I then maintained, "blessed be the Lord day by day," (Ps.68:20) and I consequently spent my money on whatever took my fancy. Whether on gifts to the poor or on teaching fees for my sons, may they be spared, for I maintained a tutor for them in my home. Then I spent my money liberally on the publication of my first book, and on buying a house. With the Almighty's help I also bought some silverware and ornaments both to adorn a Sefer-Torah as well as for ordinary use. At that period I gained the privilege of performing the Mitzvah of Brit Milah (though I rarely had new suit made for I fulfilled the Mitzvah of maintaining my wife and family more than caring for my own needs) at the homes of many members of the

CHAPTER ELEVEN

community. In particular, when a son was born to a poor family they sought my services as a Mohel; such an event occurred almost every week. Occasionally, I had the privilege of performing Brit Milah twice a week, since I was liberal with my money. I also contributed (to a fund) which made loans to the poor, or I acquired the bills of indebtedness of those people who had to borrow on security.

In the early days people sang praises especially when I obtained money from L.Norden in London to distribute among the poor, I have already mentioned the details of this. But the last two good deeds I have mentioned also had ill effects, for as the ancient proverb has it, "Every good bears the deeds of ill-fortune." This was true of my situation; for as Iong as I enjoyed the abundance of things and was in the position to do good to other people through this abundance all was well and every stratum of the community sang my praises. But when this situation ended and my purse was empty, then my enemies and ill-wishers increased for they believed I really had money but was loath to spend it. These people thought the Nordens and their purses were at my disposal. This had indeed been the position for some years, for when I interceded (with the Nordens) on behalf of another person they would listen to me and immediately make liberal gifts (of money) to that unfortunate person. This was their practice even when the needy person showed them my signature appended to a note from me, for even then they (the Nordens) would show their munificence. In fact I learned this from a local needy person who was about to leave Altona. I gave him a note with my signature since he happened to be a member of my Minyan. When this man arrived in Amsterdam he called on the Nordens who, on reading my note welcomed this man and gave him seven gold pieces, for at that particular time the Almighty had blessed them immeasurably. However, their liberality gradually diminished and consequently I had little contact with them for I had no wish to overburden them. In fact from 1740 I would not accept the money they had obligated themselves to give me for I realised they were no longer as wealthy as before but were now beset with many problems. Hence in I740, after my second marriage, both the maintenance,

MEGILAT SEFER

(from the Nordens) and the business I had previously transacted with them ended. However, I still gained some income in business (through the good offices) of Leib London. In fact, in that very same year he sent me some money, but henceforth this source of income also dried up. Nevertheless, for some subsequent years he (London) continued to assist me in trading in tinware and tinsels, but this business too dried up like overripe harvest fruit and all my business with him also terminated.(cf. Song of Songs 2:11) Finally I found myself in financial low-waters he (London) refused to help me even though he would have suffered no financial loss: this is a true example of a Sodomite principle (i.e. justice without charity cf. TB. Bava Batra 12b).

In the earlier days of my resettlement in Altona when I earned a regular income and therefore had some capital, my first wife began to make an income by lending money to local neighbours on security. I was not altogether pleased with this idea for I was not really in need of this extra income. However, my wife who was an intelligent woman argued that we did not know what the future held out for us and it would therefore be in our interest to pursue this business in loans, so that, with the Almighty's help, we might increase our livelihood. I therefore raised little objection. However, this activity immediately aroused the envy of professional money-lenders who were jealous of our involvement in the business. One of them was my neighbour Hayyimkhi who used to borrow money from me free of interest which I used to make him as a gesture of goodwill since I was always on good terms with my neighbours. Subsequently however, he became my enemy and publicly expressed terrible curses against my wife and me in the hearing of both Jew and Gentiles because he thought I had deprived him of business. In fact the community (in general) wanted me to sue him for the humiliation he caused us, but I took no such measures. Ultimately however, he received his due punishment because of his behaviour towards me. During the period my wife was involved in money-lending she achieved a measure of success with the capital I had laid aside for

CHAPTER ELEVEN

this purpose which incidentally was never more than about two hundred Reich Thaler. For apart from the fact that I did not lose any of that original capital we made a comparatively tidy profit.

But when I married my second wife about two thousand Reich Thaler of mine were invested in loans which, as I shall shortly describe were finally lost. Moreover, my original business in jewellery eventually decreased so that I had to abandon it and hand it over to another person. For David Vermesh, who used to obtain this jewellery on credit came to an agreement with me whereby the Nordens should trade directly with him and dispense with my services as a middleman. In return, I would receive a commission on all the goods he bought from the Nordens i.e. he would give me a fee proportionate to the value of the goods he had obtained (from the Nordens). He complied with his part of the contract on two or three occasions but then swindled me as I subsequently discovered for myself, for no-one informed me of his treachery. In fact he wanted to hide his cheating and to deny his complicity, but finally his trickery became known and he was compelled to give me my due commission, though even then he did not give me the full amount to which l was entitled. Subsequently, I did not receive a penny from him; who knows how much of my money he kept for himself?

Then certain swindlers prevailed upon me to lend some money to local Jews on bills of indebtedness, but I lost a great deal of this money. Then I was again swindled when certain people gave me pledges belonging to other Jews and stated that they (the pledges) were their neighbours' property, then they said the pledges were really theirs or that they belonged to a third party. Sometimes they told the truth; at other times they lied, but because of this business I was involved in any number of disagreements and quarrels. Then another person forged receipts of Iottery tickets and gave me them as a pledge for a loan of about four hundred Shock Heller, for those tickets were very expensive. When l initially showed those receipts to people who knew something about them they said the receipts were genuine, but later they proved to be forgeries and I lost all my money. Yet it was indeed miraculous I had not tried to redeem those pledges

MEGILAT SEFER

from the lottery office for I would have been accused of forging those receipts. Blessed be the Lord who saved me from those (forged) receipts. In the same way I lost several thousand Reich Thaler that I had invested in loans (on bills of indebtedness) to local people whom I did not really know (or see), but simply relied on the integrity of agents (who acted on behalf of the borrowers). Then the latter simply took the money (from me) and shared it equally with the persons they purported to represent or divided the money according to some previous arrangement. I spent a hundred Reichthalers for every hundred I received so that my income was cancelled by my expenditure. I also tried my hand at lottery and in the early period when I used to make an annual flutter I did not lose, in fact I made a little profit. On one occasion I won a hundred ducats which was quite apart from other small winnings.

In fact over several years I hardly lost a penny. However, when I began to spend more than one Reich Thaler far more than frequently I finally lost everything. In this way I forfeited a considerable sum of money during that period when cash was readily available. Later however, when I returned to Altona from my exile in Amsterdam I found things very difficult. I then remained   at home for some considerable time, with no visible means of livelihood. I tried to dabble in the sale of lottery-tickets but suffered a considerable loss. In fact I'm still repaying that money for I had to pay interest on a loans of eight hundred Reich Thaler which I borrowed from a Gentile (for them lottery business) as I shall explain later, with the Almighty's help. Yet despite all this I sing praises to Him who gives and takes; may His Name be blessed for evermore. Upon Him did I cast my burden; may He fulfil my needs and bless my worldly possessions.

To return to my adventures in Altona. In the previous Kislev my wife gave birth to a boy whom I named Tzvi Hirsch, after my father, z"l for I dearly desired to perpetuate his name in my family. I had already had a son in Broda to whom I had give the same name. This child did not survive. Since my wife, may she rest in peace, had

CHAPTER ELEVEN

ceased to give birth to any other children I paid little attention to the advice of R.Judah he-Hassid (not to name a son in memory of his deceased brother) and consequently the second son too didn't survive, a fact I have already stated. However, the birth of this second son was a source of great joy to me, for as I have already stated my wife had not had any children for several years. Hence I arranged a sumptuous banquet on the day he was circumcised for at that time I could afford it, and since I had recently settled in Altona, I decided to invite the most important members of the Three Communities, which was duly arranged. R. Ezekiel the Presiding Rabbi of the Bet Din was Sandak (godfather) and all the guests were extremely pleased. Nor did I forget to invite some poor folk whom I considered worthy people and who (incidentally) attended my Minyan. I also arranged a dinner on the third day (subsequent to the circumcision) and for a group of students to study daily a chapter of Mishnayot both in the morning and evening. Throughout this period I gave them all a fee out of the memory I had received from London, with the proviso that they studied regularly. I continued this arrangement until they failed to meet the conditions I had stipulated. Nevertheless they still demanded the fee, but I sent them packing and distributed the cash (previously reserved for those scholars) to a deserving charity.

As long as I had young children who required tuition in Torah-learning l employed a resident teacher and paid scant attention to what this arrangement would cost me, for this had been my practice in the past, both in Broda and Emden, and I now continued it in Altona. After an interval of two and a quarter years my wife gave birth to my daughter Esther, may she be spared. She was so named since she was born during Purim. Subsequently my wife gave birth to another daughter who, may God spare us, was born deformed and died within a month of her birth. Then my wife gave birth to a perfectly normal girl whom I named after her mother, my first wife, who died a week after the birth of this child.

At the birth my wife was attended by three doctors at great expense to me. She came from illustrious priestly stock and was a woman of valour and strong personality. In fact, I can say of her what Rabbi Judah said to his son respecting the latter's mother, "she was quick-tempered, but was quickly pacified." (TB. Yevamot 63b) For on many occasions I found her temper more bitter than death (cf.Eccles.7:26). Sometimes she would be cantankerous because I had invited an important guest for a meal, and on another occasion when I had secured the services of a resident tutor for my son and daughter who would also act as a scribe, she was so incensed that I was compelled to send that person away before the agreed period (for his services) had concluded and to rent a room for him elsewhere, for that man was in a turmoil. Although at that period I earned a livelihood comparatively easy she had proved cantankerous when I was badly off and searched around for a livelihood. When she lived in Broda she secured the services of a tutor for my eldest son the cost of which proved far beyond my means, yet I agreed to virtually all she did. Indeed, not only did I refrain from humiliating her but, on the contrary, I was pleased with her. This had always been my attitude, so that when she now protested (over my hiring a tutor) I kept quiet for the sake of domestic peace. In fact, there were many similar domestic squabbles. She was particularly cantankerous with the home-helpers, so that relations between them were never peaceful. Again, when I bought the house in which I presently live there was so much strife between us that I was almost sick of life, but I realised I was to blame for all these troubles. But apart from her cantankerousness she was a fine and intelligent lady who involved herself in charitable activities, caring for the poor and afflicted. When I was away from home she helped rear her children in the ways of Torah and conducted her home according to the highest standards of our Faith. Moreover, she worked hard in her business activities and for a few years in Altona acted successfully as a money-lender, though she began with very little capital not only did I not lose anything from this business activity but it received the Almighty's blessing as I have previously described. Her one fault was her tendency to lose her temper for the slightest thing.

On the day of her death Rosh Chodesh 1739 I had my first

CHAPTER ELEVEN

quarrel with the lay-leaders of Altona. For when a few years preceding her death we buried my baby daughter, a fact I have previously mentioned, the leaders of the community requested the usual fee imposed on all members of the community (for burial), for the Communal Council regarded me as a bona-fide member of the community. In fact, I paid my share of the communal meat-tax. But when it came to my first wife's burial I was asked for a surety to cover the cost. This increased my sorrow and anguish over the loss of the wife of my youth. Yet I was compelled to give this surety so as not to delay her being laid in her final resting place. However, after a time they returned my security to me and made no further demands. They behaved in the same way when, for my many sins, I lost my second wife and some of my children. May the Almighty blessed be He remove his wrath from me and from His people; "may death vanish in life eternal ".(Is.25:8)

After the incident-subsequent to the death of my first wife I attended a meeting of the Communal Council and asked them how they proposed-to consider my status (in the community). Was I to be regarded as a visitor or a fully-fledged member to which I had a presumptive right in that my fathers, z"l, had lived in Altona. "Nevertheless," I continued, "should you require earnest-money from me please let me know and I will pay it." At that Yokel Hausen jumped up from his seat and asked me most impudently as to my intention; was I planning to eject him from his respected position? (If the latter were true) then who he asked wanted this to happen? Alternatively (he continued) by whose permission had I come to the Council meeting in order to obtain the right to live in Altona? Although his colleagues (on the Council) reprimanded him (Y.Hausen) and told him to hold his tongue, my answer was that when I had arrived in Altona there was no record of my being one of the community's lay-leaders (Yokel Hausen was a recent arrival in the Council). For after the death of his uncle, Joel Shaw, Yokel had assumed his uncle's place on the Council and for some time he emulated his uncle's foolish attitude of manifesting baseless hatred towards me. Then when R.Eibeschuetz arrived in the community

MEGILAT SEFER

Yokel lost the privilege of being elected to the communal leadership. With the Almighty's help I will describe later how Yokel became my friend. Ultimately the lay-leaders of the community at the time of my re-settlement in Altona granted me permission to live in the community and consequently exempted me from any fee. They returned my security to me and henceforth treated me as a fully-fledged member.

A few years before the death of my (first) wife, may she rest in peace, I sent away my dear son, Meshullam Zalman, who was the apple of my eye, just as I had done with my eldest son whom I had sent away from Emden. I was compelled to act in this way with this fine boy (Meshullam Zalman) who when only eleven years old began to study the Tur with the commentary of the Bet Yosef. He was a highly intelligent person and of most comely appearance, but I saw little future for him in this spiritually arid region, particularly regarding arranging a suitable marriage that would enable him to continue his Torah-studies. Consequently, much against my will I finally agreed to send him away, initially to Glogau and subsequently to Poland. His departure caused me as much pain as a nail embedded in the flesh, though I had spent a considerable amount on his behalf. For I had maintained a tutor for him in my home, and even when he was living away from home I spent more than was necessary on his behalf. Moreover, I expended a hundred ducats towards his dowry and handed this amount (for which I had obligated myself) to the lay-leader David Leverdin (See "She'elot Ya'avetz Pt.2.No.44) when he was on his way to the fair at Pressburg. However, on his return Leverdin informed me that he had lost the hundred ducats with which I had entrusted him butt, he said, he wanted to repay that sum and immediately gave me twenty ducats (on account). After some years had elapsed I pressed him for the balance as he had promised, for by his own admission he had acted negligently regarding the money with he had been entrusted. But he was prepared to give me another twenty ducats on condition that he wouldn't have to pay any more and I was forced to agree so as not to incur a greater loss for he would have proved a hard opponent (in litigation) nor was I inclined

CHAPTER ELEVEN

to be involved in the degradation of a law-suit. Ultimately therefore I had to accept forty ducats (in total) from him. I now had to make up the balance of the hundred ducats that I had promised my son.

He (my son) had made a fine marriage in Brody (Galicia) to the daughter of a God-fearing Talmid Chacham but till now he has not been blessed with children. May the Almighty grant me the privilege of seeing Meshullam the father of a fine family! But, thank God, my eldest son had a family, though none of his sons survived. However his two daughters made successful marriages. May the Almighty in His kindness grant R.Meir (my son) the privilege of seeing fine grandsons.

(N.B. R.Meir's two daughters were Miriam and Rachel; the younger one was married to the Rabbi of Medzibezh, Dov Behr Cohen Rappaport.)

In 1738 I acquired a fine house a fact which provoked further envy and enmity. Firstly, the previous occupant contended with me although initially I had agreed not to pursue the purchase of the house if he wanted to acquire it. In fact there was no need to make this arrangement since the house in question belonged to a Gentile and was being sold by public auction. Nevertheless I acted beyond the line of strict justice and even enquired of several people: whether he (the Jewish tenant) declined to buy the house. Previously another Gentile had made a particular offer for the house and the owners had agreed to it. However, when that Gentile himself assured me that he considered the price he had offered was too high (and that he was no longer interested) I made a bid to acquire it from the Legal possessor by increasing the previous offer and it was accepted. But when purchase had been completed the Jewish tenant accused me of buying his property and thus gave the impression that I was God forbid transgressing a Torah principle. However, I had witnesses to support my contention and even his (the Jewish tenant's) children denied their father's allegation so that he failed to deprive me of the house on which I had to spend a considerable sum. For it was in a very bad state of disrepair when I first bought it from the Gentile who had owned it for several years. It had been built by a religious Sephardi who had inscribed the Tetragrammaton on the wall, miraculously this had not been deleted. Had the house come into the possession of another Gentile then that certainly would have happened. I therefore regarded its purchase of religious significance, especially since I had arranged to gather a minyan there (under certain conditions) and a room for my own studies. I therefore spent thousands of Reichthalers before it (the house) had the appearance of being newly constructed. I also had a Mikveh constructed in the house and this was filled by rain water. In fact this Mikveh had to be repaired at least on three occasions before it was sufficiently cemented so as to retain the water. In addition, with God's help, I built a fine Succah adjoining the house and a proper toilet on the top floor. I had to bear the cost of all this apart from many other internal and external repairs.

Some eighteen years ago (1739) the local Chevra Kadisha wanted to buy my house and offered me seven thousand Shock Heller, but I insisted on one thousand golden ducats and negotiations ceased. Subsequently on my return from Amsterdam, I spent a good deal more on further improvements and repairs to this house. My first wife lived in it for nine months and left me with a baby girl for whom I had to hire a wet-nurse. The child at first appeared to be perfectly healthy but, for our sins, it died a few months later. During the period I was a widower I published my book "Iggeret Bikoret" which had been lying around since I first wrote it (1736). It was published in 1739.

From the very moment I became a widower I was inundated with proposals of marriage to respectable and wealthy ladies, but I was not interested in money. Now let me relate some remarkable facts which are hardly credible. Yet let Heaven be my witness if my story is not true. For my sole intention is to relate the events as they occurred and thereby clearly illustrate our Sages' sentiment viz. that "Marriages are made in Heaven" and that "there is no wisdom nor understanding nor counsel against the Lord."(Prov.21:30). This is what happened; when it came to my two marriages after the death of

CHAPTER ELEVEN

my first wife, a considerable number of people wanted to arrange a marriage for me whereby I could have obtained a dowry of many thousands of Reichthalers. For example, some wanted to arrange a marriage for me with a widow of Prague who would have brought a dowry of ten thousand gold pieces. Yet I was not interested in such a figure (if it meant) acquiring a wife from a distant country about which I knew very little. Incidentally regarding my second wife who was widowed in the same year in which I lost my first wife, and who had a dowry of more than three thousand gold pieces, my marriage to her was initially so arranged that I would be given the above-mentioned sum in ready-cash. Then R. Hertz who was the Presiding Rabbi of the Bet Din of Mannheim wanted me marry his daughter and to give me two thousand Reich Thaler as a dowry. Moreover, he promised to obtain the Rabbinate of Glogau for me but I was not interested. The widow of Prague whom I previously mentioned was reputed to be attractive in person, character and piety, apart from being a youthful personality and a member of one of the finest families in German Jewry. Consequently she had many suitors who were most keen to marry her but they were unsuccessful. I too had no desire to marry her, for at that time I was not interested in marrying a widow since such a person, was denied me (cf. 1.Sam. 21:6 & TB. Pesachim 112a) indeed, virtually forbidden to me for the reason stated by our Sages. Moreover, I did not believe the marriage-broker who seemed to exaggerate the lady's virtues.

It was about this time that my brother, R.Ephraim, may he be granted life, had travelled from Lvov to Glogau where my brother-in-law, R.Aryeh Leib (later appointed to the Rabbinate of Amsterdam. Ed.) was the Presiding Rabbi of the Bet Din. This was the first visit my brother had made to Germany. When the news of my (first) wife's death reached Glogau both R.Ephraim and R.Aryeh Leib proposed I should marry my niece (my present wife) and informed me of their suggestion by the post. They both praised the young lady (my niece) highly for indeed she had a fine reputation. Consequently I wanted them to proceed with finalising arrangements (for the betrothal) since I was finding it difficult to be a widower with little children to care for. My brother however, returned to Lvov without mentioning the proposed marriage. I was not sure whether this was because he had actually forgotten all about it, or whether he had changed his mind. Hence, the matter was left in abeyance and I too thought no more about it, particularly since many people had warned me against marrying a young lady from Poland because, they argued, German Jews did not find the character and nature of Polish Jews agreeable.

During these events the Almighty took a hand in my affairs. A rabbinic scholar arrived in Altona from Halberstadt named R. Ephraim Apstrod, a member of the Halberstadt Bet-haMidrash and presently a Dayan of the province of Hesse. I had known this man from the time I had journeyed through Hesse and when he arrived in Altona he again made my acquaintance. I knew him to be a fine Talmudic scholar and a Godfearing individual. He had never visited these parts until now when he was the guest of the lay-leader Yokel Hausen. I had no idea why he was visiting Altona, nor had I heard that he had achieved anything during this visit, except his friendly visit to me when he behaved like an old acquaintance. We first conversed in Torah-learning and of affairs in general when we touched upon the subject of Sarah, the daughter of the lay-leader Haftali Herz of Halberstadt who, it seemed, was still unmarried. His praises of her were far more exaggerated than those of the marriage-broker to whom I have already referred. She was (he stated) possessed of the highest feminine virtues but above all, she was a deeply religious lady and therefore deserving of much praise. To confirm his observations he (R.Apstrod) proceeded to my Ark which contained a Sefer Torah and taking an object he raised his hand (as was the procedure for taking an oath) and swore that what he had said(about Sarah Herz) was true and in no way exaggerated. On the contrary, (he asserted) he really had not done justice to her many virtues and sterling qualities of character.

In this way R.Apstrod won me over and bound me with such bonds of affection (for Sarah) that I acceded to his request to be

CHAPTER ELEVEN

affianced (to Sarah Herz). I ignored all the promises that the other marriage-brokers had made saying all this is the Lord's doing, she indeed, is the wife whom He has designated for me and henceforth I did not swerve from this belief. In fact I was so eager to marry Sarah that I paid no attention to what she was bringing me (as a dowry) except the sum mentioned when this marriage was first mooted when I was promised three thousand gold pieces by her family, a fact I have already stated. This was the sum originally promised, but ultimately because of the high reputation in which she was held I agreed to half that sum. For the original capital (three thousand gold pieces) had depreciated to that level in the period she had remained unmarried. Moreover, she had spent a considerable amount of the original capital, quite apart from the money for the loans she had contracted. In the end therefore, she only had half of the sum first mentioned for a dowry. Indeed I did not even receive that amount, yet I paid little attention to this but was agreeable to all conditions (laid down) since love disregards the rules of dignified conduct. Hence I argued, I am agreeable to having a fine God-fearing lady as my wife. When previously I had sought the name of the lady whom the Almighty had designated as my wife I learned (through a dream) that her name was Sarah consequently I now agreed to this marriage with the assistance of the Almighty, particularly since it was my own niece (Sarah) who had been waiting for me.

On Rosh Chodesh Nissan 1740 I married my second wife (Sarah) who brought me fifteen hundred Reichthalers as a dowry, as had been promised. But not all this sum was in ready cash, for she brought (as a dowry) movables which had been valued at fifteen hundred Reichthalers. Nevertheless when the dowry was finally delivered into my hands I paid little attention to all this for I had no wish for anything which had been acquired unjustly, hence I accepted half the amount I had originally been promised. I was therefore ready to overlook this deficiency though in fact, it was really less than the half I had finally agreed to accept. I must admit however, that this business caused me some annoyance and provoked some discord between my wife and me. For though there were other conditions stated in the second document of our betrothal there was one item I had no wish to forgo viz. a condition whereby I was to receive an additional third of the assessed dowry. For it seemed unfair that I should suffer a double penalty for my kindness and generosity in not insisting on the original dowry. If my wife could not have brought me half of what she had promised, or if all her worldly goods had been lost between the completion of the document of betrothal and our marriage God forbid that I should cause her embarrassment because of this. But (on the other hand) why should I be made to suffer an additional financial loss for which I was in no way obligated.

On the contrary according to the Mishnah when a wife brings a dowry (in kind) which must be assessed, then the corresponding sum (in the Ketubah) for which the husband is obligated is reduced by a fifth (of that assessment). Moreover, when our Sages enjoin the husband to reduce his obligation (when the dowry is in kind) he must not increase the latter, for the maximum addition to the statutory sum in the Ketubah must not be more than a third of the dowry (when the latter is already in cash). My agreement to the betrothal did not involve such conditions. Because they had forced me in the knowledge that I would not humiliate my wife, should I be expected to suffer financially? I never thought they would behave in this way, but the iniquitous middlemen who were members of my wife's family, adopted a bellicose attitude towards me because of this situation even though my wife seemed to show little concern. But this business caused some ill-feeling between us, for l felt she was looking for a financial advantage (God forbid!) since her family were most concerned about my financial obligations even though it was uncertain whether I would collect the promised dowry. On the other hand, I myself paid little attention to what should have demanded my attention viz. the real value of the dowry. Consequently, in no way was I prepared to obligate myself to more than eighteen hundred Reich Thaler which included the additional third of the value of the dowry in ready-cash which my wife brought.

But despite all this my wife never lacked for anything, for I denied her nothing she desired, though as a consequence, I imposed

CHAPTER ELEVEN

on myself a heavier financial burden than I could afford. Still, I gave way to all her caprices believing she had been so treated by her first husband who was a wealthy man. I therefore accepted an inordinate financial burden hoping (thereby) that in place of this the Almighty would show as kindness by reimbursing my losses.

Initially, things seemed to augur well, for the Nordasi family helped me with a present of cash when I had agreed to the marriage whilst Leib (of) London sent me two hundred and ten pounds after the marriage. Henceforth, however, their kindness towards me ceased. Yet I had to bear considerable expenses as well as. having to provide a large and expensive wedding reception for the communal dignitaries and the many members of my family.

Consequently, whatever cash I possessed proved insufficient. Moreover, even if I made some profit from one source of income, I suffered a proportional loss from another source. But despite this everyone thought I was a very wealthy man, particularly after I had married my second wife who was reputed to be extremely wealthy and (so it was believed) had brought me a considerable fortune far more than the dowry for which she was obligated. Hence I found I had many friends who sought their self-aggrandisement, whilst all the swindlers gave me securities (for loans) which were really the property of their friends. Many falsely claimed the sureties to be their own property apart from which the market-value of these sureties was far less than the loan made on them.

Miraculously I suffered no more than the loss of the loan, for I could have been placed in a most hazardous position. For as time elapsed and the debt had failed to pay either the capital or the increasing interest but simply deferred payment, I wanted to realise the cash value of the securities from the Lombard agent. In this way I thought I would retrieve my money since the assessed value of those securities was quite considerable. I was therefore prepared to redeem them, but had I done so that Gentile (the Lombard agent) would have falsely accused me of falsifying those securities and who knows whether, God forbid all my possessions would have sufficed to save me from the punishment which the royal court would have meted out to me. When however, the swindler learned of my intention he came to me and disclosed his deception saying he had forged these documents and consequently cautioned me against demanding payment on the securities for (in fact) he held no security whatsoever against the Lombard agent, and never had any knowledge of it. The swindler too, was in a hazardous position but my liabilities were far greater than his, for the local judiciary had directed their attention to the rich viz. those from whom they realised they could extort cash, and those were certainly not the young and penniless. I must therefore recite a blessing thanking God for a calamity which turned out to be a blessing, since I had to suffer the loss of the capital I previously mentioned. Yet Blessed be He who delivered me from the grasp of the local (Gentile) judiciary.

This incident was comparatively minor in the context of my other losses which amounted to many thousands (of Reichthalers). I incurred the latter because of the fraudulent sureties which were handed to me by swindlers who were only concerned with their own gains when they encouraged me to lend money to Gentiles whom I did not really know. I therefore suffered considerable (financial) loss through this type of business. (Indeed) words cannot do justice to these deceptions and were I to give a full account of the latter it would require a separate book.

Nevertheless I must mention a few facts One incident I now re-call was particularly distressing to me for through it I learned the character of the (Gentile) judiciary, may the Almighty deliver us from, their hands. This incident I will now describe. As a security one of the swindlers gave me some Lombard Notes which emanated from Hamburg. For six months this swindler had paid daily visits to me urging me to lend money on that security, but I constantly reprimanded him saying, "Just leave me alone, I do not want to lend money to Gentiles for I have already suffered much financial loss through such transactions." But despite my protestations he (the swindler) behaved like a raging sea and without respite he made every effort to persuade me to accede to his request though I had previously sent him packing. He obtained the support of a number

CHAPTER ELEVEN

of his friends to get me to agree to lend the money (on these securities) to which was added a Bill of Indebtedness of the Gentile who was a skilled manufacture of sugar. Being outnumbered I agreed to send one of my trusted friends on whom I could rely and to whom I paid a fee, to visit the factory of that Gentile. Thereby my objections were removed and I was promised a definite profit. Consequently I redeemed the securities which were lying in a chest. Subsequently the Gentile (of Hamburg) the source of the Lombard Notes appeared with the authority of the (Gentile) Judicial authorities and issued a summons against the Jewish middle-man since it was claimed the latter had fraudulently obtained the receipt of the Lombard Notes and that he (the Gentile) had not received any payment from me. Consequently the local Judiciary summoned me (to appear before them) and declared that the Jewish middle-man had to compensate the Gentile for the losses he had sustained whilst the security should remain in my possession as a surety for the money owing to me. For the Judiciary realised I was not the guilty party but had acted with complete integrity. Hence the court ruled that I should not incur any fine but I was duty bound to retain the security and not return it to the Jewish middle-man until he had repaid the money which I had originally given him on that security. These facts were recorded in the ledger of the Judiciary and I had to pay a fee for this registration.

Now let me tell you what occurred on the following day, an incident which is virtually incredible. It was the week in which Passover fell so on that particular day my family were involved in house-cleaning. My wife, may she rest in peace, with a servant, were in the back-yard whilst I was resting upstairs. There was no one on the ground floor except a Gentile who had been employed to plaster the rooms of that floor which led onto the street. It was at this precise moment that the Gentile who was the owner of the security entered my house together with his wife and stole the chest (which contained the security) with the assistance of some other Gentiles. (The chest was lying in the passage-way which led on to the main street, and because its weight was equivalent to the total weight of several people we had not worried about its safety).

The Gentile and his wife were also assisted by some of our neighbours in effecting this theft. (As I have already stated) none of the family were around at the time so that no one saw or had any idea of the theft except the Gentile who had been employed to plaster the ground floor of the house. He realised what had happened but did not raise the alarm until the thieves had taken the chest and had left the house. He then hurried to the backyard and informed my wife, may she rest in peace. His behaviour can be explained by the fact that he did not want to be suspected of the theft and therefore by acting as he did he would be cleared of any suspicion. He said to my wife, "there were some people upstairs whom I didn't recognise and they took the chest which was standing near the front door" My wife and family quickly hurried upstairs and saw that the chest had in fact been removed despite her weight (she was with child at that time) she rushed into the street with such alacrity that she had already reached the next street before the rest of the family caught up with her. Many fellow-Jews came to her aid, but the Gentile fought with every one of them hitting and wounding anyone who tried to retrieve the chest from his possession. One of his victims nearly lost his eye and I forthwith compensated him to the tune of two Reichthalers. My wife, may she rest in peace, was also injured by the staff of the thief. But thank God no one involved in this affray sustained any fatal injuries, though this might easily have happened but for a special act of Providence by the Almighty blessed be He, who protects and delivers (from danger). Finally a group of guards was summoned and they took the Gentile and his wife as well as the chest into custody. Subsequently we appeared before the local court which was then presided over by Schumber, and claimed we had been burgled. The presiding Judge (Schumber) knew what had transpired on the previous day when the Court had decided I should be held responsible for the chest (which contained the security) and that it should remain in my possession until I had been repaid the capital and interest which I was legally entitled. Now (I complained) these people had come from a foreign region to one under Imperial

CHAPTER ELEVEN

jurisdiction and forcibly removed the chest from my possession just like a common burglar. Indeed, (I continued) if we had not learned of the theft soon after it had occurred I could have been sued for returning the legal owner's security before I had been repaid (which would have been contrary to the ruling of the Court). Moreover, (I argued) the defendant could have put any value he placed on that security (since with its theft, there would have been no way of confirming that valuation). Then, (I continued) to crown it all, he (the defendant) had attacked my wife and friends in the street and had almost killed some of them.

The Presiding Judge assured me he would deal with the thief according to the dictates of justice and that the defendant would have to compensate us on five counts. Moreover until this compensation had been paid the defendant and his wife would remain in custody. Soon after we celebrated Pesach firmly convinced that all was well and that the defendant would not be released from custody until I had received compensation. So soon after Pesach I went to the Court to demand justice from the thief but learned he had already been released. For the (Presiding) Judge, acting as he pleased, had appropriated the compensation (made by the defendant) and then released him. I protested at this injustice but no one paid any attention to me. Thus the principle of Justice was subverted in several ways. For now (it would appear) our homes were no longer safe from the marauding of foreigners and how much less safe would we be from the misdemeanours of the local inhabitants, for they had been accomplices in this misdeed. It were better (I complained) to live in a desert than in an Imperial city where there was no justice against thieves who venture forth to kill, a city in which "the tents of the robbers prosper" (Job 12:6) while its innocent inhabitants lie in fear and terror. The Judge however, shut his ears to my cries of protest and then was no redress for his misdeed. All that was returned to us was the chest which was later sold, though not without some difficulty, before I returned home.

Then there was the case of the Gentile of Hamburg who

owed me six hundred Reichthalers (this loan was effected through some Jewish middle-men and was one of the ways I tried to do business with the dowry my second wife had brought me and who had advised me to make this particular loan). I had obtained permission from the Hamburg authorities to take some of the contents of the debtor's home as a security and had delegated a Gentile to perform this function on my behalf. This person however, impaired my position by advising me to delay the debtor's repayment and eventually I forfeited the capital outlay. When later I met the Gentile who had been my debtor and reprimanded him for his behaviour he replied, "the loss of the loan was entirely your responsibility, for you thought the delegate you appointed was a man of integrity. But he accepted a bribe I offered him and I was free of him." It was by such business transactions with Gentile debtors that the dowry of my second wife, may she rest in peace, was eventually lost. Again I lent another Gentile of Altona about one hundred Reichthalers and when he defaulted in payment I had him imprisoned; I was then obliged to pay him five Schock-Heller per week for his food. I maintained this payment for almost six months until a point where I could no longer tolerate it and had to request the local Judiciary to release the debtor (and I had to forfeit repayment of the loan).

Then a Jewish swindler from London masquerading as a wealthy man took two rings from me on credit. These rings which my wife, may she rest in peace, had given me (as part of her dowry) were worth one hundred Reichthalers, but that swindler absconded with them. In the same way the greater part of my income from abroad was lost through loans to both Gentiles and Jews, this quite apart from cash which was stolen from me. Thus on one occasion a gold watch was stolen from me in my own house. Previously I had been offered eighty Reich Thalers for it, but had declined to accept this sum. I searched high and low for this watch but failed to find it. Indeed, I lost many items through such thefts, for example, one night I was burgled of all the tin utensils of my kitchen, and these were worth a tidy sum. On another occasion thieves took all the washing

CHAPTER ELEVEN

which was hanging at the back of the house. Similarly I suffered the loss of several brass and silver items, so that "I was robbed and oppressed" (cf.Deut.28:33) for the greater part of my life. Indeed, I was persecuted in so many ways that it would be impossible for me to put it all in writing!

In 1740 I was bereaved of my son Tzvi Hirsch, may he rest in peace. When he was only seven years old he had studied Talmud with Rashi and Tosefot. I think his teacher who took him on a trip to Hamburg on a cold winter's (day) caused his death. For he was perfectly healthy when he left home, but during the journey there was a sudden storm followed by snow and a heavy frost which badly affected the boy. Though his illness did not occur immediately after a cold, he gradually became weaker and when asked what was wrong he just cried and could not say what was ailing him. Apparently his internal organs were so badly affected by this journey that ultimately he became seriously ill and, may the Almighty spare us, as the result of a burst blood-vessel he suffered a nose-bleed which lasted several days. All treatment proved of no avail, for though there was a slight respite (in the loss of blood) the bleeding continued until his unblemished soul departed, for our many sins, at the termination of Shabbat Parashat Mishpatim and my funeral oration for him was based on that text. It was then that I published my "Yetiv Pitgom" in memory of my father, and I mentioned my son's passing in that work.

Subsequently my son, Meshullam Zalman, may the Almighty spare him, was married and I sent him a gift worth a Hundred ducats through the agency of Reb David, may he rest in peace. However he (Reb David) lost this gift so that I had to send my son another gift of a Hundred ducats in cash. In the meantime I was involved in the publication of my book "She'elot Ya'avetz" which I had begun to write in 1739. Then my second wife gave birth to twin girls one of whom died when she was nearly six. Her twin sister was Nechama, may she be spared for many years. Subsequently my (second) wife gave birth to another girl who lived for a few months and suddenly died. Then my wife lost a son from her first husband. Four years after our marriage my second wife died on Rosh Chodesh Adar 1743. At that time all my family was struck with illness and I likewise became so dangerously ill that the doctors despaired of my recovery. In fact, those who tended me, as well as the doctor, thought my end had come. This occurred at the termination of Shabbat Parashat Shirah (Beshalach) which corresponded to the fifteenth of Shevat 1743. On that Shabbat everyone knew that I was dangerously ill and the entire membership of the Three Communities were concerned, for at that time I had no enemies and was beloved by all. They demonstrated their deep affection for me by offering special prayers in all the Synagogues and promised donations to charity for my recovery. On the night of the termination of that Shabbat I was tied to the bed, having been give a medicine to produce perspiration. That medicine proved so excessive that I became terribly weak and was almost on the point of death. The people around my bed were frightened that this would indeed occur and that I would die. However, I was, thank God, fully conscious and gazed at them though I did not realise who they were for I felt terribly weak. They then called the doctor who despaired of my recovery for he could not discern any pulse, and because my situation appeared hopeless he had no compunction in giving me a full cup of wine. When I drank this I felt revived, with of course the help of the Almighty. So that in the early hours of the morning "he who was bent down was speedily loosed" (cf.Is.51:14) and the Holy One Blessed be He did not permit me to descend dying in to the pit" (ibid.)

Thus, the "spirit of Jacob was fully restored"(cf.Gen.45:27) and I was a living miracle both in the eyes of those who heard and those who saw it; indeed, they felt they had virtually witnessed the revival of the dead; Blessed be He who revives the dead and who heals the sick. I vowed to observe this night as an annual Yom Tov, and for some years at the termination of Shabbat Shirah as well as on the 15th of Shevat I used to arrange a special meal for the poor and arranged a minyan in order to thank the Almighty, Blessed be He for His kindness to me. This custom continued until I became involved

CHAPTER ELEVEN

in the struggle with Eibeschuetz which deprived me of friends quite apart from the fact that I could no longer afford it. Thus "all joy is darkened" (Is. 24:11) and consequently I have had to temporarily abandon the observance of this special Yom Tov. When however the Almighty will look upon my affliction (Ps.119:159) and grant me the privilege of experiencing consolation I will fulfil my promises before all his people. (cf.Ps.116:14) So that in my glory I may sing praises to You and not be silent, 0 Lord my God, and I will give thanks to Thee for ever. (cf. Ps. 30:12)

After the Holy One Blessed be He had restored me to health and I had abandoned my sick-bed my wife too, became ill, but then her illness passed and she began to regain her strength. So much so that everyone thought she was out of danger and so it appeared to those who were taking care of her during her illness. However, these very same people actually caused her death by giving her a chocolate drink to strengthen her. I knew nothing of this for I was still very weak as a result of my own serious illness and was resting in a room on the second floor of my house, whilst my wife was lying in a room on the ground floor. Hence I knew nothing of her situation though I had been informed that she had survived her illness and was on the mend. This was the actual situation for the doctor had assumed that she was fully recovered and no longer attended her since he maintained she required no further treatment. But she suddenly became very ill and lapsed into unconsciousness, may the Almighty spare us. When the doctor was summoned he was shocked and asked what had happened for as he said, "only a few days ago I left her fully recovered." Subsequently, the facts about the above-mentioned (chocolate) drink emerged and (we learned) that this particular type of drink was highly unsuitable for a sick person shortly after their recovery from a serious illness. Indubitably, this had caused her sudden relapse and her subsequent death may the Almighty spare us!

This occurred during the trade-fair at Frankfurt-on-Oder and the sad news of my second wife's death soon reached there. It so happened that my brother R. Ephraim (Ashkenazi) was visiting the fair at that time. In fact, this was his second visit to Germany since

1740 when, as I have previously stated, he visited Glogau following the death of my first wife. He was now paying a second visit to Germany because his daughter, who is presently my third wife was bespoken to the late Rabbi Joseph, the Presiding Rabbi of the Bet Din of Hanau. My brother felt obliged to entrust the dowry he had promised R. Joseph with certain conditions, to a trustworthy person in Frankfurt. The marriage however did not take place, and it was God's will that my brother was prevented from retrieving the money he had given as a dowry, after arrangements for the marriage had not materialised. Moreover, R. Joseph of Hanau had subsequently passed away and my brother was visiting Frankfurt to retrieve the dowry which he intended to trade and then return home to Lvov. In fact he almost had one foot on the coach for the return journey together with other merchants of his community who likewise had visited the fair at Frankfurt-on-Oder, when the news of the death of my second wife reached that city. Some of my brothers' associates informed him of the sad news and suggested that he could do nothing else but go to Altona with the people who hailed from that city and who had visited the fair. "You must go," they said, "to your brother the Rabbi of Emden who has just lost his (second) wife." "Moreover", they continued, "your eldest daughter is still unmarried, and it seems God's will that she was destined for your brother. So hurry and make a suitable settlement for your daughter for the Almighty has destined this match and the time has come for it to materialise." My brother took their advice and hastened to visit me here (in Emden). I had not expected him, but the Almighty had brought him to my very doorstep, for the Almighty's plan had to be fulfilled. "He spoke and it happened," refers to a lady of my family, "He commands and it was fulfilled," refers to children. "O Lord by these things men live." (Is.38:16) (I prayed) from her may I establish a perpetual fabric.

When I realised that all this was divinely ordained my brother and I agreed to draw up a document of betrothal on the seventh of Nisan,1743, a day of good omen for, (according to Num.7:48) it was the day on which the Prince of the children of Ephraim brought his offering for the dedication of the Altar of the Sanctuary. My brother

CHAPTER ELEVEN

promised me a generous dowry of seven hundred ducats and also undertook to supply his daughter with fine clothes; for this was customary in this part of the world. Regarding the dowry, my brother kept his word, but deducted twenty ducats for charity. However, he failed to keep his promise concerning my wife's clothes, but brought her almost bereft of such clothing and other articles that a lady requires. I therefore had to give her the clothes of my second wife and consequently I could not leave my daughter any memento from her mother, either one of her mother's dresses or any jewellery. For in order to avoid any ill-feeling I had to give the jewellery to my brother's daughter, my third wife, and we were married mid-way through Kislev,1744. I was so delighted with her since I realised the Almighty had destined me for this highly intelligent lady who was deeply religious, learned as well as being a member of my own family, quite apart from her fine lineage on her mother's side, that I lost the copy of my wedding speech which I had entitled "Shemesh Zedakah." In it I acknowledged the Almighty's righteousness in curing me of my illness, and He made the sun of my righteousness arise "with healing in its wings." (cf. Mal.3:20)

It was at my marriage to my brother's daughter that I again experienced the avariciousness of Rabbi Ezekiel (Katzenellenbogen) which was insatiable, for he felt no embarrassment in again demanding a fee for the erection of the Chuppah even before I had received any dowry from my brother. R. Ezekiel was quite aware that I was marrying (a third time) for religious reasons yet he showed no deference for Torah seeing that my Rabbinic forebears were among the founders of the community. He also chose to forget how I defended him in my book "Iggeret Bikoret", for although he did not deserve such consideration I spent a considerable amount of money in having it published though I made no profit whatsoever. In fact until the present time I have not realised a tenth of my capital expenditure (on that publication). Moreover, both he and his children had gained financially from me, particularly since on my second marriage he had received a tidy sum of money from me so that he was like a "publican who is not limited by legal stipulations" (cf. Bava

MEGILAT SEFER

Kama 113a). I gladly and unhesitatingly gave him that money for he (R. Ezekiel) believed I had become more affluent than I was formerly reputed to be. He (presumably) based this belief on the text in Proverbs, "there is he who makes himself rich, yet he has nothing" (Prov.13:7) consequently I made no fuss about it.

However, on this (my third marriage) when he must have known for some time that I had sustained severe financial losses through the swindlers in his community, and that I was now marrying my brother's daughter, a marriage in which there could have been no presumption of wealth, therefore I thought this was an occasion when respect for my family's reputation would conquer his avariciousness and he would not make any financial demands of me even if he were inconvenienced. Moreover, (I thought) in respecting me he would be showing respect for Torah I might have given him his usual fee and perhaps an additional sum. These were my very words to the official who demanded the marriage: fee from me,(for I wanted) him to leave me alone and not display such behaviour to me. For my brother would not have considered it to my credit should he have learned that R. Ezekiel should regard me so disrespectfully. This was not the way a person such as I would have been treated in Poland. Consequently I asked R. Ezekiel to forgo the fee so that he would be considered a generous person, whilst at the same time he would be doing something honourable in the eyes of the Almighty. Yet, despite my arguments he (R. Ezekiel) would not set up the Chuppah until I had paid the requisite fee. I was therefore forced to bow to his will so that I then understood his disparaging characteristic in financial matters viz. that he could not forgo the slightest profit and that his craving for money never ceased (cf.Is.14:4). When it was my good fortune to marry my brother's daughter I was almost bankrupt for I had no ready cash except for a few insignificant loans I had made on securities apart from some merchandise. When therefore my brother, long may he live, gave me two hundred ducats for my dowry I thought I would try my hand at some new business. Hence I forwarded this money to Reb Leib in London (with instructions) that he should buy some fancy-goods on

CHAPTER ELEVEN

my behalf. At first he declined to send me any goods but made inane excuses (for this reluctance) and retained my money for no cogent reasons, but finally he agreed to my proposal. I had previously sent him the cash on Purim, and on the Eve of Yom Kippur I received from him six dozen brass snuff tins through the agency of a certain sailor. I was terribly annoyed and made a considerable commotion, for Reb Leib had written to inform me that I was to receive some silver clocks for that was the arrangement I had originally made with him. I therefore suspected the sailor of theft and duplicity, or that he had exchanged the goods meant for me with another person's goods. Ultimately however, it transpired that the sailor was in no way remiss in the way he had fulfilled his commission but that the fault lay with Reb Leib for he had forgotten all about the clocks which were still in his possession.

Subsequently he sent me the clocks during Chanukah and with the Almighty's help I made a handsome profit from the sale of these goods. Had Reb Leib been genuinely concerned for my welfare by constantly sending me goods l required and which I had ordered from him and had he been keen to remit my orders punctually, I would easily have obtained an adequate livelihood and perhaps with the Almighty's help have made considerable profit. However, all my business dealings with him were far from easy and involved much delay. Moreover, he occasionally forwarded me goods which I had not requested; for example, he sent me some gold watch-cases which were of old manufacture and for which there was no ready market. Consequently some of the goods he sent me remained untouched though they cost me a tidy sum. Yet I had merely asked him for new watch-cases which could be sold quickly. For this reason I was often unable to meet my financial obligation to him, which I deeply desired. Finally he turned his back on me altogether. This was my experience with that Reb Leib who at first, as I have already stated, was most kind to me and befriended me before I had the opportunity to think about it. Indeed, he made every financial effort to assist me but essentially he was not a generous person who would favour me even though it entailed no financial loss to him. He merely made a slight gesture by granting me some credit which was negligible to a man of his means; no, he was not a generous person. What he did for me was done without real kindness yet he did not want to refuse me at a time he held me in considerable esteem. So I did not prosper from my business dealings with him although initially things seemed favourable and when he sent the goods I ordered my business prospered, but when he failed to do this I was the loser. Had he acted generously and more readily supplied me with the goods I requested I could have made a considerable profit and would have had no need of his generosity which he finally manifested to reduce the effect of his misdealing. Truly, the Almighty is righteous, for all this was an example of His mighty acts.

At the outset of my third marriage I planned to put my mind to the Almighty's work by the publication of Sefarim and for this purpose I endeavoured to obtain a royal licence. I succeeded in this with the assistance of the lay-leader, R. Meir Emden, may he rest in peace who hailed from Hamburg. The latter was always prompt in acting on my behalf and to do all I asked of him even though it meant spending his own money. Though he acted promptly and at considerable personal expense he did not ask to be reimbursed. In fact, he did this on two occasions. For when the Emperor died and was succeeded by his son, I had to renew my application for a licence to publish books. This, again, involved Reb Meir in some considerable expense. Moreover, may he be remembered for good, he always proved to be prompt in fulfilling my requests (of him) when I requested his assistance in business, and would send me merchandise from Hamburg. He would immediately expend his own cash (on my behalf) in buying from a local company tea and pepper the value of which amounted to many thousand Reichthalers. He would forward me these commodities without asking for a commission, and always acted generously and with every goodwill.

However my sins caused the failure of this enterprise, though I obtained some small benefit from it since I made a quick sale of the pepper which brought me a profit of one hundred Schock Heller. Moreover, at my request Reb Meir allowed me to retain this money as

CHAPTER ELEVEN

a loan over a period of years, for I had to pay a debt on my house which amounted to a thousand Reichthalers for which a Gentile creditor was pressings. So this generous lay-leader gladly left the money with me, as I had requested. I regarded this as a great favour for thereby I was freed from the payment of a considerable sum, to the tune of forty Reichthalers per annum, which was the annual fixed interest and for which no moratorium was permitted. It was because of Meir's kindness that my house was freed of this financial burden. Over the years in which I repaid that generous individual every penny I had borrowed he suffered no loss, whilst I did not regard the repayments as any imposition. In short this was an act of true kindness on Meir's part.

Regarding the sale of the tea which I had likewise obtained through the generosity of Meir. I had some heart-breaking experiences, for having kept that merchandise for several months in the hope of selling it at a profit, I was concerned whether I could keep it any longer, but the goods remained with me as there were no purchasers. Hence I regarded it as a bad deal (cf. TB. Nedarim 31a) and feared I would lose out. I therefore asked Meir to allow me to transfer these goods to another person who understood the tea-business. This man would take the goods and sell them, for I had little experience in this type of business but had to rely on other people to act on my behalf. Meir consequently arranged for his relative, Jonathan Aberle to take the casts of tea from me. In that very same week the price of tea appreciated so that I wanted to retain the casts and sell them to my advantage, for this was why they were originally sent to me. Moreover I did not think it was fair that J.Aberle should make so much profit at my expense. However, Jonathan Aberle put much pressure on me through an agent of the Bet Din, whilst I was not prepared to suffer the humiliation of confronting a Bet Din even though I felt sure Meir Emden would not coerce me for he had made the original arrangement at my request. Again, I felt certain Meir would not force me to transfer the fruits of my labour to a person who had not toiled to gain such profits. Nevertheless to silence the protestations of Jonathan Aberle, may he rest in peace, I handed him the goods with the proviso that he should give me (a commission) of ten Reichthalers irrespective of the profit he made. This arrangement did not harm me so much as the fact that my business connection with Meir Emden ended since he realised that I was not a good business-man. I did not have the courage to ask for further merchandise from him on a commission-basis. Indeed, it was my honesty which had resulted in all this distress, for I was very worried in case the whole deal would be adversely affected, either because of any depreciation in the price of tea, for it had slightly depreciated, or because the cases of tea would remain in my possession for some considerable time and I would therefore be retaining Meir Emden's money without any benefit to either him or me. It was these considerations that precipitated my request of Meir (that he should permit me to transfer the castes of tea to another party) although none of the considerations I have mentioned appeared to bother him.

CHAPTER ELEVEN

MEGILAT SEFER

CHAPTER TWELVE

I now revert to my efforts in publishing books. Were I to attempt a description of all my experiences in that field there would be insufficient space (lit. the couch would be too narrow for two people. cf.Yalkut Is.302) for it would virtually require a separate volume and even then I would be unable to describe a fraction of the events. For who can do justice to a description of all my experiences in that endeavour? For example, my first book "She'elot Ya'avetz" I have previously described my experiences regarding that matter. Then a year after my third marriage l incurred considerable expense in acquiring the Hebrew lettering (square characters) as well as vowels and punctuation marks from Amsterdam. Apart from that expenditure I had already spent a considerable sum for new tools and new Rabbinic script. In 1745 I began working on my Prayer book and postponed the publication of other works which had been left with me. I now concentrated all my efforts on the Prayer book which was an onerous and holy task. Until now I had hardly written anything except my "Luach Eres" and I had set that aside so as not to be involved in any polemics with a person who did not share my

CHAPTER TWELVE

religious faith.(a reference to Shlomo Zalman Hanau, author of Zohar ha-Tevah). In fact, I had merely written indices to my work on the Prayer book, which I called "Amudei Shomayim" into which I incorporated important rules and customs for the whole year, as well as the procedure of the various sacrifices which were performed in Temple times, as well as all the history of our Patriarchs together with the prophecies which were expressed by our Prophets at a particular time.

I set out all the observances and customs in the Written and Oral Torah which were dependent of a fixed time together with the relevant months of the year when (many of them) were observed, and I even noted the hour of the day in which some of those Observances were to be practised. In addition I mention the rules to be observed on the night of an ordinary and Holy day. Every Observance and/or rule was mentioned together with the relevant day and time, and I managed to do this without confusing the dates. Moreover, with the Almighty's help, I commented on all the prayers, benedictions, and the different versions of various supplications attributed to early generations. I did my best to elucidate the latter on the basis of either the literal or esoteric meaning or on corrected versions of the texts of those supplications. My initial efforts in getting up this work were intensive and extensive both in quantity and quality, for I considered it my duty to even record the number of words of every benediction and to embellish the words with fine allusions. In the same vein I incorporated into the work many pleasant and lucid interpretations of important Scriptural texts, quite apart from stating their common-sense meaning. With the Almighty's assistance I adopted the same approach to those sentiments of our Sages, z"l, which were ostensibly strange and irregular and by so doing they proved to be acceptable to the rational mind.

I did all this and neglected nothing in adorning "my Temple". Moreover, in my attachment to the House of my Lord I incorporated (into this work) many ethical and moral exhortations which I felt were necessary to stir the reader's heart. This was particularly required by our fellow German Jews and these exhortations would help keep Gentile influences and criticism at bay and so keep our fellow Jews happy and contented.

However the enemies of morality were to repay my efforts for their genuine benefit with evil. But at the outset my work on the Prayer book was well acclaimed and was so favourably received by all its readers that when they took it into their hands they became absorbed in it. Indeed, when the first part was ready they already craved to buy the next section. But this proved to be to my detriment. For by the publication (of the first part) I encountered (cf.Is.28:4) a brood of sinful men (cf.Num.32:14) who libelled me (by stating) that in perusing my work they had discovered that when I had noted the principle regulations governing trade and commerce and had stated our Sages opinion in the Mishnah (Kiddushin 4:14) viz. that a father should not train his son to be a shopkeeper. I had added my own observation that among the proscribed vocations contemporary bankers should be included. This so incensed the brazen bankers that they were ready to destroy me for no real cause.

In fact, they were so enraged that they publicly stated that had they met me in the street they would have attacked me physically. I learned this fact quite indirectly from trustworthy people. Therefore I thank the Almighty who delivers the needy from the power of evil-doers.

But those evil people engineered a wicked conspiracy against me and on a certain occasion they entered the communal centre and raised a hue and cry against me in the presence of the Communal authorities alleging that I was jeopardising their lives. They amplified those allegations and requested the authorities to order the sequestration of my recently published work (on the Prayer book) and to cut out the page (which contained my observation regarding bankers). To cover up their treacherous trickery they made further false and presumptuous accusations against me viz. that my book contained many ideas which endangered Judaism. Moreover, they made indignant protests against the variant-readings (my book contained). All this was designed to intensify opposition to me and resulted in the lay-leaders agreeing to request R.Ezekiel and his Bet

CHAPTER TWELVE

Din to examine my books for any serious defect. They made this decision although I had some time earlier sent the Presiding Rabbi of the Bet Din (R .Ezekiel) the first part of my printed work on the Prayer book in order too obtain his approbation. In fact, I had deliberately delayed requesting his approbation by showing him a few pages of this work, this was customary with many contemporaneous authors for I wanted him to give his verdict on the whole of the book which would remain with him for several weeks and thus afford him the opportunity of studying all of it before he issued his approbation. Subsequently he had returned the book to me with a personal note which was full of its praises. Since, however he was rather brief in praising the virtues of the work, I sent him (R. Ezekiel) a note requesting an amplification of his approbation to inform the reader more clearly as to the merits of my work. He complied with my request and wrote a second approbation. I therefore had two approbation's as well as a royal licence for my book, but even this proved insufficient to protect me against my enemies.

I therefore could not ignore the order of the lay-leaders which forbade me to publish my book until l received a specific permit from them. I received this order through their emissary who, at the same time, instructed me that the Council wanted me to deliver six copies of the first part of my work which I had already completed. These copies would he handed to a Bet Din comprising six members whom the Council had selected, i.e. three additional members to the usual quorum (of three) apart from the Presiding Rabbi (R. Ezekiel). Hence each member (of the augmented Bet Din) would have, his own copy to study. But the Council did not set a time limit to this procedure. Thus, every member of the Bet Din took home a copy (of my book) to examine its contents to the best of his ability and the fate of my work would depend on their (joint) decision. Though I protested (in the presence of the Council's representative) stating that I already had a double approbation from the Presiding Rabbi of the Bet Din who had studied my work some time previously so how could they ignore such a reality or (I argued) how could people revoke the decision of a Rabbi, nothing I said in my own defence was of any avail. Though I might jest with them I had no wish to quarrel with so many people. Consequently I concurred with the request of the Council and handed the number of copies (of my book) for which they had asked to their representative. I then made a voluntary statement in which I observed that I gladly complied with the request of the Communal Council and that the members of the Bet Din would do a great service on my behalf if they studied my work meticulously. Moreover, (I stated) any faults which they brought to my attention would be deleted from my work. Indeed, (I continued) I would be most grateful if by so doing they would save me from any mishap, God forbid! Consequently, (I said to the representative) I would regard it as a favour that they should not slacken in their task, for I delighted in such activities. But that day was a hard one for me for the evil people I previously mentioned had prepared to battle against me (cf.Jer.6:4) and I feared they would utterly destroy me, for I had expended thousands (of Reichthalers) in publishing this important work, I had experienced much stress and had toiled considerably before the first section (of my book) was completed. Moreover, the second section was almost complete before it was held up (by my enemies). Thus, it seemed all my efforts had been in vain. Again, I was most apprehensive of those critics who denounced my holy and religious work which would have brought me great and immeasurable repute, but now, God forbid, my book might never be completed.

Consequently, I was eager to return to my work on the following day and ordered my assistant to apply himself to his work and not to rest until with God's help, the work was completed. This was achieved without any further mishap. But my enemies thought there was still time to prevent the publication of (the second part) of my work since (they thought) the members of the Bet Din who were making a careful study of my book would comply with their wishes. Indeed they felt sure they would attain their evil purpose in a short time.

However, since I was concerned lest, God forbid, I would be

CHAPTER TWELVE

prevented from publishing (the second section) of my book I set out a considerable number of synopses in the latter half of the second section which I entitled "Sha'arei Shomayim Ve'ir Ho-Elokim" so that a large number of words were reduced by one synopsis. I worked very promptly in getting up this section of my work so that its completion did not suffer a delay. This was why parts of the second half of my book were not so comprehensible.

Thank God, my work was completed shortly before Rosh Hashonah, 1748 without any (further) mishap. But it was the week of Tisha Be'Av when this shocking business occurred (viz. the intervention of the Communal Council) and for the next six months i.e. almost to the end of Shevat 1749 the Dayanim who were involved in a critical examination of my book had not completed their task. During that period I frequently sent my agent early in the day to the Presiding Rabbi of the Bet Din and to the lay-leaders with the request that they should inform me whether any defect had been discovered, for I wouldn't permit "unrighteousness to stay in my home" (cf. Job 11:14) for a single night. But I could not understand the Bet Din or the lay-leaders, for every one of them referred me to their colleague. I therefore realised that notwithstanding certain criticisms of my work which the Bet Din had reached by either their intellectual abilities, or which were prompted by those who sought to libel me, for those people (The lay-leaders and the Bet Din) were definitely in their hire, they were actually afraid of me. Hence they (the libellers) did not feel confident that their adverse comments would prevail against me and so they (the Bet Din) concealed from me any denigration they had made of my book. The lay-leaders too, were silent and pretended they were ignorant of the conclusions of the Bet Din, for although a number of people bought my book the lay-leaders raised no objection. Indeed, I felt they (the lay-leaders) regretted their involvement in this affair now realised it would have been better if they had not interfered from the very outset. For those lay-leaders must have realised the weakness of the criticisms of me and were worried lest they would gain little prestige from the affair, on the contrary, they felt that shame and reproach would disaffect the

MEGILAT SEFER

Bet Din whose power and authority had been sorely tested. The latter in turn must have appreciated that they had no case against me. Hence, to protect their prestige they opted for silence and would not pronounce a prohibition or licence on the sale of my book to the local inhabitants. In fact there was not a single voice of protest.

Indeed, soon after they had instigated this affair the bankers themselves bought the first part of my work from me for a considerable price and some were so afraid of me that they immediately regretted their behaviour. In fact, the chief of the trouble-makers Aaron Berliner sent a person to beg my forgiveness. I however, wasn't satisfied with these people's silence and therefore did not refrain from sending my agent to the lay-leaders every week (requesting) the critical comments of the Bet Din so that if there were any substance(in the criticisms) I would make the necessary corrections or if I had done wrong they should pass sentence on me. In this way I would be acting according to the Halakhah as well as the spirit of the Torah. On the other hand, I argued (through my agent) if I were innocent and they had no complaint of my conduct how long would this slander against me be allowed to continue, I certainly could not allow such a situation to continue. The six months after the libel against me had been publicised and the subsequent examination of my work by the Bet Din the lay-leader appointed for that particular month and as a result of my earnest entreaties agreed to grant my request and inform me of my misdemeanour, if I indeed was at fault. Consequently he sent the representative of the Communal Council to me with a copy of the report the Bet Din had issued to the lay-leaders i.e. a report of the complaints and criticisms which they had of my book. I asked (the representative) if I would be allowed to reply (in writing) to the report which I assumed contained the criticisms which those wise men (the Bet Din) had levelled against me (and my work), so that we could then judge as to who was right. The representative however, did not want to give me an explicit permit but merely stated, "I know nothing about such permission." I then understood that the Communal leaders had no desire to exacerbate the situation, but merely to reject my request.

CHAPTER TWELVE

Anyhow, it suited me to conceal the outcome of this affair from all and sundry, so I too opted for silence so as not to be accused of being a cantankerous person since the lay-leaders were in no way inclined to provoke further trouble.

But privately I penned a reply to those people who had complained about my book and dealt with their deceitful and shameful conduct. For, if the truth be told, they could not distinguish their right and left hand so that whatever they wrote, though that was hardly worth mentioning, they were unable to state a single correctly reasoned complaint. Though, as I myself noted, they could have found several mistakes (in my work) and therefore given an appropriate reply to my protestations. For I noted that my book was not devoid of various mistakes which were the result of my haste to complete the work. However, those men who were struck by intellectual blindness did not observe one defect, either of a minor or major degree, so that what was distorted could have been straightened. All they did was to slander me with baseless libels thereby revealing their foul error and exposing the basis of their folly. This is how they attired themselves in their dispute with me, as I have clearly illustrated in a monograph specifically dealing with this affair which I called "Zikhron Ha-Sefer" or "Ma'ase Amalek"! In it I clearly demonstrated that they had not appreciated my book nor my real purpose in publishing it. I stored away that monograph and presently it remains in my possession for I had no wish to publish it and so increase any ill-feeling towards me. (Another reason for my reluctance to publish that monograph was because) "Just as the Almighty did not delay His vengeance of the king of Edom (cf. Amos 2:1) so did He not delay my vengeance" (cf.TB. Bava Batra 22a) For soon after the emergence of the mischief against me which was provoked by the impudent bankers, (it seems) there were two (in particular) who took the lead in zealous pursuit of this calumny. One named Aaron Berliner had been a bankrupt several times and apart from this was known as an appropriator of public funds and as one who jeopardised the Jewish community by his activities in clipping the coinage which was a long-standing prohibition. This Edomite whose hair was like the reddish hue of the Krum was likewise notorious for his hypocrisy. This thief who had what was commonly known as a guilty conscience, joined forces with a similar character called Hirsch Munden (Minden). I did not know the latter, nor had I ever set eyes on him but he was not as evil as Aaron Berliner. According to my informants Munden was very rich and a highly respected person in the community. Together these two caused the stir and mischief I have described.

In the wake of this affair Aaron Berlin's son fled taking with him a purse-full of his father's money, but was subsequently arrested. Aaron Berliner, the red-beard, regretted his behaviour towards me and sent Rabbi Isaac Tabor (see p. 30 of E. Dukes "Chachmei Altona, Hamburg, Wandsbeck" pub. Hamburg 1908) to seek my forgiveness and reconciliation, and to inform me that he (Berliner) was prepared to come and fall at my feet. However, (I replied) I had no wish to set eyes upon him unless he first stood in the Great Synagogue publicly confessed his sin and beg the Almighty's forgiveness and then declare his sin against me. For repentance,(of sin) must conform to the type of sin committed, since (other-wise) people may have learned of the wrong (he did me) but not of the repentance of that wrong. Consequently it was essential that Aaron Berliner put matters: right publicly then, and only then, would I be prepared to pardon his insult.

Regarding the second (ring-leader) Hirsch Munden. He suffered a terrible fate, for after a short time he had to flee the city because he had robbed his fellow-bankers. It was strongly rumoured that he had fled to a place where bankrupts and the like who lived in regions where the power of the Emperor held sway (i.e. the Austro-Hungarian empire) would be safe. However, the authorities pursued him to that refuge bearing letters of complaint which they had laid before his Majesty, the Emperor, and having caught up with him took him away from this place of refuge. He then sought royal protection but all the expenditure he made to this end proved unsuccessful. He was handed over to the law-enforcement authorities who put him in fetters, and on the journey back to Hamburg he passed away. Just

CHAPTER TWELVE

before Hirsch Munden fled his eldest daughter who in the previous year had contracted a marriage befitting very wealthy people, died in giving birth to her first child. Then Munden suffered the loss of a young son. Then a few years after the dispute with Eibeschuetz had erupted another son of Munden robbed a Gentile in public. He was arrested as a common thief and was brought to trial just like any ne'er-do-well. He suffered considerably and was imprisoned in iron fetters for quite a long period. In fact, he would have been condemned to death had not the court taken pity on his grandfather who was alive at the time and who had sought the court's mercy on behalf of his grandson. The verdict of the court was that he should be severely whipped, and in fact he was beaten as if he were black cumin, so that he bled profusely. Subsequently he was imprisoned and was put to hard-labour. Hence for some years he had to spin cotton and wool. Having completed his sentence he was banished from the country. Such was the situation of H.Munden that death was preferable to life. This then was the fate of the man who cursed me grievously during the affair I have just described, and who always carried in his pocket calumnious notes, i.e. lampoons against me. He failed to learn the lesson of his father's fate. Let this be the fate of all insolent men!

But regarding the affair of the bankers who plotted against me and who sought to destroy me for no apparent reason, though the Holy One blessed be He took his vengeance of them and didn't give them the opportunity of really harming me nevertheless the seeds of animosity still remained in the hearts of those impudent people and they were only frightened by the evil spirit that rattled within them. Some of them as I have already stated, were full of remorse, but I failed to destroy the animosity from the mind of every one of them. When any of them visited me I tried to prove my innocence to them by stating that I had never intended to do them any harm, God forbid!. My intention (I argued) was simply to take advantage of their presence and to state my position. I wrote a great deal to this effect in the monograph which I mentioned above. In the same way those who did business with me as well as others who were

MEGILAT SEFER

close to me were convinced by my arguments, hence they remained unaffected by this affair. However I could not address all the people involved (in the affair) so that seed of animosity was still retained by those who were ignorant of my true involvement. What was the point of adducing any number of logical arguments to the effect that the whole purpose of my activities was for the advantage (of the Jewish bankers). Hadn't I over a long period deposited my money with Joseph Pofret (a banker) from which I obtained no profit but was completely to has advantage? In fact not only did I deal with a banker as rich and trustworthy as Joseph Pofret, but I used to lend money to my neighbour the honourable Zalman Munden, the brother-in-law of Berliner whom I previously mentioned, so that he (Munden) could run his Money-exchange business and so sustain his family. Because he was poor I made no demands of him not even (to insist on) a security. Nor did I ask for a receipt of such loans since I regarded him (Munden) as a trustworthy person. Indeed I didn't, God forbid earn a penny from such loans, and though he wanted to do me certain favours I said to him, "God forbid I should take anything from you; but whenever I have any spare cash it is yours to use to your advantage. Indeed I would be pleased to do this since I have not the expertise to use the money profitably whereas you have, so why should I withhold good from one to whom it is due" (Prov.3:27) seeing it will prove to your advantage and not to my disadvantage.(cf. TB. Bava Kama 20a).

In the same way I would have said to those bankers who doubted my good intentions towards them if I really intended you harm would not I have discouraged others from making use of your cash? I have to state such arguments because of those evil men (in fact) the majority of the leading communities of Germany were affected by the corrupt practices of the bankers of that period. On several occasions the Three Communities were heavily fined because of the malpractice of those who indulged in clipping the coinage and thereby infringing the prohibition originally imposed by Rabbenu Gershon (Me'or Ha-Golah). In fact, warnings of the serious consequences of infringing that prohibition were promulgated

CHAPTER TWELVE

month after month in the Three Communities. Because of our many sins men of probity and integrity were made to suffer for that sin as Scripture illustrates in the incident of Achan for whose sin many perished (Joshua 7). Moreover the middle-classes, the poor, orphans and widows complained bitterly about those communal Robbers through whose activities the Three Communities were manacled with (additional) financial responsibilities. For if not for those evil men the Three Communities would have managed to meet their financial responsibilities reasonably easy and not at the expense of the poor. Indeed there was a distinct possibility of a surplus in the communal treasury. But those worms were like rottenness in the bones with the result that money had to be borrowed at such a ruinous rate of interest that the Communities were never free of that financial burden. Because of this the poor and down-trodden were the sufferers not only because the Three Communities were unable to meet their financial, obligations so that the poor had to beg for foods but because the Communities were forced to flay the skins off their very bones in order to meet their debts as well as those of former generations. It was particularly in the sphere of marriages which the poor contracted that the demands of the community were harsher than those of Pharaoh, for the (Three) communities would not license such marriages until they (the poor) had paid in whatever way possible, a levy imposed on them. Hence the poor suffered greatly because of those wicked Robbers and henceforth "the people of God went down to the gates" (Jud 5:11) i.e. steadily declined and, because of our many sins prosperity (in the community) ended. People's property was forfeited and the rich lived in a low state whilst, because of our many sins poverty prevailed.

All these factors prompted me to do a simple thing to arouse the hearts of honest men. (I thought) by this I might help reduce the calamity. In the same way as our Sages acted in warning us about shop-keepers and their associates for we cannot get rid of them altogether. For what difference is there between a shop-keeper and a banker, are they not brothers in crime (as Scripture says), regarding the merchant, the balances of deceit are in his hand, he loves to oppress" (Hos.12:8); one in food-stuffs, the other (the banker) with silver and gold coins. In our own day bankers' activities are even more evil and their wickedness has reached a point when life itself is endangered. Thus it was necessary to remind people of this and to arouse their conscience. Nevertheless I refrained from casting the slightest slur against any particular banker since there were bound to be some honest men among them as indeed there are in all strata of the economy. However, concerning those extortionists who were known to have been involved in that repulsive affair (in which l was a victim), their conscience pricked them and they consequently provoked that commotion against me. But they did not succeed in denigrating the integrity of my efforts and their good effect though they were successful in affecting my financial status. All my toil and effort and the many expenses I incurred in order to produce that religious work appeared to be in vain; for apart from the treacherous conspiracy they engineered among themselves to refrain from purchasing my book, these bankers discouraged both local folk and those of other localities (from buying it), by casting a slur on my reputation. Consequently, I had to distribute copies of my work by sending them to other places and countries for example Italy, Bessarabia, Poland etc. Most of these however were lost so that I have, as yet not realised a penny from their sale, may the Almighty compensate me.

Despite this I continued the religious duty I had begun and did not abandon God's work as long as I could afford to print (my book) the cost of which amounted to a considerable sum, and as long as circumstances were not (completely) against me. I again exerted every effort to accomplish God's work by adding ethical comments to my book. (Now) my previous detractors remained silent, a silence effected by shame and reproach, "pangs and sorrows took hold" (Is.13:8) of all my accusers so that those who were envious of me as well as those who condemned me completely ceased (their activities). Hence my new work was favourably received by all who studied it and these people openly praised it without demur. Though I seemed to have forgotten that the purchasers of

CHAPTER TWELVE

new books had decreased I didn't refrain from publishing my new religious work to which I had committed myself because of the spiritual benefit it would bring as well as meeting my own religious needs quite apart from the benefit it would bring to people like myself who had to consider their financial position.

I then published the second volume of my "Bet Middot Ha-Gadol" which I had not succeeded in completing for it was such an extensive work that it could not be comprehended in one volume. I therefore had to divide it into sections and sub-sections. With the help of the Almighty I had already managed to print ten pages of the second volume and was still involved with its publication when I was interrupted by that man Eibeschuetz who came into my life to violate the Eternal Law to overthrow our traditions and to uproot the foundations of our faith. "I was at ease and he broke me asunder, he took me by the neck and shook me to pieces, and set me up for his mark." (Job 16:12) For the lay-leaders of the Three Communities handed me this demon with whom to grapple, but because of the mercy of the Almighty he did not overcome me. For the Holy One blessed be He, "concealed me with the shadow of His hand, and made me a polished shaft; in His quiver He hid me."(Is.49:2) For all the world, acknowledged that justice was with me, that I was truly innocent. However, this affair caused me considerable loss of business. For not only did he (R.Eibeschuetz) fail to compensate me for all the financial and physical harm he and his evil assistants caused me but, "the treacherous one continued to act treacherously,"(Is.21:2) and "to ravage my tent."(Jer.10:20).

With God's help I will eventually give further details of all this. He (Eibeschuetz) put an end to all my business, indeed from the moment 'arrogance' arrived and up to the present I have been unable to pursue my livelihood nor to earn anything in order to maintain my family, so that 'my life became a prey to me' (cf.Jer.39:18). But the Holy One, blessed be He, has been my helper and saviour until now, in Him have I put my trust, for He has not suffered my foot to be moved (cf.Ps.121:13) "He has established goings."(Ps.40:3) and so put into my mouth a new song to our Lord. Let the whole world take note and trust in Him. I will not give a long account here of my experiences with that foolish person I have just mentioned for I had begun to write a special work about that affair which I entitled "Megilat Purim U-Milchemet Tanin" but by the time I had returned home from my travels I had only completed half of it. Moreover, because of all that has happened to me since then I have not had the time to complete the book particularly since I have been involved in publishing a work of two parts (Akitzat Akrav). In the first section I gave a clear description of the affair of the small amulet and the argument with its author, whilst the second entitled Teshuvat Haminin, was a response to R.Eibeschuetz regarding the large amulet which he gave to the daughter of the lay-leader (Eliakim) Goetchlik and which R.Eibeschuetz's pupil Karl Anton published. This was after the amulet had been translated into German and sent to Anton who having gained the consent of Eibeschuetz's father-in-law Sab (Kosov) published it as a defence of his teacher and sent it to the Emperor, long may he reign. His object was to obtain royal protection for R.Eibeschuetz, for since the latter appeared to be a good person the Emperor was obliged to save him from his persecutors. (This publication) denigrated me in the eyes of the Emperor and libelled me by stating that my wife had previously declared, before R.Eibeschuetz's arrival (in the community), "my husband Ya'akov has already sharpened the knife with which to cut his (R.Eibeschuetz's) throat." Statements such as this were published by R.Eibeschuetz in the work to which I have previously referred. I replied to all his denigrating comments and to his explanation of (the text) of the amulet. But the second section of my book Teshuvat Ha-Minim was abandoned half-way because of the actions of Karl Anton who disturbed my peace of mind. In any case, since I had no money I could not possibly publish that section. Eventually (I hope) God will find favour with my work and enable me to complete its (publication). Indeed, may the Almighty help me complete and not discourage the work of my hands.

  I now revert to the high-lights of my life as they occurred and to my life with my third wife, my brother's daughter with whom I

CHAPTER TWELVE

despaired of obtaining any domestic peace. Indeed as long as the children of my previous marriage lived with me my domestic peace was even less than I had enjoyed in previous years so that I came to appreciate our Sages' comment on the Scriptural verse "your sons and daughters will be handed over to another people" (Deut.28:32) -that this refers to a step-mother (TB. Yevamot 63b) There was no solution to that situation. I thought when I married my niece that since she was young she would be submissive towards me and show consideration to my daughters as well as respect me, but in fact in this respect she proved worse than her predecessor. In fact the sword of discord remained active throughout the period she lived with me in Altona, though apart from this she was a pious and most modest lady. This discord therefore, must surely been the result of my own shortcomings coupled with the well-known temperament of Poles and their up-bringing. Consequently I never realised her good qualities, may she rest in peace. I hope therefore, that God will grant me some joy in my old age so that I will never again suffer such worries.

In the year following my marriage to my niece which took place on the eighth of Iyar 1744, my wife miscarried but in the following year she gave birth to a boy whom I called Mordechai. But he lived for another eighteen months and died on the eighth of Marcheshvan 1748. Two or perhaps three years later my wife gave birth to a healthy boy my delightful and favourite son Judah, may he be granted many years and be a man among his brothers. Judah was born to my good fortune, on Shabbat the eighth of Cheshvan 1751. May the Almighty preserve and sustain him for His service, and may I merit to raise him for Torah, Chuppah and noble deeds. I pray I may be privileged to see worthy future generations, so may it be God's will, Amen. Following Judah's birth there began the period of my religious controversy with Eibeschuetz, a battle in which I was involved for more than seven years. In this present year, 1758 I thought I would be able to lead a peaceful life but (it seems) I was destined to wage an obligatory religious struggle which was not to my advantage. I have recorded these facts in my Megilat Purim Eidut

MEGILAT SEFER

BeYa'akov so that I will not give a full account of that dreadful affair which was worse than all the sufferings I had experienced from my very youth. I devoted a number of books to this affair but still failed to cover halve of it. Who knows what I will yet experience since, for our many sins, nothing quite like it has ever been seen or heard. (As Scripture puts it) "A wicked man does evil a hundred times" (cf.Eccles.8:I2) "yet he prolongs his life in his wickedness" (cf.ibid.7:15), but "what happens to the fool has no parallel." (cf. Eccles.2:15) May the Lord act for the sake of His glorious name, and may we merit to see the consolation of His people and His land speedily in our days.

At the end of Iyar 1751 I fled from Altona and went to Amsterdam. I have recorded in my book I previously mentioned viz. Megillat Purim all that befell me in the period of my flight and exile from my home. After living through a variety of harassing experiences in Amsterdam and after I had been declared innocent of the charges against me which had been brought before his Majesty the Emperor, long may he reign. I received a call to return home. I arrived there (Altona) in the middle of Av 1752 unharmed both physically and financially and found my family in the best of health. However I was informed that my son Judah had been ill with smallpox, may the Lord spare us, but had since recovered. But as I have already stated he suffered a further attack of this illness some years later. Thank God, now all was well, and my friends who delighted to honour me welcomed me with the utmost respect and great joy. On that day I returned home with great pomp whilst my enemies were dispirited for only a few days later the authorities of Hamburg decided to remove R.Eibeschuetz from the Rabbinate of the city. This decision was implemented so that R.Eibeschuetz lost that Rabbinate for more than three years. In fact my followers thought R.Eibeschuetz had met his fate particularly since there had been an assurance from the Imperial court that the final decision would go against him so that his defeat was inevitable. Indeed it seemed he was on the point of being declared guilty by the Imperial court and he had been compelled to answer fourteen charges. However, he

CHAPTER TWELVE

pleaded for a few months extension to collect a few outstanding debts in the Three Communities. During that period the situation which at one time was definitely not in his favour changed to his advantage.

    Generally (speaking) I did not enjoy much prosperity and when the Almighty had returned me to my family everyone maintained that R.Eibeschuetz and his party were obligated to compensate me for the damage they had caused me. My friends argued that he (R.Eibeschuetz) despaired of success and planned to reach some compromise with me. But (they argued) I was very kind and it was not right for me to seek that compensation through the non-Jewish courts so that they would make every effort with the opposing party to reach a satisfactory compromise on my behalf. My friends believed that the opposition would repent of their ways and regret their past action in supporting R.Eibeschuetz since they saw his ultimate failure and that their assistance (to him) was of no avail. Hence, these people believed that the two opposing groups and the rest of the community would now enjoy tranquillity. Consequently my friends no longer planned to approach the secular courts for they believed they had won the struggle and that the vanquished (R.Eibeschuetz) was irreparably ruined. In replying to them (I quoted the verse in Scripture) " Let not he who girds on his harness boast himself as he that puts it off."(1 Kings.20:11) and (another verse) "Boast not thyself of tomorrow" (Prov.27:1). For I felt that their hopes that justice would be done would not be fully realised and therefore warned them that the warrior must always be alert in battle. I was not speaking merely in my own interests but because I felt the need to achieve the essential goal viz. to destroy the growing tree which was constantly causing damage. For (I argued) he (R.Eibeschuetz) is twisting to and fro with his tricks, whilst those who support him in his evil designs are on the increase. Moreover (I said to my friend) you have not fully discharged your obligation in properly setting out your arguments and claims against the opposing party, so you are like raked coals in his hands or (you appear) appear to be moving in a circle but never reaching the centre. For I was not in Altona when all those events occurred, nor was I informed, whilst in Amsterdam, what the opposition were. planning when they brought their complaint before the Imperial court of justice. But they relied on their wisdom and put their trust in their intelligence, yet "there in no wisdom nor understanding against the Lord" (cf. Prov.21:30) who "turns wise men backwards and makes their knowledge foolish." (Is. 44:25) For I was saved with God's help and "from His hand my judgement was brought to light and to my advantage." (cf. Zeph3:5)

I therefore said (to my supporters), "Just leave me alone and I will argue my case with him and his supporters. Don't act over righteously nor show any pity to cruel people. I will plead my cause in the proper and most suitable way and will clearly expose the guile and trickery of that man(R.Eibeschuetz). Then with God's help, you will be successful in your endeavours." But no-one paid any attention to me and my friends in whom I trusted opposed me and prevented me from seeking financial compensation. Consequently I was forced to remain inactive. But what I had foreseen actually occurred so the Lord frustrated their machinations in order to end the tranquillity again. Certainly God would not execute justice without cause. For our many sins, they (the opposition) enjoyed the fruits of their stratagems, so that the situation was reversed, those who had been successful were no longer so, whilst those who had been on the lowest rung of success viz. R.Eibeschuetz and his clique ascended by the scale of deceit. Hence the sympathies of the Emperor veered towards him (R.Eibeschuetz) as I have previously indicated. Thus "the treacherous one deals treacherously and the spoiler spoils", (Is.21:2) that wicked sinner "'spoke as the piercing of a sword." (Prov.12:18).

All this was caused by their (my supporters) plans with the result that the in iniquitous men spoke out more so than they did initially. Indeed they were audacious enough to fall upon me and "suddenly spoil my abode."(cf. Jer.4:20) Here again though the Almighty did not allow them to destroy me, they caused me considerable financial loss and much worry. A short time after my

CHAPTER TWELVE

return home a considerable number of my well-wishers begged me to write, in the form of a responsa my struggle on behalf of the Almighty and the outcome of the Judicial inquiry which I previously mentioned. I did as they requested. They then asked me to get up a general statement (which was to be sent) to the Rabbis and scholars of various communities informing them of the way we had acted with integrity and justly towards him (R.Eibeschuetz), and requesting their support in (adding their signatures) to those of my followers. This request too, I did not decline and in no way delayed its fulfilment. My supporters however, were slothful and failed to give me their full assistance in all this. Meanwhile, as I previously mentioned, Karl Anton's book was published though I still believe the real author was R.Eibeschuetz himself. The work was addressed to the Emperor, long may he reign, and requested his support of R.Eibeschuetz, for the Emperor was friendly disposed to everyone. Finally, during Chanukah 1753, a royal decree deprived R. Eibeschuetz of the authority to compel any person to appear before his Bet Din. Hitherto, as the presiding Rabbi of the Bet Din of the Three Communities he had the authority to impose corporal punishment. But he was now deprived of this prerogative, though his other privileges remained intact. Furthermore, another (royal) decree stated that the controversy over the amulets was to cease and that a heavy fine would be imposed on anyone who (publicly) denigrated R.Eibeschuetz. My followers however, were not discouraged by all this but objected to the decision of the Imperial judiciary. Moreover, certain important members of the opposition came over to our side. For they now realised the trickery of that deceitful person (R.Eibeschuetz) in that he had initially promised his followers to prove his innocence in the eyes of God before the contemporary Rabbinic authorities provided he first obtained their (his followers) support in obtaining that same decision in the Secular courts. Once he had obtained the latter he promised to prove the justice of his cause according to the tenets of Judaism.

But the enormous amount of money and energy they (his supporters) had expended in this venture were wasted. For when they (his supporters) subsequently approached him (R.Eibeschuetz) and stated it was now incumbent on him to fulfil his part of the agreement and prove he was innocent according to the Halakhah before selected Rabbinic authorities. He laughed and scoffed at them and (finally) dismissed them in peril of their life. Now when some of these people realised how he had lied to them, and how they had wasted their money and time on his behalf, they saw how wrong they had been and that my supporters and I were truly faithful to God. They therefore turned against him and joined his enemies. Having done this they now undertook to prosecute him (R.Eibeschuetz both in the Secular courts and judiciaries. However all this came to naught, and up to the present time these people have not succeeded. Subsequently, the lay-leaders attempted to compel him (R.Eibeschuetz) to accept a compromise to which he should append his signature in the presence of the Council of Altona. (The compromise) would state that he would agree to accept the Halakhic decision which a court (Bet Din) of arbitration would make. The format of the document (stating this compromise) would be drawn up with the full authority of the Council and would contain the signatures and seal of the Bet Din. It would then be recorded in the ledger of the President of the Council's office. (Furthermore) any infringement of the agreed compromise would entail a heavy fine. We now thought that the accursed R.Eibeschuetz had been brought to justice. But he utterly spurned the lay leadership by informing against them to the Imperial authorities, with the result that the Council was fined for compelling him to submit to the decision of the Jewish judiciary. Hence he (R.Eibeschuetz) emerged unscathed.

I now revert to the events of my family life. On the eighth of Iyar 1753 my wife again gave birth, this time to a boy whom I named Levi, basing myself on the Scriptural verse, "And of Levi he said, Let Thy Tummim and Thy Urim be with Thy holy one whom Thou didst prove at Massah, and with whom Thou didst strive at the waters of Merivah."(Deut. 33:8) This alluded to the events of my being tested in the struggle on behalf of the Almighty. My friends rejoiced on the

CHAPTER TWELVE

day of his circumcision but, for our many sins, he, just like his older brother who was born on the same day and month, did not live long but died on the eighteenth of Av 1756. Subsequently my wife presented me with a daughter on the same day of my son's passing viz. the eighteenth of Av 1756. I called the child Hannah, may she enjoy a long life, and may I merit to participate in her happiness together with my other children! A great miracle occurred to this little girl only two weeks before her birth, for it was on the third of Av (1756) on the eve of the Shabbat that a group of violent men entered my home to search for my book, Sefer Akizat Akrov. At that moment I happened to be with the printers'-apprentice Moses Buen on the top floor whilst my wife and family were on the ground floor. Thinking that I would be on my own the spoilers made a sudden incursion on us about midday. They fell upon us like locusts and my wife who had no inkling of the reason for this gross impudence almost died (of shock) and required blood-letting. All the details of that incident would need a separate monograph, particularly the special praise due to God for His power and wondrous deeds which He performed on our behalf on that day. That story is hardly credible, for we experienced not merely one but perhaps ten perceptible miracles. We, who trusted in God with all our being, witnessed His wonderful and revered providence. Thank God my wife was not really harmed in any way so that my daughter whom I previously mentioned was born two weeks after that incident. She proved to be a healthy and fully-formed child and since she was endowed with a kindly disposition she found favour with everyone she met. Indeed her name befitted her character; may she enjoy a long and healthy life.

Now I previously mentioned that during this difficult period my close friends and acquaintances seemed to forget me altogether. In particular my former friend the lay-leader Judah Leib Norden, who now became estranged from me and was reluctant to do me the slightest favour even though kindness would not have affected his pocket. For previously I had persuaded some of my friends to ask him (Norden) to send me certain commodities from London in lieu of money (he owed me). For earlier on I had sent him fifteen hundred gold ducats which I had obtained by mortgaging my house, and had requested him to let me have goods to the value of that sum. However, he refused to do this and returned the money which remained frozen for some time. Since I had no idea as to what business I should now pursue I sent the money to my brother-in-law, may he rest in peace, who was then the Presiding Rabbi of the Bet Din in Amsterdam, requesting him to make every effort to purchase a hundred Iottery tickets at a third of the market price and thus enable me to make some profit. However, there was a sudden depreciation in the price of those commodities so that I could not sell any of them without incurring a heavy loss. So I sold half of them at two thirds of the price I had paid in the hope that I might perhaps recoup some of the loss when I sold the remaining half. But (it seems) the Almighty wanted me to lose out completely. "The Lord gives and the Lord takes away, may the name of Lord be blessed." (Job 1:21)

As long as I did not incur too much financial loss I had no intention of bothering anyone here (in Altona) even though people volunteered to help me. In particular, the lay-leader Meir of Hamburg who on several occasions sent his sons or others requesting me to consent to an arrangement whereby I would earn an honest Livelihood. This (too) had been the wish of a select group of people who, realising my financial plight, endeavoured to persuade me to accede to their requests. However, I absolutely refused to accept any human bounty, a situation which I managed to avoid throughout my residence here (in Altona. For I thought God would perhaps favour me with some gift of His liberality. Nevertheless those friends I previously mentioned who were so eager to help me improve my lot were certainly the emissaries of the Almighty who wanted to test them as well as wishing to discover if God forbid, I would pledge myself to human bounty. Hence when I learned of the loss I had sustained regarding the lottery tickets though it appeared almost as a death sentence to me, I felt I had no right to question the decision of the Holy One, blessed be He, for I know "He is a God of

CHAPTER TWELVE

faithfulness and without iniquity" (Deut. 32:4) So I recited the blessing ("Blessed be the true Judge") with full devotion and gave thanks to my Creator who had exacted the debt (I owed Him) through my money. My friends (who had offered me their assistance) were aware of my business with the lottery tickets and had waited with trepidation until the final withdrawal of those lottery-tickets. When these friends learned of the complete loss of the latter and consequently the complete loss of my capital they approached me and disclosed their noble resolution, assuring me that their plan would be to my advantage and would in no way affect my reputation. I then consented to their scheme, I also consented to the endeavours of some of the lay-leaders e.g. Abraham Leib and David Laverdin with respect to Mrs.N...., for I. thought I was justly entitled to some compensation for the loss of the deposit I had sustained because of her husband, may he rest in peace.

In this same period there appeared the work Luchot Eidut written by that mentally blind person (R.Eibeschuetz) who thought everyone else was blind. On this occasion he sought to exonerate himself and prove publicly his innocence by mockery and bitter lies. This was the first occasion we had witnessed any publication of his whereby we could test his knowledge of Torah and worldliness. We thought we could at least expect some intelligent statements, especially since he had been involved in writing this work for more than four years. But any new Talmudic interpretations he contributed merely covered four paragraphs in average print. Regarding the amount which was actually published at some considerable cost we were convinced it would prove of some significant literary value. But when we perused this work we were astounded to discover it was replete with inanities and inaccuracies, dross covered by earthenware. Above all his Torah novellae which he presented (in this work) were worthless and perverted attesting to the fact that he had not studied nor understood the relevant literature. By my very life I have never seen such a bad publication. It was as if an old and foolish man who having left prison in order to rule over a box of reptiles says, "I am, and there is none other besides me" (Is. 47:8)

Yet he (R.Eibeschuetz) had boasted he was one of the Kings of Torah stating, "Who is there like me?" But indeed all his statements are vanity, as if he had never seen the light of Torah nor understood the truth it convoys. The novel comments and interpretations which he wrote on the Revealed Torah were addressed either to one who has no inkling of even the general outlines of the topic or to the feeble-minded or imbecile. Moreover, all that he adduces from the Gemara, the decisors, and the verses (he quotes) are either upside down or distorted. His logical arguments are confused and his language barbarous. In short, the illustration of his foolishness and stupidity in his interpretations of Revealed Torah tells us enough about his treatment of esoteric Torah. For (in this field) there is no limit to the vain and false observations which he (often) expresses in faulty acrostics. He was certainly aware of these facts, but considered every one foolish or ignorant so they would not perceive his vain disgraceful statements. Consequently, as soon as I made a careful study of this book I was delighted in the thought that what I had seen confirmed (my earlier suspicions) that its contents were false through and through. But I was mistaken in thinking that, to say the least, he was bound to be a scholar and an intellectual with respect to Revealed Torah. But I now realised that the work had produced thistle for it was replete with foolish errors and a variety of folly. Then, "with a mouth full of laughter" (cf.Ps.126:2) I exclaimed, "is this the man of devotion who speaks so arrogantly and whose students (at Prague Yeshivah) have produced treaties dedicated to him but, like his work, are written with guile and deceit?" Yet he has not attained the perception of one who announces the dawn of day.

For unless this be so how can an intelligent person imagine that he could be so presumptuous to set before us here (in Altona) such empty and foolish statements written in such an explicit style that any literate person can understand and appreciate their true value, unless that person was so distraught that he had forgotten all his learning? Nor is there any need to mention his empty and trifling comments which he wrote in explanation of the text of the amulet

CHAPTER TWELVE

he wrote by which he planned to deceive people, as though no one could understand his many falsehoods and sorceries! Truthfully, it is very much to my benefit that a publication of his (R.Eibeschuetz) had now appeared for now he could no longer deny or refute (his verbal statements) as was his custom.

Now I knew that God was with me for he (R.Eibeschuetz) had added folly and wickedness to his previous notoriety. I therefore took up my pen to make a quick response to his final humiliation. I gave him no leeway in describing his brazen arrogance, his ignominious stupidity and his lack of knowledge, all of which I revealed to his admirers. I entitled this responsum Shevirat Luchot ha-Aven and with the Almighty's help completed it without too much effort within a few weeks, in fact just as long as it would have taken to read any book I had been handed for perusal. Within a month a number of people had read my book and came to realise that his (Eibeschuetz's) work (Luchot Eidut) was of one mould viz. a source of corruption. Indeed, he had escaped the snare only to fall into the pit. (cf. Is. 24:L8). In the following Kislev 1757 the box which contained my books and printed articles which the worthless and reckless agents of R.Eibeschuetz had plundered from my house the previous Av was examined by Professor Shtecht in the presence of three members of the Council and two of my opponents viz. Julius and Rotschild. However, they failed to discover what they were looking for just as the latter scoundrels themselves had learned when they read the articles they had originally discovered. The professor alone examined the contents (of the box) and then issued a certificate which he confirmed by oath to the effect that he had examined the contents and found nothing which the opposition claimed. My friends and I thought we would be fully exonerated in this adjudication and that my opponents would be proved guilty. Indeed this was what the whole Council believed. But subsequently the devil I previously mentioned viz. Suflik approached the city authorities and claimed that the original charge against me was not concerned with my Eidut beYa'akov only but also with my other work Torat ha-Ke'naot which I had published in my own name. I had already given away some copies of that work and sold some copies to the public and there had been no complaints. Yet they now proposed to oppose me regarding this work too. A further complaint by him,(Suflik) was that the above mentioned professor (Shtecht) was not an expert in the Hebrew language.

Furthermore, he (Suflik) had the audacity to assert that the special commission (appointed by the city authorities) had not carried out all its duties. This intrigue coupled with bribes which he (Suflik) distributed fulfilled its aim and the decision of the commission was abrogated. Previously it had been decided to restore to me the box they had purloined and to compensate me for the loss, damages and humiliation I had sustained. Now they went back on this decision and declared the box should be opened again. I had already spent more than one hundred ducats on this affair a sum which some important personalities among my supporters had willingly reimbursed me. When those people now saw the decision of the commission had been reversed they appealed to the judiciary in Gluckstadt in the belief that there they would extol the innocent and denigrate the guilty. But there too, they assisted the guilty party by stating they were duty bound to help them. Consequently they fully affirmed the decision of the Council of Altona. Nor was the recommendation (on my behalf) offered by the lay-leader Yokel Hausen of our community prove of any avail. This appeal involved the loss of five hundred Reichshocken. In fact, for our many sins, we suffered considerable financial loss from the very outset. For those involved in this affair relied on their wisdom but their plans miscarried. Much of this failure was due to sluggishness. In short, their wise counsel proved to be foolish so that they squandered much money to no avail. However, since the opposing party did not want to take matters any further my friends likewise showed no enthusiasm in pushing the matter of the enquiry.

Thus for the past two years this affair has remained dormant, just like an article to which there are no claimants. Then, in 1757 a second Imperial edict was promulgated concerning the above-mentioned business, for the lay-leaders had petitioned the Emperor

CHAPTER TWELVE

with the plea that they be permitted to terminate Eibeschuetz's Rabbinate which he had held for three years. They now wanted him to leave the Rabbinate of the Three Communities. It was therefore decided that all members of those communities should convene to decide whether he should continue in the local Rabbinate or whether he should be dismissed. The outcome would depend on a majority decision. Hence the whole community was consulted; the poor as well as the idle folk whose vote was never considered regarding spiritual matters. All this was carried out at the Emperor's ruling. (In the meantime) the followers of R. Eibeschuetz wrote a letter of recommendation to the Hamburg authorities in support of R. Eibeschuetz requesting that he be restored to the local Rabbinate. They (the Hamburg authorities) acceded to this request so that he (R.Eibeschuetz) regained the Rabbinate of which he had been deprived for more than three years. Thus the principle of a majority opinion was completely ignored for the actual number who voted in favour of R.Eibeschuetz proved indefinite.

In celebration of this he (R.Eibeschuetz) provided a banquet to which all and sundry were invited. There were trumpeters and horsemen in the streets as well as upholstered wagons (cabs); some of the revellers provided livery of Sha'atnez for the riders and thronged the streets of Altona from one end of the town to the other in order to publicise their joy at the restoration of that hypocrite and mischief-maker. They made one of the young followers who was marked out as a leader because of his considerable height ride in front of the procession just like a cavalryman of the Hungarian army known as a hussar. The choice of that person was due to his intelligence and height but he was to pay a heavy price (for that honour). For a few days later this young man happened to see a Polish Jew perusing my book, Torat haKe'naot. Whereupon this fellow began to deride that learned Jew who protested at the young man's conduct. The latter ignored this (protest) and continued to his lodgings. Suddenly he exclaimed, "O, my head, my head," and sent a message for that learned Jew to come to him since he now regretted the way he had addressed the former.

MEGILAT SEFER

He probably wanted to apologise for his misconduct, but that Jew did not come (as requested) and the young man passed away soon after. May his death be his atonement!

In the previous year (1756) there had occurred a most unseemly event in Podolia, Poland in connection with a group of Sabbataeans who had lived there clandestinely for several years and had socialised with authentic Jews. Although many were suspected of that heresy they had not been identified but managed to practise their heretical faith secretly. But in 1756 their contemptible beliefs were finally exposed moreover the fact that they still adhered to their abominable practices, for after careful investigation their hiding-places were uncovered. Then the Rabbinical authorities of Poland meted out justice, in particular the community of Brody, and they and all their adherents and anyone who had any dealings with them were expelled. These Sabbataeans then approached certain governors of Poland and asserted that they were being persecuted for their religious beliefs which had much in common with Christianity. At the same time they (the Sabbataeans) squandered a great deal of money in bribing the authorities of the Church and consequently they succeeded in obtaining residence in fortified towns to escape the vigilance of the Jewish authorities.(cf. 2.Sam.20:6) They received special support from the governor of Kamenitz and his entourage who permitted them (the Sabbataeans) to observe their peculiar religion. This governor was also responsible for ordering the most humiliating burning of the Talmud and other holy books by the public executioner. (However, a great miracle occurred the details of which I hope, with God's help, to mention later.)

The (Jewish) authorities also wanted to compel Jewish women of probity to leave their husbands since they (the women) could not tolerate their husbands' activities viz. the abominable pagan rites (practised by the Sabbataeans). I received a variety of letters from eminent Polish Rabbis who sought my advice concerning this shocking affair. I advised them of the necessity of publishing an account of those abominable practices and to confirm the disgraceful

CHAPTER TWELVE

behaviour of those Sabbataeans by even referring to Christian literature. (For I argued) from that very source a weapon could be wielded against them.(the Sabbataeans). I therefore accepted this task in order to bridle their mouth as well as the Christian priests who supported them. The Almighty enabled me to publish my Seder Olam Rabba. Hamburg, 1757). In it I also refer to the special blessing of the sun which was celebrated in that year (1756) and I appended an article about this Sabbataean affair. In the course of that monograph I alluded to R.Eibeschuetz and his trickeries as well as to his devotees Karl Anton and Magril as well as to the revelries of his (R.Eibeschuetz's) young followers which I have already mentioned, all of which made the Torah appear to be fraudulent. When he (R.Eibeschuetz) read this work it was a thorn in his sight for he realised he could not prevail over me. Then he began to libel me and wrote to various Jewish communities (asserting) that in supporting Christianity I had been infected with heresy. He also hurriedly wrote to distant communities to which he realised my book would take some time to reach for example Amsterdam in particular, to which he dispatched that idiot Samson Morno and his coterie of demons who libelled my work before it had even been perused. They fulfilled his evil plan in frightening all the people there (in Amsterdam) from reading my book and obviously from buying it. Consequently when I forwarded my work to Amsterdam it was immediately returned to me. Moreover, the agent Robbed me of seven Reich Thaler when he returned the book so that I saw no return on my expenditure. It was only here (in Altona) that I sold a few copies (of my book) when it was first published (and this) despite his (R.Eibeschuetz's) vociferous criticisms (of it) to his simplistic followers who readily accepted all his snide observations. Yet this did not deter them from buying the work, on the contrary, they were most eager to read it. But when they did study it they were filled with reproach for they realised I had set out to fight God's battles. Indeed, I risked my life (cf. Jud.9:17) in order to prove from Christian theological) works that the Jew was bound by the most powerful bonds to the Torah of Moses our teacher, may he rest in peace, whilst the Gentiles were obligated to observe the Seven Noachide laws only. I then contended with these deceitful fellows, Margil and Karl Anton referring to them as seducers of Israel.

When these people realised it was in their best interest to praise me and my new book they ceased their criticism (of my book) and remained silent. Moreover a notice appeared in the Altona Gazette regarding the nature of my book and praising it. (No doubt) it was because that wicked person (R.Eibeschuetz) should see it and be annoyed. What did he do? He bought many copies of that edition of the Gazette to destroy them, but some copies had already appeared in other localities. In the same year God was wondrously good to me in enabling me to arrange marriages for my two elder daughters simultaneously with two of the most eminent and honourable Polish Jews, nor did I have to provide any dowry. One daughter, Esther, the child of my first wife was to be married to a son of one of the lay-leaders of the Council of the Four Lands-Abraham Yoskes who from the outset regarded the proposed marriage to be most suitable. His son, my future son-in-law was Rabbi Zechariah Mendel, the Presiding Rabbi of the Bet Din of Tishvitz (Tyszowce -village in province of Lublin) and was both young and wealthy. He had no children from his first wife so may the Almighty grant him a family from my daughter.

The second marriage was arranged between my Nechama, may she be granted long life, the daughter of my second wife Sarah, may she rest in peace and the son of the communal leader Baruch Yovon. The latter had been involved in a religious struggle on my behalf with Hayyim Lublin and his father at a time when he (Yovon) was not at all wealthy but nevertheless powerful enough for his advice to be taken by the Polish authorities. He (Yovon) caused the arrest and imprisonment of Abraham of Lublin, a leader of the Council of the Four Lands, though he (Yovon) could have profited from bribery had he sided with those who opposed me. But he would not accept such bribery but acted as a sincerely religious Jew in opposing the above-mentioned people (Abraham and Hayyim Lublin). In fact, he spent some of his own money for the glory of

CHAPTER TWELVE

God's blessed name and because of his (Yovon's) zeal for His Torah. Consequently the Almighty granted him His reward by elevating his status. For about a year ago rumour had it that he had become very rich. May the Almighty grant him the greatest success for his beneficent character. Now he (Yovon) was very anxious for my daughter (Nechama) to be married to his son, a fine intelligent young human being. I concurred with the Almighty's will for I realised that these marriages had been ordained by Heaven and decreed by the Almighty.

I sent off my daughters together at the end of the summer 1757 by boat to Danzig, and was most concerned about them for on the journey their boat was buffeted by very strong storms. In fact I subsequently learned they had been in great danger for it seems that when their boat was approaching Danzig the storm threw it some miles off course, the person on watch was drowned and the ship was on the verge of foundering. We must therefore thank God for saving my daughters and enabling them ultimately to reach Danzig in safety. Esther, my oldest daughter, then continued her journey (to Poland) quite peacefully and was married last Rosh Chodesh Kislev. Her younger sister, Nechama, remained in Danzig. I was again concerned about her for she stayed there (in Danzig) about six months as she was taken ill. But I thank the Almighty for the good news that I received at the end of Adar Rishon which informed me that she had left Danzig two weeks earlier for her wedding which, with all good fortune, will soon take place. May I merit seeing her too, establish a family as is my wish that all my family will be blessed with fine sons and daughters who will be mindful of their duties towards man and God, may this be His will, Amen!

The winter of 1758 proved to be long and harsh and was burdensome both to my family, may they be granted life, and me. Moreover, I suffered considerable financial loss for my two sons, having survived the first attack fell ill once again with anaemia. But blessed be the Almighty, He cured and saved them again. However, my young son of seven Judah Shai remained listless for about three months following his recovery from the above-mentioned illness.

Throughout this period this listlessness was the cause of much distress to us (his family), to the lad and to our friends (for he was my favourite child, a loveable and pleasant character who knew two tractates of the Talmud virtually by heart) unto Shevat, so that we had despaired of his life. But now, thank God, his former vitality has returned. Praised and blessed be He who saved and restored him to health.

I too, fell ill and remained in bed for several weeks with stomach pains and catarrh. But the faithful Healer, may His great mercies be extolled for ever, restored me to my former vigour. On the eighteenth of Adar Rishon (1758) which was a Shabbat my wife gave birth to a boy and he was brought into the covenant (circumcised) on the following Shabbat (Parashat Mishpatim). I named him Joseph Shai and his godfather was the local lay-leader and, thank God, the day of the circumcision was one of joy for us. We also had occasion to rejoice on the third day subsequent to the circumcision. For on the day of the operation we were concerned for the baby for he was very weak at the termination of the Shabbat as he had lost a considerable amount of blood as a result of the "periah" (removal of the membrane of the corona) having affected the membrum virile. The women were unaware of this until they discovered an excessive amount of blood on the baby's napkin. The child required medical treatment for besides this a wound had emerged beneath the membrum virile. This period of distress lasted for some weeks, but the Almighty blessed be He, in His infinite mercies, rescued us from this anxiety. May He continue to protect us and our children and preserve us from any further distress. May He grant us peace from all who would trespass against us so that we may shelter in the shadow of His wings for ever.

My lovely daughter Nechama too, fell seriously ill in Danzig during the winter subsequent to the rough journey she had experienced. I never failed in my hope that the Almighty would help her recover and, thank God, she was eventually well enough to be married to the son of the above-mentioned Baruch. May they be happy for many years to come.

CHAPTER TWELVE

It was during that particular winter that I received a variety of letters from Poland and one in particular from Rabbi Abraham Ha-Cohen of Tarlow a devoted member of the Council of the Four Lands. (R. Abraham HaCohen of Tarlow is mentioned in I. Heilprin's "Pinkas Va'ad Arbah Aratzot". According to the latter the letter to which R.Emden refers was sent from Konstantynow, the locale of conference of the Va'ad in 1758)(In the letter) he described the serious troubles in which loyal Jews found themselves which were caused by certain people (Frankists) who had acted as informers against our people and who had made libellous statements against Judaism in general and about the Talmud in particular. This had especially aroused the wrath of the governor of Kamenets (Kaminitz) who with the assistance of some Christian clergy who supported the Frankists, condemned copies of our sacred literature to burning. To our shame this command was carried out. Then the Frankists provided him (the governor) with a sumptuous banquet which was attended by his clergy and other supporters. They raised their glasses (of wine) and toasted the man who had succeeded in achieving this (foul) deed and they (the Frankists) stated that they fully supported his decision and assured him of a long life as his reward. But shortly after this (toast) their joy was turned to mourning and their song to lamentation, their feast of wine to lees (cf. Is.25:6) and that governor was drinking the wine of trembling (cf. ls.51:17). For while drinking and rejoicing the governor exclaimed bitterly, "Alas we have permitted the Jews to observe their Torah," with that he slumped to the floor in an epileptic fit and died. The faces of all the guests, the enemies of the Jews changed to a pallor resembling the bottom of a pit.

Then in Adar I received letters from my children and brothers that stated that our people were praising God and His great power for granting them miracles similar to those they had experienced at the Exodus from Egypt. For they had been confronted with harsh enemies like Haman and Antiochus who planned to erase the name of Israel and the destruction of the Torah. (The letters) also informed us of the events leading to the burning of our Holy Literature, a fact which caused us much distress. But (the letters continued) when God saw this destruction He relented and performed wondrous miracles just as (He did) in the days of Purim and Chanukah.

This was the general gist of those letters, but my students who hailed from Danzig wrote to me in some detail of those incidents, for (it seems) that following the incident involving that foolish governor another three people who were party to that evil scheme passed away. One of them died during a journey to Altona, the second as the result of a broken leg and the third of an epileptic fit. When the Christians realised that the hand of the Almighty was turned against that sect (the Frankists) they (the Christians) allied themselves with the loyal Jews and assisted the latter by falling upon another group (of Frankists) who had planned to lead Israel into apostasy. Some of the latter were killed outright, some were banished, and others had their beards removed and were persecuted without respite. So may all your enemies perish, O Lord!

My daughter's father-in-law the honourable Baruch Yovon, also deserves special mention in this affair in which he played his part in the destruction of the Frankist sect by his persistent protests to the King of Poland and his nobles. Thus he too, helped to frustrate their evil plans against the loyal Jews and ensured that they (the Frankists) received their just punishment. Baruch willingly offered his services and his worldly goods. For this may the Almighty help him and grant him every success because of his efforts on behalf of God's glorious name. The eminent scholar, Rabbi Katz sent me a copy of their arguments and strictures which the members of the above-mentioned sect (the Frankists) had set forth against us, the Jews who held steadfast to our faith, and which they (the Frankists) had delivered to the above-mentioned governor of Kamenets. Included in their statement was their brazen and explicit acknowledgement of a belief in the trinity and the corporeality of God. They advocated rebellion against the Almighty for which there was no atonement.

Rabbi Katz asked me to write an appropriate reply to those

CHAPTER TWELVE

Frankists and though those letters I had received (from Poland) had weakened my spirit I didn't delay or avoid this religious duty, but I immediately got up a reply in the form of a skeleton responsum until the Almighty granted me the energy to deal with this matter appropriately. Thus, with the Almighty's assistance I wrote this reply which I entitled "Shimush".

I will now tell you of my experience regarding the houses which I bought in Altona. I have already mentioned the first house I bought and the considerable outlay that occasioned which amounted to more than double my capital. Then when I returned from Amsterdam where I had taken refuge, I discovered my gentile neighbour had extended his house and (in so doing) had encroached on my property but I raised no objection. But then he acted unlawfully regarding my toilet which was situated in the back-yard close to his extension. For he tore down my toilet and having erected a wall facing my house he built a toilet for his use. I could not tolerate this unlawful behaviour any longer but was compelled to sue him in the state-court. The case dragged out for more than a year and the court's verdict was that he (my neighbour) was obliged to rebuild my toilet to its original specifications, and this he did. However, he still retained half the area he had encroached on when he originally tore down my toilet. The expenses that law-suit involved amounted to about twenty Reichthalers which sum, I never recovered.

In 1754 I bought a few more houses which adjoined my house because I was apprehensive of acquiring bad neighbours. Moreover I thought (these houses) would help me obtain some income. For despite every effort to find a proper source of livelihood in some kind of business I had been unsuccessful. I have already mentioned (my efforts) regarding Leib London and how I lost the money I had obtained by mortgaging my house. I was now conscious of the sound advice of our Sages z"l, that one's capital should be divided into three parts. "One third invested in land, one (third) in merchandise and one (third) in ready cash".(TB. Bava Metzia 42a) Consequently, I resolved to buy those houses adjoining my own and invest all my capital which amounted to about fifteen hundred Schockheller. I still needed 4,000 of the original money and searched for them for half a year but did not find them. It seems that this was because of enemies who besmirched my reputation amongst the Gentile mortgage brokers. When the time arrived and had not got my requirement I was forced to ask for a short-term loan from my friends. I pleaded and troubled them to save me from the disgrace of a court case and unnecessary expenditure, but their eyes were closed although in truth it was a small thing as far as they were concerned, for there were at least four notables from whom I asked this, viz. the Parnas and communal-leader Reb Gershon Katz, may he live, the Parnas and communal-leader Reb Y. Hausen, may he live, the Parnas and communal-leader Reb M. Giska and the leader Reb Y. Gottingen, may he rest in peace.

I wanted to effect this with them by way of a Heter Iska for a limited time until I would find a Gentile loan but they did not listen to me. All of them blamed the last of the above-mentioned, for he was renowned for his wealth and everyone depended on him. (cf. Bava Batra 145b) [lit. nobody moved without him] Everyone had to pay him some ready money (a brokerage fee), although for him this was a trifling matter, to secure a loan like this (with Heaven's help!).

Nevertheless, all the requests and recommendations from myself and from others were to no avail, for he was a difficult man, quite apart from his dignity. I was left in this great anguish in which I nearly lost my money which I had already expended in this purchase, apart from the embarrassment and disgrace and the rejoicing of my enemies, until he saw that the water had reached danger point. I was on the point of drowning as the date of repayment had passed and I had been summoned to court. Then his mercy was aroused, in anger he found himself (cf. Yoma 87a) fulfilling my request on that occasion, after he had caused an unnecessary expenditure of 20 Reichthalers. Only then the above-mentioned four men, together as partners, gave (a loan of 4000 Reichthaler) for a profit of 400 Reichthaler; I repaid them 1000 Reichthaler and there remained from their loan 1000

CHAPTER TWELVE

Shockheller from the four people mentioned above without profit.

During this period a row of bricks fell from the top of the wall of my residence on the side of the street and I expended a large sum on my house to renew it totally, outside and in, and to have placed on the edge of the roof facing the street, eaves of hewn stones with beautiful iron balustrade rails instead of the wooden eaves and balustrade that I had before. This alone cost 100 Reichthaler of additional new expense, apart from my expenditure on the houses that I had recently purchased in order to strengthen their structure as was necessary. In the first two years of purchasing these houses they made a tidy income, thank God, so that I was able to repay the interest from the first sum on time and to leave over on deposit between 400 and 500 Shock per year after outgoings on repairs and land-tax. In this way during those two years I had an income from my money which I had invested in the above-mentioned property of between four and five hundred Shock per year with ease.

However in 5517 and winter 5518 I lost much of that investment, may God make good my loss and send blessing to my house and activities and strengthen my health and wealth to His blessed service, to honour God from my wealth and money and to increase Mitzvot and charity as is my desire/ and may He be extolled, fulfil the desires of my heart to do His will.

In the winter of 5519 I sold, without loss, (thank God) five houses which I had bought 4 years earlier. That is four years after the burglary and damage mentioned above that had occurred in my home. During that period Moza Julius had a great delivery (after he had been ill for a whole year (Heaven forfend) in Altona from weight-loss (?); he went to from Altona to Friedichia the place of an asylum for those escaping NOSHIM. Before Tisha B'Av 5519, the low-life who had exploited Jews and gentiles fled from here with a huge sum of money. In the week before his flight he took by stealth a sum of money from the Jews of Hamburg who deal in exchange and swindled them by showing them forged papers from many businesses in which he was to receive by sea goods which are called

MEGILAT SEFER

"Consignments". Relying on this they lent him several thousand. He also falsified signatures on the bill of debt to a gentile in Altona a sum close to 50,000 Shockheller guaranteed ready money (a bank draft?) besides his debts to merchants for produce. May all Your enemies be destroyed! Afterwards the low-life Mendel Speir sent me a letter asking for forgiveness, with a great flurry.

By the way the great enemy who bothers to do evil with the Jews and their religion, the enemy of God, His people and His Torah, the evil sectarian, the abhorrent villain, the like of whom had never before arisen, to deceive and defile the virgin (of) Israel with hidden apostasy and to raise a hand against the Torah and to rebel with a strong hand and an outstretched arm to rebel against the Eternal God by praying to "gods"- not only does he go about up to now, walking erect with cheek against Heaven, but his temporary successes increased greatly.

That summer he married his daughter, mentioned in the second letter, to Rabbi Malutringen, after despairing of having a husband, and after having married a young lad with plenty of money who ran away. He also married off his grandson, the son of his oldest son, Natsh, (Nota Eibeschuetz), to the daughter of Elijah Yarok with great honour. He purposely made the wedding on the day before the 17th (Fast) of Tammuz [which is the Yomtov of Shabbetai Tzvi] in such a way that the Feast of the Near-relatives was on the Eve of the Fast. All the 7 days of feasting continued through Bein Hametzarim (the 3 weeks of semi-mourning from 17 Tammuz to 9 Av) with great celebration. On 21st Tammuz Yehialchi Wolfe made a great dinner for himself, his children and in-laws at which they drank to excess.

At the same time his son, the lad Wolf returned from the journey and brought with him much silver and gold and regal opals, fabulous wealth with precious articles, as was rumoured unceasingly about that he had brought with him. He also bought immediately a holding in Altona, houses with a large garden. When that (month of) Av arrived the Simcha increased [c.f. TB. Taanis 26b "when Av arrives one decreases in merriment"] He uprooted many fruit trees

CHAPTER TWELVE

the kind of which did not exist in Altona. Many and goodly - they were destroyed and uprooted to make way for the planting of rejoicing - he desired trees for timber and a shaded summer house in the days of Av. He also placed figures sculpted from marble in them. Thus the lad established hid home; then, on Shabbat Chazon he dedicated his house in that month. His father (the enemy) was with him at the dedication party on that Motzei Shabbat. At the outgoing of that holy Sabbath when they imbibed and got drunk with an abundance of wine, they made a noise and acted in a debauched fashion. More than that it seems that they established a Bet Midrash at the head of which they placed Moshe David Ba'al Shayd (lit. Master of the Demon, instead of Ba'al Shem =Master of the (Divine) Name). This person studied there Chabbalah (=destruction. Instead of Kabbalah, mysticism) with unmarried students who go and meet there every day to be involved in Chabbalah with this Ba'al Shayd whom Eibeschuetz and son dressed in silk for years and fed with delicacies and saturated with juice and new wine, whereas those who fear God are in pain and desolate at the desecration of the Great Name, who are filled with bitterness and have their fill of hemlock.

The members of this sect justify themselves saying in their righteousness and the uprightness of their hearts they have done this and that they are in their eyes the simple, good and upright, whilst we the just seekers of God who seek the honour of His Torah, believers who tremble at his word and who are desolate at the desecration of His Name, because of our many sins are considered in their eyes unclean and sinners, mad stupid and simple. Woe to the generation in whose days this (situation) arose! Concerning all this mourning - the ideal has been reversed. The upright are below and the low-life is up to the highest heaven. Its summit was raised really to heaven amongst the stars- there was its dirge (by the ones who serve Him) and above the stars the mountains covered His throne.

Last year I brought my book "Shimush" to the printers and when it was nearly completed there entered a spirit of folly in to the worker Moshe Bun, so that he did not want to complete it which caused me great anguish, for I had made a great outlay on this for God and to establish His Law \ so that the Torah should not be hidden\ so that heresy should not prevail\. This occurred close to its completion, it stopped and still was lying incomplete (viz. printed) Until Hashem was pleased with my work\ Hashem will compete on my behalf\ He will strengthen my hands\ the work of my hands do not tear.

At this point the manuscript ends [Ed. Note]

CHAPTER TWELVE

MEGILAT SEFER

ca so
END NOTES
ca so

MEGILAT SEFER

CHAPTER ONE

(1) Rabbi Yaakov Emden commences the work with the Hebrew word "Avi" lit. my father. He probably intended to allude to both God (his Heavenly Father) and the Chacham Tzvi his earthly father whose biography this is. However the meaning is an invocation to find favour as in Job 34:36. hence the translation "May he who...."

(2) i.e. the final outcome which will undoubtedly be good. cf. TB.Berachot 64a. A person cannnot of course wait until the end of his life in order to tell his story.

(3) "ZaK" is a mnemonic of "Zera Kodesh" holy seed indicating that the person is the descendant of a martyr. Hence the not uncommon Jewish surnames - Zaks,Sacks etc.

(4) Vilnius the capital of Lithuania.

(5) The Chemielnicki massacres 1648-9 known in Hebrew Literature as Gezerot Tach veTat viz. the decrees of 5408-9.

(6) Rabbi Ephraim Cohen, the Rabbi of Uban Yashan (see note 12) The Chacham Tzvi's maternal grandfather who died in 1638.

(7) Hebrew mnemonic z"l =zichrono livracha of blessed memory. Emden uses other mnemonics such as zatza"l etc...so for brevity. I have reduced them all to z"l.

(8) Ba'al Shem lit. Master of the Name. A not uncommon term for a wonder-worker or miracle-curer from the 16th to the 18th century.

(9) Flourished mid 16th century.

339

(10) Responsa Chacham Tzvi first published in Amsterdam 1712 (5471)

(11) Autonomon, a robot made from clay. Perhaps the most famous was that made by the Maharal of Prague on which Shelley based the story of Frankenstein, but see TB.Sanhedrin 65b for the talmudic origin.

(12) Known as Abuda (Heb.Uban Yashan) a large village which became part of Buda later Budapest.

(13) 1644-1737, Chief Rabbi of Prague.

(14) Rabbi Samuel Kaidinover known by his initials MaHaRSHaK.

(15) Rabbi Shabbtei HaCohen author of "Sifsei Cohen" a classic commentary on the Tur Yore Deah and Chosen Mishpat.

(16) Rabbi Hillel, Chief Rabbi of Zolkova and then the Three Communities of Altona, Hamburg and Wandsbeck (A'H'U), died 1690.

(17) Requiring only one witness.

MEGILAT SEFER

CHAPTER TWO

(1) Cf. Isaiah 28.4. R.Ya'akov's father was the Chacham Tzvi.

(2) R. Yaakov Emden's grandparents viz. R.Ya'akov b. Benjamin Ashkenazi and Nechama the daughter of R. Ephraim Ha-Cohen.

(3) R.Elijah b.Judah Kovo (c.1620-1689) was a native of Salonika where he studied in his father's Yeshivah. While acting as rector of the latter institution he was appointed Av Bet Din of the community (1670) and his "Aderet Eliyahu" was published together with the Responsa of his son-in-law R.Joshua Handali, under the title "Shnei Me'orot ha-Gedolim" (Constantinople 1739). See "Korot ha-Yehudim beTurkiya ve-Artzot ha-Kedem" by S.E.Rosanes Vol.4 p.120 (Sofia 1934-35) also the Introduction to R.Elijah b. Judah Kovo's "Shnei Me'orot ha-Gedolim" - Constantinople 1739.

(4) Jews came to settle in this city from the middle of the 16th century.

(5) The Jewish community had sided with the Turks.

(6) cf. 2 Sam. 3.34.

(7) This is a reference to (responsum) No.61 in the Responsa of Chacham Tzvi.

(8) Provisions for the return of dowries are already recorded in the Talmud Yerushalmi Ketubot chap.9 at the end of Halakha 1. (I am grateful to Rabbi Dr. N. L. Rabinovitch for pointing out this reference). Further problems concerning the return of dowries can be traced back to the period of the Crusades (11th-13th centuries), during which Jews suffered death at the hands of

Christian mobs or by martyrdom. As a consequence some of the great contemporary Rabbinic authorities were frequently confronted with questions regarding the dowry of a young wife and/or husband who were victims of those medieval pogroms. Thus a Takkanah (Rabbinical Ordinance) associated with the name Rabbenu Tam (R. Yaakov b.Meir 1100-1171) states as follows: "if a man marries a woman and then she dies within a year of he marriage without being survived by any permanent issue, he shall then return to the giver of the dowry or his heirs, all that is left of his wife's dowry or her jewels." (p166). L.Finkelstein "Jewish Self-government in the Middle Ages" 1924) It was presumably on the basis of the proceeding Takkanah that an Ordinance of the thirteenth century emanating from a Synod comprising of the principal Rabbinic authorities of Spiers, Worms and Mainz (Takkanat Shu"m) required the husband to return to the family of his wife one-half of what he received (as a dowry) from them. (ibid. p.58) According to Chacham Tzvi's responsum (No.61) it would appear that neither of the aforementioned Takkanot was in force in 17th century Buda, but they followed the custom whereby it was the husband's duty to draw up a legal document which provided for the return of the dowry to the wife's family should she or her husband die without being survived by any permanent issue. The circumstances surrounding this responsum were reminiscent of the tragic experience of the Chacham Tzvi in Buda during the period of the Imperial siege.

(9) The invasion and capture of Buda by the Imperial forces occurred in 1686 so that the duration of Chacham Tzvi's rabbinate of Sarajevo must have been very short, but he remained there in a private capacity.

(10) October 1697. However in his Torat ha-Kena'ot (1752) R.J.Emden observes that his father was forced to leave Sarajevo because of the machinations of the notorious Sabbataean Nehemiah Hayyun. (See note to p.370 Vol. Graetz-Rabbinowitz

"Divrei Yemei Yisrael" Warsaw, 1916).

(11) Rabbi Emden cannot mean R. Samuel b. Abraham Aboab for he died in 1694 and Chacham Tzvi did not leave Sarajevo until 1697 (see previous note). Presumably he means R.Samuel's son Yaakov (died c.1725) who succeeded his father to the rabbinate of Venice.

(12) TB.Makkot 10b. See Maharasha ad loc. for a novel interpretation of this Rabbinic adage.

(13) W. Germany, where a Jewish community already existed in the 14th century.

(14) A marriage prohibited by rabbinical enactment e.g. marriage to a grand-mother. (See Shulchan Arukh- Even Ha-Ezer Ch.15).

(15) According to Jewish law an agency for the fulfilment of a wrongful act is invalid. (TB.Kiddushin 42b).

(16) i.e. Ansbach

(17) Kiddush HaShem - a sanctification of God's name which is effected by some noble deed or through martyrdom.

(18) The prohibition is stated in Lev.25:36-37 incl. and in Deut. 23:20-21 incl. (19) See Lev 19:13.)

(20) A "chamsan" like a "gazlan" takes forcibly, but unlike the latter, he pays for the object he has extorted. (see TB. Bava Kamma 62a).

(21) i.e. a false oath which incorporates the name of God and thus infringes the negative precept, Lev 19.11.

(22) (God) repays them that hate Him to their face, destroying them i.e. during their lifetime God pays them (the wicked) their recompense in order to cause them to perish from out of the

future world. See Rashi ad loc.

MEGILAT SEFER

CHAPTER THREE

(1) see supra Note (20)

(2) R. Yaakov b. Joseph Reischer (Backofen) c.1670-1733, author and Halakhic authority. After holding important Rabbinic positions in Prague, Ansbach (1709) and Worms (1715) he was appointed as Av Bet Din and Rector of the Yeshivah of Metz (1718). In the course of time he was accepted by contemporary Rabbis as the final Halakhic authority as his Responsa, Shevut Yaakov (3 Parts) indicate.

(3) It was only in the last quarter of the 16th century that the first, Portuguese Jews, later German Jews gained admittance to Hamburg, Altona and Wandsbeck, adjoining communities united with Hamburg (1664) under the supervision of a joint Chief Rabbi to provide care for the poor and for burial. Chacham Tzvi Ashkenazi served as Chief Rabbi of the Triple communities in the period 1707 - 1709.

(4) R. M Z Neumark (Mirels) was born in Vienna (c.1620) and came of a family which formed a branch of the famous Fraenkel (Frankel) family. (Encyc. Judaica 7 pp. 1-2) following the expulsion of Jews from his native city (1678).

(5) Kloiz (Yiddish), Klaus (German) or Hesger (Hebrew) means literally "enclosed", and refers particularly to small Yeshivot where the teachers were enclosed. These institutions were usually endowed by wealthy patrons.

(6) The Talmud lit. "Six Orders"(of the Mishnah)

(7) The (four) Pillars, the monumental Law Code by Rabbi Yaakov ben Asher (1270 - 1343)

(8) Tenach is a mnemonic for Torah (Pentateuch) Nevi'im(Prophets) and Ketubim(Writings), the three parts of the Hebrew Bible.

(9) In the first decades of the eighteenth century the Reichthaler was governed by the provisions of the Leipzig Convention of 1690 which laid down that the Thaler was to consist of 19.35 g. of pure silver. In terms of the early eighteenth English currency, which was then of silver 92.5%, rather than 100%, fine. 19.35g. of pure silver was the equivalent in monetary terms of about 3 shillings and sixpence. What did 3/6 mean in c.1700? J.E.Thoreld Rogers in "A history of Agriculture and Prices in England" (Vol.5. Oxford 1887.pp.670) lists the weekly wages of a carpenter and bricklayer in 1701-2 at an average of 2s.6d. per week, a mason also at 2s.6d, a plumber at 3s 0d and a "labourer to artisan" at 1s.8d. In other words a Reich Thaler represented something in the order of the weekly wage of a highly skilled worker or one-and-a-half week's wages of a tradesman.

(10) Possibly a descendent of Nathan Nota Hanover (d.1683), the author of Yeven Mezulah, an account of the Chmielnicki pogroms in Poland (1648-52).

APPENDIX A: PHOTOS AND ILLUSTRATIONS

מגלת ספר

כולל

יעקב ישראל עמדן הנקרא יעב"ץ. אשר כתב בעצמו על ספר

מאת

דוד כהנא

ווארשא

שנה תרנ"ז לפ"ק

Мегилатъ Сеферъ

т. е.

Автобіографія Р. Якова Эмдена

Изданіе „Ахіасафъ".

ВАРШАВА

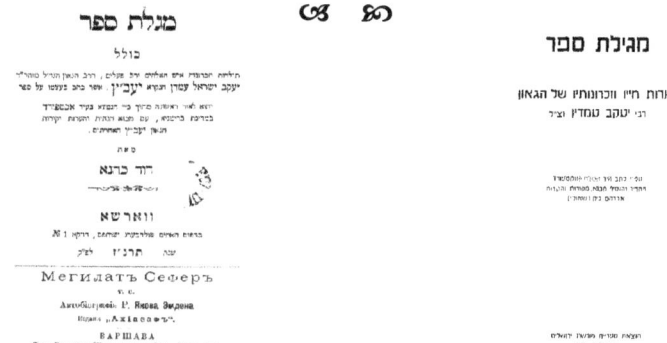

Illustration 1: Title page from the 1897 edition of Megilat Sefer – Kahane Edition

מגילת ספר

קורות חייו וזכרונותיו של הגאון

רבי יעקב עמדין זצ"ל

Illustration 2: English title page from the 1979 edition of Megilat Sefer (Bick Edition)

ספר

תולדות אדם

ואל תתמיצו הבא לידכם:

ווילמרש דארף

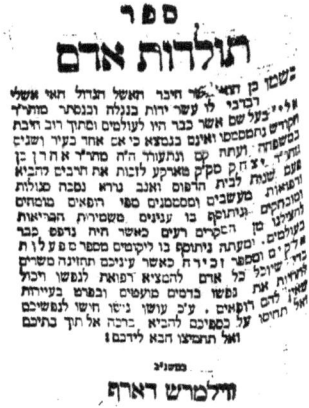

Illustration 3: Title page from Sefer Toldos Adam, authored by R' Elijah Baal Shem, great-grandfather of R' Jacob Emden

ספר

שער אפרים

בשאלות ותשובות להרב הגדול.

נדפס פה קק ווילצבאך

Cum Licentia Serenissimi.

לבן שמח

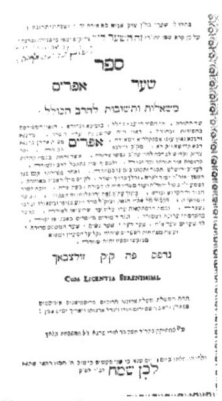

Illustration 4: Title page from Sefer Shaar Ephraim, written by great-grandfather of R' Jacob Emden

APPENDIX A: PHOTOS AND ILLUSTRATIONS

Illustration 5: Portrait of the Chacham Tzvi from the 1897 Kahane Edition of Megilat Sefer

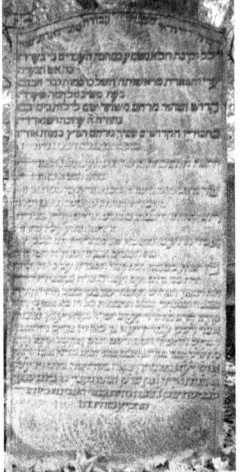

Illustration 6: Gravestone of R' Jacob Emden (courtesy of Steinheim Institut)

Illustration 7: Portrait of R' Jonathan Eybeschutz from the 1906, Sefer Chachmei Ahu by Eduard Duckesz

Illustration 8: Gravestone of R' Jonathan Eyeschbutz (courtesy of Steinheim Institut)

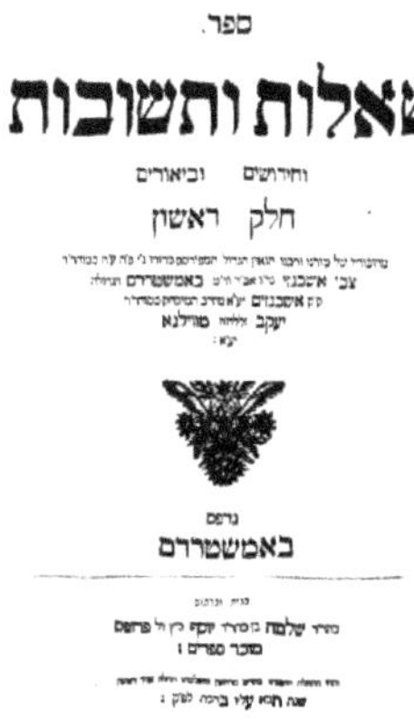

ספר

שאלות ותשובות

וחידושים וביאורים

חלק ראשון

באמשטרדם

Illustration 9: llustration 6: Title page from Responsa of the Chacham Zvi, Amsterdam

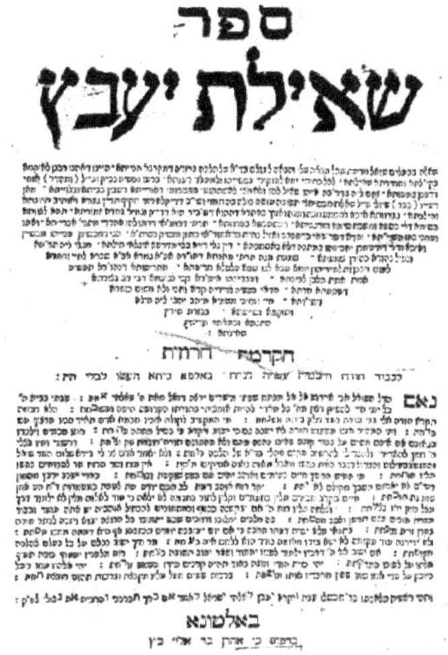

ספר

שאילת יעבץ

באלטונא

Illustration 10: Title of Page of Sefer Sheilas Yaavetz, the responsa of R' Jacob Emden; Altona

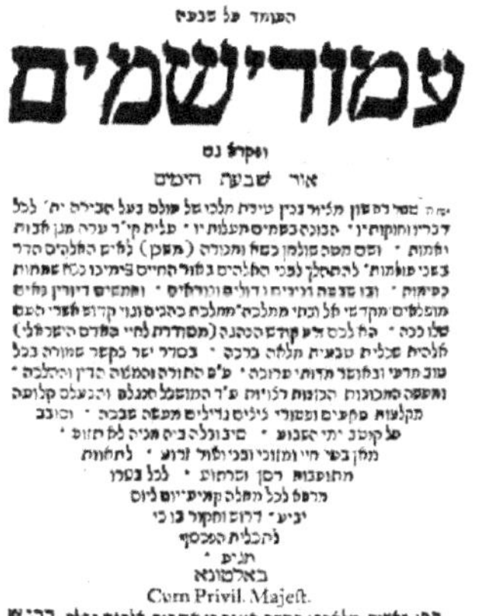

עמודי שמים

ונקרא גם

אור שבעת הימים

באלטונא

Cum Privil. Majeft.

Illustration 11 Title Page from Siddur Yaavetz by R' Jacob Emden, Vol 1; Altona

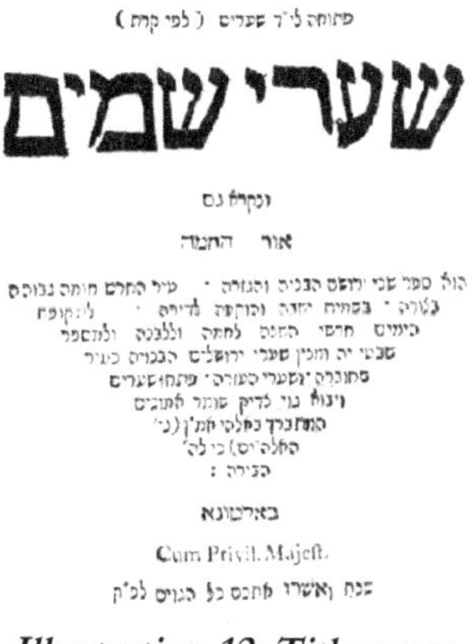

שערי שמים

ונקרא גם

אור החמה

Cum Privil. Majeft.

Illustration 12: Title page from Siddur Yaavetz by R' Jacob Emden, Vol 2: Altona

APPENDIX A: PHOTOS AND ILLUSTRATIONS

Publisher's Note: Title pages are courtesy of HebrewBooks.org. The photographs of the tombstones above were obtained from the Steinheim Institut under CC-BY 2.0 license as follows:

1. Tombstone of Rabbi Jacob Emden:
Digitale Edition - Jüdischer Friedhof Hamburg-Altona, Königstraße (1621-1871 / 5937 Einträge): Inv.-Nr. 1586
URL: http://www.steinheim-institut.de/cgi-bin/epidat?function=Ins&sel=hha&inv=1586 (2010-09-27)

2. Tombstone of Rabbi Jonathan Eyeschbutz:
Digitale Edition - Jüdischer Friedhof Hamburg-Altona, Königstraße (1621-1871 / 5937 Einträge): Inv.-Nr. 1593
URL: http://www.steinheim-institut.de/cgi-bin/epidat?function=Ins&sel=hha&inv=1593 (2010-09-27)

MEGILAT SEFER

APPENDIX B: GLOSSARY

Av Bet Din
lit. "Father of the Court" President of the Court, Presiding Rabbi

Ashkenaz
lit. "Germany" hence Ashkenazim Central and East-European Jews.

Bet HaMidrash
House of Study, Study hall often doubling as a synagogue

Bet Din
Jewish Court of Law

Brit/Brit Milah
lit. "covenant of" circumcision

Chacham
lit. "Sage" title used for Sephardi rabbis

Chametz
leaven forbidden to be eaten on Passover (see Matzah)

Chazan (pl. Chazanim)
cantor

Dayan
Ecclesiastical Judge. Two Dayanim (pl.) would assist the Rabbi and form a Bet Din

Eretz Yisrael
the Land of Israel

Gaon
Genius, Eminence. Title reserved for world renowned Rabbinic authorities

Halakhah
Jewish Law

APPENDIX B: GLOSSARY

Kiddush Hashem
Sanctification of God's name, martyrdom

Matzah (plural Matzoth)
Unleavened bread eaten on Passover (see Chametz)

Mikveh
ritualarium, ritual bath

Mitzvah pl. Mitzvot
commandment, loosely a good deed

Pesach
Passover, a Spring Festival celebrating the Exodus from Egypt

Rav
lit. "great one" Rabbi (title used amongst Ashkenazim)

Reb
Mr. a title used for adherents of Rabbinic Judaism (as opposed to Karaites)

Rosh Chodesh
the New Month (commencing at the new moon)

Sephardim
lit. Spanish Jews also used for Oriental Jews (non-Ashkenazim)

Shulchan Arukh
lit "set table" authoritative Code of Jewish Law by Rabbi Yosef Caro, 16th century Safed

Shavout
lit. "Weeks" Festival of Pentecost, 7 weeks after Passover, celebrating the Giving of the Law on Mount Sinai

Sukkot
Festival of booths, a harvest festival celebrated in Autumn

Yeshivah (plural Yeshivot)
Talmudic academy/Theological college

MEGILAT SEFER

œ ഉ

APPENDIX C: BIOGRAPHICAL NOTES
œ ഉ

Rabbi Yaakov Emden (known as the Yavetz) was born on the 4th of June, 1697 in Altona and died there on 19th April 1776. He was the son of the Chacham Tzvi Ashkenazi, the foremost Halachik authority of his age and the father of Rabbi Meshullam Solomon, Rabbi of the Hamboro' (Hamburg) Synagogue in London from 1765 to 1780.

Emden studied with his father firstly in Altona and then in Amsterdam (1710-1714) until the age of 17. In 1715 he married Rachel, the daughter of Rabbi Mordechai Hakohen, rabbi of Uhersky Brod in Moravia and continued to study in his father-in-law's yeshiva. Besides a wide and deep knowledge of Talmudic and Rabbinic Literature, Emden studied Kabbalah, philosophy, grammar. Besides Yiddish and Hebrew, he studied Latin, Dutch and some Spanish.

He had lectured in Talmud in Brod, but became a dealer in jewellery which required him to travel. He generally avoided the rabbinate, adding the beracha "shelo asani av bet din" every morning but was induced to accept the rabbinate of Emden in 1728 from which he took his name.

He returned to Altona in 1733 and received a permit to open a small private shul. He was on friendly terms with Rabbi Moshe Chagiz, the head of the Sefardi community. However, his relationship with Rabbi Yechezkiel Katzenellenbogen, the Rabbi of the Ashkenzim was strained from the outset. He considered every successor of his father as an intruder.

Some time later he obtained permission from the King of Denmark to establish a priting-press in Altona and began to publish what turned out to be over fifty works!

Some of the his most famous works are:
- Siddur Tefillah (now known as Bet Yaakov) in three parts. Altona 1745-48
- She'elat Yavetz, 372 responsa, Altona 1739-59
- Lechem Shamayim, commentary on the Mishnah. Altona 1728
- Etz Avot, a commentary to Pirkei Avot, Amsterdam 1751
- Mor u-Ketziah, notes and comments on Orach Chayyim section of the Shulchan Aruch
- Tzitzim u-Ferachim, a collection of articles on the Kabbala in alphabetical order. Altona, 1768
- Edut beYaakov on the supposed heresy of Yonatan Eibeshutz, Altona 1756

353

APPENDIX C: BIOGRAPHICAL NOTES

- Shimmush, in three parts against the Sabbateans and other heretical groups. Amsterdam 1758-62
- Amongst his many works, unpublished by him, is Megilat Sefer, the manuscript of which is in the Bodlean Library, Oxford, England.

Emden is also famous for the controversies in which he was involved. His attacks were mostly directed against the followers of Sabbatai Zevi or those he suspected of Sabbatean tendencies. In 1756 the members of the Synod of Constantinov asked Emden to help them repress the Sabbatean movement. The most prominent controversy was with Yonatan Eibeshutz, whom Emden accused of being a secret Sabbatean. This was based mainly on the interpretation of amulets which Eibeshutz had written. The controversy lasted several years, split the European rabbinate into two, and continued even after Eibeshutz's death. Interestingly, Emden and Eibeshutz are buried in the same cemetery with a gap of only one grave![7]

Emden's property and his very life were often under attack from the opposition and at one point in May 1751, he had to flee, taking refuge in Amsterdam where he had many admirers, in the house of his brother-in-law Aryeh Leib Saul, the rabbi of the Ashkenazim. Later the court of Frederick V of Denmark issued a ruling on 3rd June 1752 in favour of Emden and against the Council of the Three Communities (Ah"u that is Altona, Hamburg and Wansbeck) fining them 100 thalers. Emden returned to Altona, and re-opened his shul and printing-press.

The truth or falsity of his accusation against Eibeshutz cannot be proved. However, it is interesting to note that Eibeshutz's son openly declared himself to be a Sabbatean, after his father's death.

Emden's works show him to be possessed of critical faculties rarely found among his contemporaries. His opinions were sometimes extremely unconventional, nevertheless he was a strict traditionalist never deviating from the established custom, even when a change in time and circumstances might have warranted it.

Emden died in Altona, aged 79 and leaves many descendants in England and Israel to this day.

ෆ ෩

Rabbi Dr Shlomo Benzion Leperer was born in London in 1922. He attended the Jewish Free School and the Etz Hayyim Yeshiva where he studied under the famous Talmudists Rabbi Nachman Shlomo Greenspan, Rabbi Elya Lopian and Dayan Abramsky. He then studied at Jews' College under Rabbis Koppel Kahana and Isidore Epstein whilst simultaneously completing two first class BA degrees in Hebrew and Aramaic at University College and in History at Birkbeck College. He won the literary prize of the entire University of London for

---

7   See appendix A above for photos of their gravestones

MEGILAT SEFER

an unprecedented three years in a row.

The professor of history at Birkbeck wanted him to pursue an academic career but the then Chief Rabbi, Sir Israel Brodie, stepped in, creating the post of Chaplain to the Jewish Students at Oxford University, thus saving this rising star for Anglo-Jewry.

He was rabbi to several communities in London and taught at Carmel College before joining the staff of his alma mater in 1975 as Professor of History and Talmud. He often arrived at the College before 8am for morning services and was seen at 10pm at night supervising doctoral candidates. He was in demand as a speaker and lecturer by synagogues and organisations throughout Anglo-Jewry and rarely failed to enthrall his audiences. His appearance and general demeanour hid his vast and deep rabbinic knowledge. His love of humanity was matched only by his love of God.

Dr. Leperer remained at his post, at one point serving as acting Principal, until his death in December 1995.

ଓଃ ଛ

Rabbi Dr. Meir Wise was born in Manchester in 1956. He arrived at Jews' College, London on the same day, 6th October 1975, as his great mentor Rabbi Leperer. He also studied under the famous Talmudists Rabbi Nahum L Rabinovitch, Rabbi Simcha B Lieberman and Rabbi Moshe Turetsky.

After graduating with an honours degree in Jewish Studies and a post-graduate degree in Education, he was ordained by Chief Rabbi Jakobovits and awarded a Fellowship of the College. Rabbi Wise was elected rabbi of the Central Synagogue, East London and the Hillel chaplain for London and region and later was the last rabbi of the Western Synagogue before its amalgamation.

He maintained contact with Rabbi Leperer for over 21 years and was the last talmid to see him alive and was asked to eulogise him in the College and in the Jewish Press.

He has taught at the JFS, Carmel College in Oxford, Yakar Educational Foundation and in the kollel of Yeshivat Od Yosef Hai in London.

Married with four children and five grandchildren, Rabbi Wise continues to research, teach, lecture and write and is in great demand as a public speaker whilst planning his aliya to Israel.

ଓଃ ଛ

APPENDIX C: BIOGRAPHICAL NOTES

[This page has been intentionally left blank]

www.ingramcontent.com/pod-product-compliance
Lightning Source LLC
Chambersburg PA
CBHW052010070526
44584CB00016B/1694